"The Catholic Commentary on Sacred Scripture richly provides what has for so long been lacking among contemporary scriptural commentaries. Its goal is to assist Catholic preachers and teachers, lay and ordained, in their ministry of the Word. Moreover, it offers ordinary Catholics a scriptural resource that will enhance their understanding of God's Word and thereby deepen their faith. Thus these commentaries, nourished on the faith of the Church and guided by scholarly wisdom, are both exegetically sound and spiritually nourishing."

—**Thomas G. Weinandy, OFM Cap**, United States Conference of Catholic Bishops

"This could be the first commentary read by a pastor preparing a text and could be read easily by a Sunday school teacher preparing a text, and it would be an excellent commentary for a college Bible class. . . . The Catholic Commentary on Sacred Scripture will prove itself to be a reliable, Catholic—but ecumenically open and respectful—commentary."

—**Scot McKnight**, *Jesus Creed* blog

"The Word of God is the source of Christian life, and the Catholic Commentary on Sacred Scripture is an ideal tool for living our faith more deeply. This extraordinary resource feeds both the mind and the heart and should be on the shelf of every committed Catholic believer. I highly recommend it."

—**Charles J. Chaput, OFM Cap**, Archbishop of Philadelphia

"When the Scripture is read in the liturgy, it is heard as a living voice. But when expounded in a commentary, it is too often read as a document from the past. This fine series unites the ancient and the contemporary by offering insight into the biblical text—verse by verse—as well as spiritual application to the lives of Christians today."

—**Robert Louis Wilken**, University of Virginia

"There is a great hunger among Catholic laity for a deeper understanding of the Bible. The Catholic Commentary on Sacred Scripture fills the need for a more in-depth interpretation of Scripture. I am very excited to be able to recommend this series to our Bible Study groups around the world."

—**Gail Buckley**, founder and director, Catholic Scripture Study International (www.cssprogram.net)

Catholic Commentary on Sacred Scripture

2022

James,
First, Second, and
Third John

Kelly Anderson
and Daniel Keating

B **Baker Academic**
a division of Baker Publishing Group
Grand Rapids, Michigan

© 2017 by Kelly Anderson and Daniel A. Keating

Published by Baker Academic
a division of Baker Publishing Group
P.O. Box 6287, Grand Rapids, MI 49516-6287
www.bakeracademic.com

Printed in the United States of America

Library of Congress Cataloging-in-Publication Data
Names: Anderson, Kelly (Assistant Professor of Biblical Studies), author. | Keating, Daniel A., author.
Title: James, First, Second, and Third John / Kelly Anderson and Daniel Keating.
Description: Grand Rapids : Baker Academic, 2017. | Series: Catholic commentary on sacred
  scripture | Includes bibliographical references and index.
Identifiers: LCCN 2016042288 | ISBN 9780801049224 (pbk.)
Subjects: LCSH: Bible. James—Commentaries. | Bible. Epistles of John—Commentaries. | Catholic
  Church—Doctrines.
Classification: LCC BS2785.53 .A53 2017 | DDC 230/.2—dc23
LC record available at https://lccn.loc.gov/2016042288

Printed with Ecclesiastical Permission
Most Reverend Earl Boyea, Bishop of Lansing
December 7, 2015

The *nihil obstat* and *imprimatur* are official declarations that a book is free of doctrinal or moral error. No implication is contained therein that those who have granted the *nihil obstat* or *imprimatur* agree with the contents, opinions, or statements expressed.

Except as otherwise specified, Scripture versification and quotations are from the *New American Bible, revised edition* © 2010, 1991, 1986, 1970 Confraternity of Christian Doctrine, Washington, DC, and are used by permission of the copyright owner. All rights reserved. No part of the New American Bible may be reproduced in any form without permission in writing from the copyright owner.

Scripture quotations labeled ESV are from The Holy Bible, English Standard Version® (ESV®), copyright © 2001 by Crossway, a publishing ministry of Good News Publishers. Used by permission. All rights reserved. ESV Text Edition: 2011

Scripture quotations labeled NIV are from the Holy Bible, New International Version®. NIV®. Copyright © 1973, 1978, 1984, 2011 by Biblica, Inc.™ Used by permission of Zondervan. All rights reserved worldwide. www.zondervan.com

Scripture quotations labeled NJB are from THE NEW JERUSALEM BIBLE, copyright © 1985 by Darton, Longman & Todd, Ltd. and Doubleday, a division of Random House, Inc. Reprinted by permission.

Scripture quotations labeled NRSV are from the New Revised Standard Version of the Bible, copyright © 1989, by the Division of Christian Education of the National Council of the Churches of Christ in the United States of America. Used by permission. All rights reserved.

Scripture quotations labeled RSV are from the Revised Standard Version of the Bible, copyright 1952 [2nd edition, 1971] by the Division of Christian Education of the National Council of the Churches of Christ in the United States of America. Used by permission. All rights reserved.

In keeping with biblical principles of creation stewardship, Baker Publishing Group advocates the responsible use of our natural resources. As a member of the Green Press Initiative, our company uses recycled paper when possible. The text paper of this book is composed in part of post-consumer waste.

21 22 23   7 6 5 4 3

Contents

Illustrations

Editors' Preface

The Church has always venerated the divine Scriptures just as she venerates the body of the Lord. . . . All the preaching of the Church should be nourished and governed by Sacred Scripture. For in the sacred books, the Father who is in heaven meets His children with great love and speaks with them; and the power and goodness in the word of God is so great that it stands as the support and energy of the Church, the strength of faith for her sons and daughters, the food of the soul, a pure and perennial fountain of spiritual life.

Second Vatican Council, Dei Verbum 21

Were not our hearts burning [within us] while he spoke to us on the way and opened the scriptures to us?

Luke 24:32

The Catholic Commentary on Sacred Scripture aims to serve the ministry of the Word of God in the life and mission of the Church. Since Vatican Council II, there has been an increasing hunger among Catholics to study Scripture in depth and in a way that reveals its relationship to liturgy, evangelization, catechesis, theology, and personal and communal life. This series responds to that desire by providing accessible yet substantive commentary on each book of the New Testament, drawn from the best of contemporary biblical scholarship as well as the rich treasury of the Church's tradition. These volumes seek to offer scholarship illumined by faith, in the conviction that the ultimate aim of biblical interpretation is to discover what God has revealed and is still speaking through the sacred text. Central to our approach are the principles taught by Vatican II: first, the use of historical and literary methods to discern what the biblical authors intended to express; second, prayerful theological reflection to understand the sacred text "in accord with the same Spirit by whom it was written"—that is, in light of the content and unity of the whole Scripture, the living tradition of the Church, and the analogy of faith (*Dei Verbum* 12).

The Catholic Commentary on Sacred Scripture is written for those engaged in or training for pastoral ministry and others interested in studying Scripture to understand their faith more deeply, to nourish their spiritual life, or to share the good news with others. With this in mind, the authors focus on the meaning of the text for faith and life rather than on the technical questions that occupy scholars, and they explain the Bible in ordinary language that does not require translation for preaching and catechesis. Although this series is written from the perspective of Catholic faith, its authors draw on the interpretation of Protestant and Orthodox scholars and hope these volumes will serve Christians of other traditions as well.

A variety of features are designed to make the commentary as useful as possible. Each volume includes the biblical text of the New American Bible, Revised Edition (NABRE), the translation approved for liturgical use in the United States. In order to serve readers who use other translations, the commentary notes and explains the most important differences between the NABRE and other widely used translations (RSV, NRSV, JB, NJB, and NIV). Each unit of the biblical text is followed by a list of references to relevant Scripture passages, Catechism sections, and uses in the Roman Lectionary. The exegesis that follows aims to explain in a clear and engaging way the meaning of the text in its original historical context as well as its perennial meaning for Christians. Reflection and Application sections help readers apply Scripture to Christian life today by responding to questions that the text raises, offering spiritual interpretations drawn from Christian tradition or providing suggestions for the use of the biblical text in catechesis, preaching, or other forms of pastoral ministry.

Interspersed throughout the commentary are Biblical Background sidebars that present historical, literary, or theological information, and Living Tradition sidebars that offer pertinent material from the postbiblical Christian tradition, including quotations from Church documents and from the writings of saints and Church Fathers. The Biblical Background sidebars are indicated by a photo of urns that were excavated in Jerusalem, signifying the importance of historical study in understanding the sacred text. The Living Tradition sidebars are indicated by an image of Eadwine, a twelfth-century monk and scribe, signifying the growth in the Church's understanding that comes by the †grace of the Holy Spirit as believers study and ponder the word of God in their hearts (see *Dei Verbum* 8).

Maps and a glossary are included in each volume for easy reference. The glossary explains key terms from the biblical text as well as theological or exegetical terms, which are marked in the commentary with a cross (†). A list of suggested resources, an index of pastoral topics, and an index of sidebars are included to enhance the usefulness of these volumes. Further resources, including questions for reflection or discussion, can be found at the series website, www.CatholicScriptureCommentary.com.

It is our desire and prayer that these volumes be of service so that more and more "the word of the Lord may speed forward and be glorified" (2 Thess 3:1) in the Church and throughout the world.

Peter S. Williamson
Mary Healy
Kevin Perrotta

Note to Readers

The New American Bible, Revised Edition differs slightly from most English translations in its verse numbering of Psalms and certain other parts of the Old Testament. For instance, Ps 51:4 in the NABRE is Ps 51:2 in other translations; Mal 3:19 in the NABRE is Mal 4:1 in other translations. Readers who use different translations are advised to keep this in mind when looking up Old Testament cross-references given in the commentary.

Abbreviations

†	Indicates that a definition of the term appears in the glossary
//	Indicates where the same episode occurs in two or more Gospels
AB	Anchor Bible
ACCS 11	Ancient Christian Commentary on Scripture: New Testament 11, *James, 1–2 Peter, 1–3 John, Jude*, edited by Gerald Bray (Downers Grove, IL: InterVarsity, 2000)
ANTC	Abingdon New Testament Commentaries
BDAG	W. Bauer, F. W. Danker, W. F. Arndt, and F. W. Gingrich, *A Greek-English Lexicon of the New Testament and Other Early Christian Literature*, 3rd ed. (Chicago: University of Chicago Press, 2000)
BECNT	Baker Exegetical Commentary on the New Testament
BST	The Bible Speaks Today
c.	circa
Catechism	*Catechism of the Catholic Church*, 2nd ed. (New York: Doubleday, 2003)
CSS	Cistercian Studies Series
CWS	Classics of Western Spirituality
d.	died
DS	H. Denzinger and A. Schönmetzer, *Enchiridion Symbolorum: Definitionum et declarationum de rebus fidei et morum*. 33rd ed. (Barcelona: Herder, 1965)
DSBS	Daily Study Bible Series
ESV	English Standard Version
FC	Fathers of the Church
ICC	International Critical Commentary
ISB	Ignatius Study Bible
KJV	King James Version
Lectionary	*The Lectionary for Mass* (1998/2002 USA edition)
LXX	Septuagint
NAB	New American Bible
NABRE	New American Bible (Revised Edition, 2011)
NIGTC	New International Greek Testament Commentary
NIV	New International Version
NJB	New Jerusalem Bible
NPNF[1]	*Nicene and Post-Nicene Fathers*, First Series

NRSV	New Revised Standard Version
NT	New Testament
OT	Old Testament
OWC	Oxford World's Classics
PL	Patrologia Latina [= *Patrologiae Cursus Completus*: Series Latina], edited by J.-P. Migne, 217 vols. (Paris, 1844–64)
PNTC	Pillar New Testament Commentary
RSV	Revised Standard Version
SHBC	Smyth & Helwys Bible Commentary
SNTW	Studies of the New Testament and Its World
SP	Sacra Pagina
TWOT	R. L. Harris, G. L. Archer Jr., and B. K. Waltke, *Theological Wordbook of the Old Testament*, 2 vols. (Chicago: Moody, 1980)
v(v).	verse(s)
WBC	Word Biblical Commentary
WSA	The Works of Saint Augustine: A Translation for the 21st Century

Books of the Old Testament

Gen	Genesis	Tob	Tobit	Ezek	Ezekiel
Exod	Exodus	Jdt	Judith	Dan	Daniel
Lev	Leviticus	Esther	Esther	Hosea	Hosea
Num	Numbers	1 Macc	1 Maccabees	Joel	Joel
Deut	Deuteronomy	2 Macc	2 Maccabees	Amos	Amos
Josh	Joshua	Job	Job	Obad	Obadiah
Judg	Judges	Ps(s)	Psalm(s)	Jon	Jonah
Ruth	Ruth	Prov	Proverbs	Mic	Micah
1 Sam	1 Samuel	Eccles	Ecclesiastes	Nah	Nahum
2 Sam	2 Samuel	Song	Song of Songs	Hab	Habakkuk
1 Kings	1 Kings	Wis	Wisdom	Zeph	Zephaniah
2 Kings	2 Kings	Sir	Sirach	Hag	Haggai
1 Chron	1 Chronicles	Isa	Isaiah	Zech	Zechariah
2 Chron	2 Chronicles	Jer	Jeremiah	Mal	Malachi
Ezra	Ezra	Lam	Lamentations		
Neh	Nehemiah	Bar	Baruch		

Books of the New Testament

Matt	Matthew	Eph	Ephesians	Heb	Hebrews
Mark	Mark	Phil	Philippians	James	James
Luke	Luke	Col	Colossians	1 Pet	1 Peter
John	John	1 Thess	1 Thessalonians	2 Pet	2 Peter
Acts	Acts	2 Thess	2 Thessalonians	1 John	1 John
Rom	Romans	1 Tim	1 Timothy	2 John	2 John
1 Cor	1 Corinthians	2 Tim	2 Timothy	3 John	3 John
2 Cor	2 Corinthians	Titus	Titus	Jude	Jude
Gal	Galatians	Philem	Philemon	Rev	Revelation

Introduction to James

The brilliance of the Letter of James lies in its understanding of faith, the human person, and salvation. While at first glance the letter seems to contain simply a collection of counsels and exhortations about proper conduct, its message is actually much more profound. James holds that a person's change of behavior begins with a change of heart. Because inner attitudes affect outward behaviors, he probes the interiority of the person, explaining where evil tendencies arise, how to fight them, how to progress along the way to maturity, how to tell whether one is progressing or regressing, and, ultimately, how salvation is attained. Although the letter is not a systematic theological treatise, James manifests a beautiful understanding of the Christian life and provides a strong support for all those limping painfully along the path of perfection.

Who Is James?

The name "James" is the English rendering of the Greek *Iakōbos*, itself a Greek rendering of the Hebrew *Yaaqob*, which is translated as "Jacob" in English versions of the Old Testament. Jacob was the ancestor of the twelve tribes of Israel, and his name was common among Jews in the first century. Besides giving his name, the author of this letter identifies himself only as "a slave of God and of the Lord Jesus Christ" (1:1).[1] The lack of further introduction suggests that James is already well known to his readers. It also might indicate that he is an authoritative figure, since Church leaders like Peter, Paul, and Jude also refer

1. The Greek term *doulos* can mean either "slave" or "servant." Most English translations, such as the NRSV, NJB, and NIV, translate *doulos* in James 1:1 as "servant," but the NABRE translates it as "slave."

1

to themselves as slaves of Jesus Christ, and the Old Testament refers to Moses as a slave (in most translations, servant) of God.

Three important figures bear the name "James" in the New Testament, two of whom were among the original twelve apostles. The first, traditionally called James the Greater, was a son of Zebedee and brother of the apostle John (Matt 10:2; Mark 1:19–20). He was beheaded around AD 44 by Herod Agrippa I (Acts 12:1–2) and therefore probably died too early to have written the letter. The second, traditionally called James the Lesser, is referred to as the son of Alphaeus (Mark 3:18; Luke 6:15; Acts 1:13), but the New Testament says nothing more about him. The third James, who became a major leader of the church in Jerusalem, is referred to by Paul as "the brother of the Lord" and a "pillar" of the Jerusalem church (Gal 1:19; 2:9). Later writers, including the Church historian Eusebius (263–339), refer to him as the first †bishop of Jerusalem.[2] This James has traditionally been considered the author of our letter.

Saint Jerome took the view that the apostle James the son of Alphaeus was the same person as James the brother of the Lord. Because of

Wikimedia Commons

Figure 1. A nineteenth-century Russian Orthodox icon of James the Just

the respect accorded Jerome, this identification became a common though not authoritative opinion in the Western Church. However, today most scholars do not identify James the brother of the Lord with James the son of Alphaeus on account of the lack of evidence in the New Testament and other early Christian sources.[3]

A number of scholars have questioned the traditional attribution of the letter to James the brother of the Lord and have proposed that the epistle was written pseudonymously in the late first or even second century by an admirer

2. *Ecclesiastical History* 2.1.2.
3. Luke Timothy Johnson, *The Letter of James: A New Translation with Introduction and Commentary*, AB 37A (New York: Doubleday, 1995), 93.

of James who wished to perpetuate his teaching.[4] This position is suggested for three reasons. First, the slow pace at which the Church accepted this book as part of the †canon of Scripture implies that there were doubts regarding its authorship. The Letter of James is not included in the Muratorian Canon (a list of approved books, c. 170), it is not mentioned by name by ecclesiastical writers before Origen, and its canonical status is described as disputed in the early fourth century by Eusebius.[5] Second, some scholars have doubted that a Galilean peasant could write such polished, elegant Greek as is found in James. Third, some have doubted whether enough time had passed before AD 62, when James was martyred, for a letter to have been written in response to Paul's teaching about faith and works.[6]

Recent commentaries, however, have generally moved away from the view that James is a pseudonymous composition. Some suggest that the letter presents the oral teaching of James the Lord's brother, written down by a disciple and circulated as a letter.[7] Others find no compelling reason to reject the tradition that the letter was actually written by James. The late acceptance into the New Testament canon could be due to the mistrust of Jewish Christianity that characterized the predominantly Gentile Church during the second to fourth centuries. As to the letter's polished language, the example of the Jewish historian Josephus shows that a first-century Jew could learn to write excellent Greek; even a humble background in Galilee would not necessarily exclude a gifted person from acquiring facility in that language. Finally, it is quite likely that an important figure like James would have made use of an amanuensis (a writing assistant), which could likewise account for the letter's fine Greek style. As regards the date of James in relation to Paul's writing on faith and works, Galatians is generally dated in the early to mid-fifties, which would have allowed adequate time for James to have responded to problematic interpretations of Paul before his death in AD 62. Also, the letter appears to have been written earlier than the advocates of pseudonymous authorship suggest, since it shows no knowledge of the Roman conquest of Jerusalem and destruction of the temple in AD 70, nor does it mention the more highly developed Church

4. See Martin Dibelius, *James*, rev. Heinrich Greeven, Hermeneia (Philadelphia: Fortress, 1976), 17–21; Udo Schnelle, *The History and Theology of the New Testament Writings*, trans. M. Eugene Boring (Minneapolis: Fortress, 1994), 388; Raymond E. Brown, *An Introduction to the New Testament* (New York: Doubleday, 1997), 741–42.

5. *Ecclesiastical History* 3.25.3

6. J. A. Motyer, *The Message of James: The Tests of Faith*, BST (Downers Grove, IL: InterVarsity, 1985), 18.

7. Ralph P. Martin, *James*, WBC 48 (Waco: Word, 1988), lxxvi–lxxvii; Patrick J. Hartin, *James*, SP 14 (Collegeville, MN: Liturgical Press, 2003), 24–25.

structure depicted in 1 Timothy and Titus. The letter also contains references to Jesus' ethical teaching without using the formulations found in the Synoptic Gospels, suggesting that James may have written prior to the solidifying of the tradition in written form.

What do we know about James the brother of Jesus? There are a few indications in the Gospels that Jesus' relatives did not initially accept him as the †Messiah (Mark 3:20–21; 6:1–4; John 7:5), although nothing explicit is said about James in this regard. James later became the leader of the Jerusalem church (Acts 12:17; 21:18; Gal 2:9). His most important contribution recorded in the New Testament was his leading role at the Council of Jerusalem, where he taught that converted †Gentiles need not follow the regulations of the Mosaic law (†Torah) and proposed instead that they merely abstain from eating meat of animals offered to idols, from unlawful marriages, from the meat of strangled animals, and from consuming blood (Acts 15:13–21).

Paul mentions James in both Galatians and 1 Corinthians. In Gal 1:19 Paul recounts his journey to meet Peter, noting, "I did not see any other of the apostles, only James the brother of the Lord," suggesting that Paul regarded James as an apostle, although the Greek text here is ambiguous.[8] Paul considered James one of the "pillars" of the church in Jerusalem (Gal 2:9) and presented his preaching of the †gospel to him, along with Peter and John, seeking their confirmation (Gal 2:2–6). In 1 Cor 15:3–7, Paul lists James alongside those to whom the resurrected Jesus appeared, indicating his importance to the first generation of Christians.

In the early Church, Origen (d. 253), Clement of Alexandria (d. 215), and Jerome (d. 420) referred to him as "James the Just," a testimony to his righteous and devout conduct.[9] Eusebius of Caesarea recounts a tradition from the writing of the chronicler Hegesippus (110–80) regarding James's holiness and solicitude for his flock:

> He was in the habit of entering alone into the temple, and was frequently found upon his knees begging forgiveness for the people, so that his knees became hard like those of a camel, in consequence of his constantly bending them in his worship of God, and asking forgiveness for the people.[10]

Two important accounts of the martyrdom of James at the hands of Jewish authorities in Jerusalem have come down to us. The Jewish historian Josephus

8. See Johnson, *Letter of James*, 94.
9. Origen, *Against Celsus* 1.47; Clement, quoted in Eusebius, *Ecclesiastical History* 2.1.4; Jerome, *On Illustrious Men* 2.1, 3.
10. *Ecclesiastical History* 2.23.6.

(d. AD 100) recounts that James was put to death in AD 62 under the high priest Ananus II, a Sadducee, whom Josephus describes as arrogant and harsh in his judgments.

> Ananus saw he had the opportunity to act since Festus [the Roman prefect] was now dead and Albinus [Festus's replacement] was but upon the road. So he assembled the Sanhedrin of judges, and brought before them the brother of Jesus who was called Christ, whose name was James, and some others . . . ; and when he had formed an accusation against them as breakers of the law, he delivered them to be stoned.[11]

Some of the leading Jewish citizens of Jerusalem objected to the killing of James and appealed against Ananus to Albinus on his arrival. The result, Josephus reports, was that King Agrippa removed Ananus from his post as high priest after he had held that position for only three months.[12]

Eusebius provides a longer account:

> After Paul, in consequence of his appeal to Caesar, had been sent to Rome by Festus, the Jews, being frustrated in their hope of entrapping him by the snares which they had laid for him, turned against James, the brother of the Lord, to whom the episcopal seat at Jerusalem had been entrusted by the apostles. The following daring measures were undertaken by them against him. Leading him into their midst they demanded of him that he should renounce faith in Christ in the presence of all the people. But, contrary to the opinion of all, with a clear voice, and with greater boldness than they had anticipated, he spoke out before the whole multitude and confessed that our Savior and Lord Jesus is the Son of God. But they were unable to bear longer the testimony of the man who, on account of the excellence of ascetic virtue and of piety which he exhibited in his life, was esteemed by all as the most just of men, and consequently they slew him.[13]

Audience

James addresses his letter to "the twelve tribes in the dispersion" (1:1). "Twelve tribes" seems to indicate those Jews who had accepted Jesus as the Messiah and were dispersed or scattered away from Palestine, the promised land. But Gentile Christians also considered themselves to be part of the renewed Israel, and

---

11. *Jewish Antiquities* 20.200.
12. *Jewish Antiquities* 20.201–3.
13. *Ecclesiastical History* 2.23.1–2. Although Eusebius's version simply says that "the Jews" turned against James, Josephus's account indicates that many leading Jews in Jerusalem were unhappy enough about Ananus's execution of James to appeal successfully for his removal.

1 Peter, which is written to Gentile Christians, begins "to the chosen sojourners of the dispersion" (1:1). Thus the Letter of James could be addressed to either Jewish or Gentile Christians. But given that the letter does not address the vices that Jews typically associated with Gentiles (idolatry, sexual promiscuity) and focuses attention on the Mosaic law and refers to the community as a "synagogue" (2:2 [literal translation]), it is more likely that the letter was written to Jewish Christians.[14] What is most probable is that James the Just, bishop of Jerusalem, heard of problems in the Jewish Christian communities around the Mediterranean and sent a circular letter to these churches to encourage them to amend their ways and persevere in the midst of trials.

James addresses his audience as "brothers" and even "beloved brothers," but he has no qualms about sternly rebuking them, using words such as "ignoramus," "adulterers," and "sinners." He consistently uses the second personal plural "you." When addressing the problem of favoritism, he says, "If a man with gold rings on his fingers and in fine clothes comes into *your* assembly . . ." (2:2); on the necessity of works he says, "If a brother or sister has nothing to wear and has no food for the day, and *one of you* says to them, 'Go in peace, keep warm, and eat well' . . ." (2:15–16). Admonishing them for factions and divisions, he asks, "Where do the wars and where do the conflicts among *you* come from?" (4:1).[15] James's pattern of addressing his readers as "brothers," coupled with his honest, straightforward criticism, indicates his concern for the holiness and salvation of his audience. The letter is not a generic writing on holiness but a letter written by a pastor-teacher who is very aware of the concrete problems in the Christian communities to which he is writing.

It seems that the intended readers of James are struggling with both internal divisions and external pressure. The first verses of the letter indicate that they are undergoing temptations and trials (1:2–5). While this might refer to persecutions by outsiders, James also makes it clear that there are problems within the community, since he chastises his readers for flapping their tongues, showing favoritism toward the rich, and allowing factions to develop. But the latter part of the letter also suggests that these Christians are suffering oppression at the hand of the rich and powerful. In reference to these people, James adopts the tone of the Old Testament prophets who announced judgment, warning the rich of their impending condemnation because they are oppressing the righteous poor (5:1–6). In response to the painful situations caused by the Christians' own lack of faith and charity, James counsels deeper conversion by repentance

14. Brown, *Introduction to the New Testament*, 742.
15. See Dan G. McCartney, *James*, BECNT (Grand Rapids: Baker Academic, 2009), 32.

and humble reception of the word that has been planted in them. In response to oppression at the hands of rich and powerful outsiders, James counsels patient perseverance and prayer, and he reminds his audience of the fate of the wicked.

Genre

Scholars debate whether the Letter of James can rightly be called a letter since it lacks some typical characteristics of letters at that time, such as a prayer-wish at the beginning, a personal greeting at the end, and the names of at least some of his addressees. Some suggest that the letter originally circulated as a written sermon and was later put into the form of a letter by the addition of an opening greeting.[16] However, the presence of the standard Greek salutation in 1:1, "greetings" (*chairein*), and the concluding exhortation to call a brother or sister back from sin, without any final greeting, suggest that the work was always a letter. This ending, which seems strange to us, is quite similar to the endings of 1 John and Jude. The First Letter of John finishes by exhorting the community to pray for sinners, and the Letter of Jude challenges readers to act on behalf of an erring brother or sister, indicating that early Christians had an alternative way of concluding letters that was different from that of Paul.[17] Finally, the letter's lack of personal greetings of individuals by name is similar to other "diaspora letters." These were letters that were sent from Judea by someone of recognized authority for circulation among Jews living outside the land of Israel and that offered advice on how to maintain integrity as the people of God in a foreign land.[18] If, as seems likely, James's letter was meant to serve the needs of Jewish Christians in a variety of places, it is perfectly natural that no individuals are singled out for a personal greeting.

Literary Features

James is a master teacher and uses a variety of literary techniques to keep his readers' attention and make them reflect more deeply. He likes paradoxes, teaching that those suffering temptations should rejoice (1:2) and that the poor should exult in their high standing while the rich should boast of their lowliness (1:9–10). James employs a lively array of similes and metaphors drawn from ordinary life, including the waves of the sea (1:6); sun, grass, and flowers

16. Brown, *Introduction to the New Testament*, 726.
17. Hartin, *James*, 286.
18. McCartney (*James*, 39) points out other diaspora letters in 2 Macc 1:1–2:18; Bar 6; Acts 15:23–29.

(1:10–11); mirrors (1:23); dead bodies (2:26); horses and ships (3:3–4); fire (3:5–6); fresh and salty water (3:11); and corroded metal (5:3). These techniques engage readers and allow them to enter more fully into what is being said.

Since James is written as a letter of exhortation, it is natural that imperative verbs predominate. In 108 verses there are some 59 imperatives, more than in any other book. These usually are followed by reasons why the instructions should be followed.[19] James's sentences usually are short, producing a staccato rhythm and a sober tone.

Theological Themes

Faith, Works, and the Law

A predominant theme of this letter is the strict relationship between faith and works (especially 2:14–26). For James, a saving faith does not consist in simply believing that God exists, but must be "completed by the works" (2:22) that accord with faith. Mere belief without corresponding action (2:15–16)— "faith alone" (2:24)—does not justify, but is "dead" and "useless" (2:17, 20, 26). Instead, faith must be accompanied by conduct that manifests the new life in Christ.

James seems to be responding to a misinterpretation of Paul's important teaching that Christians are justified by faith rather than works (Rom 3:28; Gal 2:16; Eph 2:8–9). It is clear from the Pauline Letters that faith should be completed by works, and that Christian conduct is crucial.[20] Paul's emphasis on faith arose from two concerns. First, he needed to counter the Judaizers, who taught that Gentile Christians needed to be circumcised and observe the ritual elements of the law of Moses. Second, he considered it important for everyone to realize that salvation in Christ is a gift from God, not something that anyone can earn or achieve by human effort (Eph 2:8–9; Phil 3:9; 2 Tim 1:9).

Far from contradicting these points, James himself identifies the gospel, the "word of truth" (1:18 [see 1:21]), as the means of our salvation. And even though he writes to Jewish Christians who probably continue to practice circumcision and observe the dietary laws, James focuses on the ethical aspects of the law, especially the "royal law" that Jesus himself prioritized, "You shall love your neighbor as yourself" (James 2:8; Lev 19:18; Mark 12:31), which Paul also teaches (Rom 13:8–10; Gal 5:14).

19. Johnson, *Letter of James*, 8.
20. See Rom 6:12–23; Gal 5:6, 19–21; Eph 2:10; Titus 2:7, 14; 3:8.

Ethical Conduct in Daily Life

Which works illustrate that one has saving faith? For James, "religion that is pure and undefiled before God and the Father is this: to care for orphans and widows" (1:27). James advocates care for the poor and warns of the danger of riches. God has chosen the poor in the †world (2:5), but the rich will suffer the judgment of God (5:1–6). A Christian ought to care for the material needs of the poor and not show favoritism to the wealthy. In keeping with this theme, James says that one should not be greedy or a lover of the world (4:1–5), and that employers should pay their workers' wages promptly (5:1–5).

When it comes to personal comportment, the height of perfection is evidenced when a person controls the tongue. Mastery over speech indicates spiritual maturity; the life of a person whose words are uncontrolled burns with the fire that his or her speech produces. James devotes a great deal of the letter to admonishing his readers against sins of the tongue such as cursing (3:9–10), slander (4:11–12), and boasting (4:16). Finally, James instructs his readers to conduct themselves with gentleness and mercy (2:13; 3:17) and to pray, no matter the circumstances they find themselves in (5:13–18).

Humility and Double-Mindedness

James's explanation of the lack of charity among some who profess to love Jesus is simple: they are unfaithful in their relationship with God ("Adulterers!" [4:4])—that is, in their hearts they have not fully surrendered to him and been transformed by his love. According to James the primary way to overcome this defect is to embrace an attitude of humility before God.[21] The alternate path that James warns against most is that of being double-minded (1:8; 4:8; 5:12). The double-minded person has not completely submitted to the will of the Lord (4:7) and thus is a slave of personal passions (1:14–15) and someone whose prayers focus on material gain (4:3). The person's lack of interior unity is manifested in exterior conflict. Wars, factions, bias toward the rich, speaking evil of others, boasting, disorder, and "every foul practice" indicate a person who is divided within.[22]

James's strategy for overcoming these behaviors is not to recommend a rigorous program of self-discipline, but rather to urge his readers to humbly welcome the word of the gospel that has been planted within them, to ask God

21. See James 1:9, 21; 3:13; 4:6, 10.
22. See James 2:9; 3:14, 16; 4:11, 16.

for the wisdom they need, and to repent (1:5, 21; 4:7–10). Through humility and repentance, we can obtain God's grace and be lifted up by God himself (4:6, 10). Thus, James makes it clear that a good relationship with God is a gift to be received, and not something earned. Only by turning to the Lord can a person reach spiritual maturity, and this requires profound humility and thoroughgoing repentance.

The Two Ways

Sharp contrasts inform not just James's view of a faith-filled life but all aspects of his worldview: there is a wisdom from above and a wisdom from below (3:13–18), self-exaltation or submission (4:7, 16), a way to life and a way to death (1:12–18). For James, a person either has saving faith or does not: one keeps the whole law or is guilty in respect to all of it (2:10); one is a friend of God or an enemy (4:4); one is a doer of the law or only a hearer (1:22–25); one blesses or curses (3:10); one produces pure or salty water (3:11); and one is either filthy or pure (1:21, 27). There is no middle road; waffling and indecision amount to choosing against God. Faith requires a total commitment to the ways of God, and one's charitable actions demonstrate one's faith.

Anointing of the Sick

In keeping with an apostolic practice mentioned in Mark 6:13, James 5:14–15 teaches the importance of anointing the sick with oil. Largely on the basis of this passage, the Church recognizes the anointing of the sick as a sacrament instituted by Jesus Christ.[23]

The Timeliness of James

While still a young abbot, Bernard of Clairvaux said, "There are more people converted from mortal sin to grace than there are religious converted from good to better."[24] What the saint noted among the monks of his community could be applied to many of us today and is cause for reflection. Some people go to Mass every Sunday year after year and say rosary after rosary yet never become holy—that is, spiritually mature. Wholehearted disciples seem to be few and far

---

23. Council of Trent Fourteenth Session (1551), "Doctrine on the Sacrament of Extreme Unction," 1.1 (DS 1695).
24. Thomas Dubay, *Deep Conversion, Deep Prayer* (San Francisco: Ignatius Press, 2006), 12.

between, and Jesus' call to holiness is brushed off as too lofty and unrealistic. But James insists on spiritual perfection for *all* his listeners and shows that the way to get there is a deep conversion that flows from humility and repentance. The Letter of James echoes Jesus' words, "Be perfect, just as your heavenly Father is perfect" (Matt 5:48). James invites us to make an honest interior search to see where we are double-minded, where we have not submitted to Jesus, and where we are seeking the things below instead of the things above.

James's challenge to confront the sin in ourselves is provocative, and even painful. Who doesn't need to bridle the tongue? Who can claim to have never judged anyone? Who never shows favoritism? And who consistently acts with gentleness and mercy? Human nature, sin, and temptations do not change, and the interior battle for holiness that James's audience fought then is the same that we Christians fight today. James, like Jesus, taught that holiness is not only possible but is an imperative for every Christian. The Letter of James, written by a godly man who knew, spoke with, and touched Jesus Christ and who walked the arduous path to perfection before us, can serve as a beautiful guide for all who want to live a deeper life with Jesus, a life where charity and peace reign, where wisdom and mercy abound, and where holiness becomes possible.

Special thanks to Sr. M. Ancilla Matter, FSGM, who was a true handmaid of the Lord in the preparation and writing of this manuscript. To her I dedicate this writing.

Kelly Anderson

Outline of James

Greeting

James 1:1

---

¹James, a slave of God and of the Lord Jesus Christ, to the twelve tribes in the dispersion, greetings.

OT: 1 Kings 8:53, 66; Ps 90:13, 16; Isa 11:1–10; Ezek 47:13
NT: 1 Cor 15:3–8; Gal 2:9; Acts 12:17; 15:1–31
Catechism: perpetual virginity of Mary, 499–501, 510

Letters written in Greek in the first century typically began with three elements: **1:1** the sender, the addressee, and the greeting. This letter begins with all three. The sender is **James,** one of the most prominent figures in early Christianity, known as "the brother of the Lord" (Gal 1:19) and leader of the Jerusalem church (Acts 12:17; 15:13; 21:18), whom the fourth-century Church historian Eusebius refers to as the first †bishop of Jerusalem (see introduction). But James identifies himself as **a slave of God**. The fact that James does not stress his familial relationship with Jesus or his leadership position in the Jerusalem church, but identifies as a slave, shows a profound humility.[1] The term "slave" (*doulos*) refers to a person who is the property of another. The Old Testament refers to the Israelites as "slaves" or "servants" of God (Pss 90:13, 16; 102:15, 29) and uses the term as a title of honor for Moses, David, and the prophets (1 Kings 8:53, 66; Jer 7:25). In the New Testament, Christian leaders sometimes refer to themselves by this

---

1. Many translations render this phrase as "servant of God" to avoid associations with the degrading enslavement of Africans in the seventeenth to nineteenth centuries most familiar to American readers. Generally speaking, the practice of slavery in ancient Israel and Rome was more humane, as evidenced by the fact that when offered their freedom, it was not uncommon for slaves to choose to remain in that condition, motivated by love for their master or the desire for financial security.

term (see introduction). By calling himself "a slave of God," James emphasizes his position as one who belongs to God and lives in humble obedience to him.

James also identifies himself as a slave **of the Lord Jesus Christ**, indicating his aim to follow in the footsteps of Jesus, the servant of the Lord par excellence, who through his obedient suffering ransomed many (Isa 53:11). By pairing Jesus with God, James places the two on the same level. James uses two titles for Jesus: "Lord" and "Christ." The first title, "Lord," was the title for God in the Greek Old Testament, and in the New Testament it is applied to Jesus to acknowledge him as God (1 Cor 8:6; Phil 2:11). James uses "Lord" both for Jesus (2:1) and for God the Father (3:9). The second title, "Christ," is the Greek form of the Hebrew word "†messiah," which means "anointed one." In the Old Testament, "messiah" originally referred to Israel's anointed king, but it came to refer to the descendant of David who would come and save his people from their enemies (Isa 11:1–10; Luke 1:69–75). In calling Jesus the Messiah, James, with the early Church, confesses his belief that Jesus is the promised one whom the prophets foretold, and that the fulfillment of the messianic hopes of Israel is realized in him.

The recipients of the letter are **the twelve tribes**, which is a reference to Israel. The nation Israel was composed of twelve tribes descended from the patriarch Jacob. Ten of those tribes virtually disappeared from history after being exiled by the Assyrians in 721 BC, but the Old Testament and later Jewish writings speak of the hope of the restoration and reconstitution of the twelve tribes.[2] James understands the Church as the fulfillment of this restoration, which Jesus Christ has initiated (see 1:18).

The **dispersion**, or diaspora, refers to the large number of Jews who resided outside the land of Israel. Faithful to their religion, they built synagogues and sought to follow the teachings of Moses. The first Christians were Jewish, and the †gospel message was first preached in their synagogues. James, whose pastoral ministry was directed to Jewish Christians (Acts 21:18–25; Gal 2:9), seems to be writing a letter for Jewish Christians scattered throughout the Mediterranean world.

Finally, James finishes his salutation by offering **greetings**—literally, "rejoice" (Greek *chairein*). The typical greeting among Jews was "peace" (Hebrew *shalom*). James's word choice is more typical of the Hellenistic world; perhaps he chooses this greeting to lead into his exhortation to have "joy" (*chara*) in the next verse (1:2).

---

2. Ezek 47:13; *Testament of Benjamin* 9:2; *Psalms of Solomon* 17:26; *War Scroll* 2.1–3. See Dan G. McCartney, *James*, BECNT (Grand Rapids: Baker Academic, 2009), 79.

Trials and Joy

James 1:2–11

What question would you most like to ask God? When I pose this to a parish or prayer group audience, people invariably bring up the problem of suffering. God's goodness seems incompatible with the presence of evil and suffering in the †world, and intense suffering sometimes tempts people to abandon their faith. The next-most-common topic concerns unanswered prayers: it sometimes seems that God does not listen or care. I find it interesting that it is precisely with these two heart-wrenching issues that the Letter of James begins. Without ceremony, the author dives into two of the most profound difficulties of Christian life that we share with readers two millennia ago. James does not attempt a comprehensive treatise on the problem of suffering or on unanswered prayer. Rather, he teaches how suffering can be beneficial to a person's growth and why some prayers may not be answered.

James's thought is not always easy to follow, but if we pay close attention to his words, his logic begins to emerge. The first section of his letter features a series of six imperatives: the first two concern trials and how one should cope with them (vv. 2–4); the second two teach on prayer (vv. 5–8); and the last two shed light on how to regard one's social standing (vv. 9–11).

Trials, Testing, and Perseverance (1:2–4)

²Consider it all joy, my brothers, when you encounter various trials,
³for you know that the testing of your faith produces perseverance. ⁴And

let perseverance be perfect, so that you may be perfect and complete, lacking in nothing.

OT: Pss 34:19–20; 119:69–71; 138:7–8; Sir 2:1–6
NT: Rom 5:3–5, 20; 8:28; 12:12; Eph 6:18; Col 1:22–23; Heb 3:14; 1 Pet 1:6–7
Catechism: providence and the scandal of evil, 309–14

James begins his letter by offering startling advice on how to respond to suffering. He leads off with two imperatives: "consider it all joy" (v. 2) and "let perseverance be perfect" (v. 4). After each exhortation he offers a reason: "testing . . . produces perseverance" (v. 3), and perseverance will make us "perfect and complete" (v. 4). Each movement points to the next: trials lead to perseverance, perseverance should be perfect, so the person can reach spiritual maturity. In short, trials can lead to human perfection.

1:2–3   James's first directive is **Consider it all joy** when encountering **trials**. By using the word **encounter**, he suggests that trials are met, stumbled upon, or even bumped into in the course of our lives. They are of **various** kinds, including sickness, poverty, abandonment, death—in a word, the full range of painful human experience. "To consider" means to take a certain view of reality. Difficult situations often have different causes or meanings than what appears on the surface, so if we are able to view them in the light of God's plan, we will be able to see them in true perspective.[1] When James asks his readers to consider their trials as joy, he is not urging them to play mental games or force themselves to think absurd thoughts. For James, suffering really can be considered "all joy." But how can that be? Let us examine James's logic.

James equates the trials with a **testing of your faith**. James could mean that suffering is a test because it tempts us to doubt God's goodness and love when we are suffering. But more likely he means that the trials have another purpose, which is the strengthening of our faith. For James, faith means more than just belief in God; faith means a life lived in fidelity, commitment, and truth; it entails an interior commitment to God that is expressed in concrete behavior. According to James, a person's faith is tested, proven, and fortified through trials. Since faith is so important for a Christian, anything that strengthens our faith must be considered as positive, even trials and suffering. So James's idea is not that trials are a cause for joy, but that their *fruit* is.

For James, the **perseverance** or "steadfastness" (RSV) that trials produce is one of the most desirable qualities that a Christian can have, and it is a key theme

---

1. Paul tells us that Jesus did not consider his equality with God something to be held on to (Phil 2:6); Paul himself considers everything as a loss in light of Jesus Christ (Phil 3:7–8); and Peter teaches his readers to consider the delay of the †parousia as God's patience (2 Pet 3:15).

of his letter. To persevere means to endure whatever comes without allowing distress or any external circumstances to sway one's convictions, thinking, or way of life.[2] Throughout the letter James reproves those who "change," who are unstable (1:8), double-minded (1:8; 4:8), tossed about by the wind (1:6), or whose lifestyle causes them to fade away in the midst of their pursuits (1:11) (see sidebar, "The Wise Person and the Fool," p. 76). These descriptions refer to people who lack a firm faith and passively allow external circumstances to direct their lives. James, however, praises the person who perseveres with Job-like patience (5:11), the one who stays the course no matter what comes, because this person has come to a firm inner conviction to follow Jesus Christ and evidences such commitment by endurance. Such stalwart perseverance, according to James, is the fruit of trials.

Building on the previous verse, James gives his second exhortation: **let per-** **1:4**
severance be perfect. "Perfect" (*teleios*) expresses the idea of completeness or wholeness, so perfect perseverance means to be entirely committed to following Jesus to the end, no matter what trials arise.

James employs three nearly synonymous expressions to describe the desired effect of perseverance: **that you may be perfect and complete, lacking in nothing**. In the New Testament the adjective "perfect" (or its verbal cognate) is sometimes used to describe a person who is spiritually mature, someone who has an undivided heart for God.[3] This is the opposite of being double-minded. A person who is complete and lacking in nothing is one who is pleasing to God and is ready to meet Jesus when he returns (5:7–12).

Saints Peter and Paul also teach the value of perseverance in trials. Peter says that "for a little while you may have to suffer through various trials, so that the genuineness of your faith, more precious than gold that is perishable even though tested by fire, may prove to be for praise, glory, and honor at the revelation of Jesus Christ" (1 Pet 1:6–7); and Paul says, "We even boast of our afflictions, knowing that affliction produces endurance"—the same Greek word translated here as "perseverance"—"and endurance, proven character, and proven character, hope" (Rom 5:3–4). All three saintly men—James, Peter, and Paul—teach that sufferings can prepare a person for his or her final destiny, an encounter with Jesus Christ. Hebrews 5:8–9 teaches that Jesus himself had to suffer to become perfect: "Son though he was, he learned obedience from what he suffered; and when he was made perfect, he became the source of eternal salvation for all who obey him" (see also Heb 2:10).

2. Dan G. McCartney, *James*, BECNT (Grand Rapids: Baker Academic, 2009), 87.
3. See Matt 5:48; 19:21; Phil 3:12; Heb 2:10.

James's bold teaching is not easy to accept and requires a considerable amount of faith. He asks his listeners to revamp their entire way of looking at suffering and to consider it in light of our final destiny: eternal life with God. James considers nothing more important than an interior commitment to God that is lived out consistently, and since trials can help produce that commitment and bring spiritual maturity, they should be regarded as an occasion for joy. To accept James's teaching entails seeing every aspect of life as part of God's mysterious plan of love. This means believing that our every moment is contained within the sovereign plan of a God who tenderly keeps track even of the sparrows (Luke 12:6–7), and in whose hands even suffering and evil become instruments to bring about a greater good (Rom 8:28; Catechism 309–13). But James is a realist. He appreciates how challenging it is to view trials positively, and so he addresses this issue in the next section.

Asking in Faith for Wisdom (1:5–8)

---

[5]But if any of you lacks wisdom, he should ask God who gives to all generously and ungrudgingly, and he will be given it. [6]But he should ask in faith, not doubting, for the one who doubts is like a wave of the sea that is driven and tossed about by the wind. [7]For that person must not suppose that he will receive anything from the Lord, [8]since he is a man of two minds, unstable in all his ways.

OT: 2 Chron 1:7–12; Prov 2:1–8; Isa 55:6–9
NT: Matt 7:7–11 // Luke 11:9–13; Mark 11:22–24; Luke 18:1–8; Phil 4:5–7
Catechism: persevering in prayer, 2742–45; desire for God, 2560–61

James finished the previous section by saying that the person who is perfect in perseverance will not lack anything. He begins this section advising readers who might lack wisdom that they can ask for it.

1:5   James implies that in order to consider trials as all joy and to become perfect, a person needs wisdom (James will describe wisdom in 3:13–18). Wisdom supplies the divine perspective that enables a person to withstand trials without giving up.[4] Wisdom enables a person to live in a godly, virtuous manner, especially in moments of suffering. This spiritual maturity is a gift from God that we cannot attain by our own efforts, so our task is to **ask God** for the gift of wisdom. Since wisdom can be obtained only through prayer, James strongly

---

4. Peter H. Davids, *The Epistle of James: A Commentary on the Greek Text*, NIGTC (Grand Rapids: Eerdmans, 1982), 70; McCartney, *James*, 138.

exhorts his readers who are enduring trials and who know that they lack wisdom to turn to God. God's nature is to give, and he gives wisdom **generously and ungrudgingly**. No one need be concerned about stinginess or reluctance on the part of God because God wants us to turn to him for the help we need (Luke 11:9–13; 12:30–32; 18:7–8). First Kings 3:5–12 tells how Solomon asked for and received wisdom; the book of Wisdom affirms that God will give wisdom to anyone who seeks it ardently and with a pure heart, as Solomon did (Wis 8:2,

Wisdom

BIBLICAL BACKGROUND

The Old Testament has much to say about wisdom and the wise, devoting an entire corpus of books to the subject. Wisdom is associated with discernment (Gen 41:39; Deut 1:13), understanding (Exod 36:1; 1 Kings 5:9), experience (Deut 1:13), and knowledge (Job 34:2). It is also related to training, discipline, and discretion (Prov 1:2–5). Wisdom is practical and enables a person to succeed in life; the opposite of conducting one's life according to wisdom is to be a fool (Prov 12:15).

The Old Testament also teaches that wisdom cannot be acquired solely by human effort (Job 28:1–28) because it is a gift from God (Prov 2:6; Dan 2:21). In one of the earliest mentions of wisdom in the Bible, God gives this gift specifically to prepare for liturgical worship: the metalworkers, embroiderers, weavers, and builders of the tabernacle receive "a divine spirit of skill and understanding and knowledge" (Exod 31:3). A repeated theme of Scripture is that wisdom is grounded in a right relationship to God and manifests itself in righteous conduct; for example, "The fear of the Lord is wisdom; / and avoiding evil is understanding" (Job 28:28).

James uses the term "wisdom" only in 1:5 and 3:13–18. He follows the Old Testament by reiterating that wisdom comes from God (3:17), that one must pray in order to be wise (1:5), and that wisdom leads to success in life, success measured in terms of fidelity and perseverance in doing God's will. When James speaks of wisdom in 1:5, he especially has in mind the divine help that sustains a person in trial, the ability to trust in God's goodness in the midst of suffering and pain. Pope Benedict XVI eloquently describes this kind of wisdom:

> In the presence of suffering and grief, true wisdom is to allow oneself to acknowledge the precariousness of life and to read human history with God's eyes. He always and only desires the good of his children; in his inscrutable plan of love he sometimes allows them to be tested by sorrow to lead them to a greater good.[a]

a. "On the Suffering the Lord Allows," Sunday Angelus, March 7, 2010.

9, 21; 9:18). James continues this tradition and teaches that a person can obtain help from God to navigate life's stormy trials simply by asking.

1:6–8   James now turns to his second instruction, which concerns prayer. One should **ask in faith**, with the confident expectation of a child who knows that the Father always and only gives good things (Luke 11:13). Those who ask in faith—that is, those who ardently desire wisdom to live well in their times of trial—will not be denied. The faith that is necessary is an act of trust in God's character and promises; it is holding fast to God as sons and daughters because God is trustworthy. There is no duplicity in God, and he wants only our good and salvation (John 10:10; 1 Tim 2:3–4). Since God is faithful, we can trust him even in adversity and misfortune. Faith, then, is to entrust ourselves to God's care and providence, knowing that his will is perfect for us. James assures us that God will never refuse the gifts we need to live out our Christian vocation. God desires our eternal salvation and will give to us everything we need to walk the path to that destination.

At this point, James uses three expressions to describe the kind of person whose prayers will *not* be answered. In referring to the person **who doubts**, James does not condemn someone who struggles with intellectual uncertainty about some point of Christian doctrine, or someone like Job, who in the midst of his suffering passionately questions God. Rather, the word translated as "doubt" (*diakrinomai*) refers to being undecided between alternatives and here describes someone whose fundamental allegiance is not firmly fixed. It refers to a person who has not come to a firm, interior decision to trust in God's character and promises. James compares such a person to a sea wave **driven and tossed about by the wind**. The passive verbs indicate that the doubter is moved and persuaded by exterior forces because he or she is not steadied by inner convictions. James also describes the person as being **of two minds** (*dipsychos*, literally, "of two souls"). This could refer to a hypocrite, one who pretends to hold a certain position but actually does not; however, in the context of the letter it probably refers to someone who has not settled on a course of life and wants both to live a Christian faith and to embrace the †world (4:4; see 1 John 2:15–16). Such a person is divided and not whole (1:4). Consequently, this person is **unstable**—that is, easily swayed from living as a Christian by disordered desires or false teaching. This person's hesitancy or indecision, which is the opposite of faith, indicates an unwillingness to place all trust in God. In such a condition, he or she is the opposite of the one who perseveres (see 1:3–4).

To sum up, in this section James teaches that wisdom is necessary to successfully navigate trials. Wisdom is available for the asking, but asking requires faith, an interior opening to †grace, and a wholehearted adherence to God's will.

Believe in God

Saint Augustine explains the meaning of faith in a sermon on the Creed:

> "I believe in God, the Father Almighty." In the first place, beloved, note well with what word the Creed begins: "I believe." . . . It does not say "I believe God is truly God" nor "I trust in God," though these are necessary for salvation. . . . To trust that what God has said is true is possible for many, even for evil people. They believe it to be true, but they refuse to follow it because they are lazy. And it is possible even for demons to believe that God is indeed God. But to believe in God is possible only for those who love him.[a]

a. Author's translation.

Reflection and Application (1:5–8)

Jesus is both the teacher and model of prayer. Pope John Paul II said, "Human history knows of no other personage who was so fully—and in such a way—absorbed in prayer with God, as was Jesus of Nazareth."[5] The Gospels show prayer to be thoroughly woven into the fabric of Jesus' life: he withdraws to pray in the course of his ministry (Mark 1:35; Luke 5:15–16; 9:18); he prays before decisive actions (Luke 6:12–13; John 11:41–42) and at significant moments of his life (Matt 4:1–2; Luke 3:21; 9:28–29; Mark 14:32–42).[6]

Jesus' prayer during his agony in the garden (Mark 14:32–42) can teach us something of the prayer that James advocates. Distraught before his impending suffering (v. 33), Jesus turns to God and makes his appeal as Son: "Abba, Father" (v. 36). Then Jesus makes his request: "All things are possible to you. Take this cup away from me." Jesus knows that God can do anything. Surely, the Father must be able to free humans from sin and death without Jesus having to experience the terrible suffering that he is about to endure. Nevertheless, Jesus finds strength through his prayer to fulfill God's will, for his request is followed by his consent: "But not what I will but what you will." In prayer, Jesus submits himself to the will of his Father. Pope Benedict XVI explains, "The human will finds its complete fulfillment in the total abandonment of the I to the You of the Father, called Abba."[7] Adam and Eve reached for autonomy by disobeying

5. Pope John Paul II, *Jesus, Son and Savior: A Catechesis on the Creed* (Boston: Pauline Books and Media, 1996), 181.

6. Ibid., 181–82.

7. Pope Benedict XVI, General Audience, February 1, 2012.

God's will, but instead they found themselves alienated from God and learned that the consequence of sin is death. But Jesus in the garden of Gethsemane, fully sharing our human nature, stands before God and with his yes becomes the first human being to adhere perfectly to the divine will. He not only teaches us by his example how to say yes to God, but also, by uniting us to himself in baptism, gives us the grace to say yes to God.

The *Compendium* of the Catechism says,

> The prayer of Jesus during his agony in the garden of Gethsemane and his last words on the Cross reveal the depth of his filial prayer. Jesus brings to completion the loving plan of the Father and takes upon himself all the anguish of humanity and all the petitions and intercessions of the history of salvation. He presents them to the Father who accepts them and answers them beyond all hope by raising his Son from the dead.[8]

Through Jesus' passion and resurrection we can see that God's mysterious will for us is life and not death. Although God allows trials and suffering, his purpose is our eternal good.

The Poor Exalted and the Rich Humiliated (1:9–11)

[9]The brother in lowly circumstances should take pride in his high standing, [10]and the rich one in his lowliness, for he will pass away "like the flower of the field." [11]For the sun comes up with its scorching heat and dries up the grass, its flower droops, and the beauty of its appearance vanishes. So will the rich person fade away in the midst of his pursuits.

OT: Pss 41:2–3; 49:6–13; 113:7–8; Prov 29:7
NT: Matt 19:24 // Mark 10:25 // Luke 18:25; Matt 5:3 // Luke 6:20; Matt 6:30–34 // Luke 12:29–34
Catechism: poverty of heart, 2544–47; freedom from riches, 2548–50; love for the poor, 2443–49

At first glance, this passage is puzzling, since there does not seem to be a logical connection to what preceded it. But further consideration suggests that James is teaching how those aspiring to wisdom should view their lives. When a person sees the †world with God's eyes, his or her values are turned upside down, and what once was important often becomes unimportant. James describes two situations, that of a lowly person and that of a rich one.

8. United States Conference of Catholic Bishops, *Compendium: Catechism of the Catholic Church* (Washington, DC: United States Conference of Catholic Bishops, 2005), 161 (no. 543).

The first is a **brother in lowly circumstances**. By specifying a "brother,"   1:9
James indicates someone—male or female—who has accepted Jesus as the
†Messiah, does the will of his Father, and thus belongs to the family of Jesus'
disciples (Matt 12:48–50). The word describing the brother, "lowly" (*tapeinos*), can have an external or internal aspect. On the one hand, it can describe
a person who is economically poor and, consequently, has few rights or
privileges, perhaps oppressed or overlooked. But "lowly" can also describe
an interior quality, humility, the attitude of a servant. Jesus refers to himself
as "lowly" or "humble" (*tapeinos*) in heart (Matt 11:29). James invites such
a person to boast, to rejoice, to **take pride in his high standing**. This is another stunning paradoxical statement, like considering trials to be a reason
for joy (1:2–3). But James helps us see that a person considered lowly by the
world may be blessed in the eyes of God and can rejoice because he or she
will share in Christ's glory.

The rich person, on the other hand, is called upon to take pride in **low-**   1:10–11
liness (*tapeinōsis*). James does not use the word "brother" here; rather, he
emphasizes that the rich person is destined to **pass away** and **fade away in
the midst of his pursuits**. "Pursuits" is more precisely "journey," the path
one has chosen in life. James quotes Isa 40:6–7 to make his point, a prophetic
text which teaches that *all* humankind is ephemeral. Nevertheless, James
singles out those who are wealthy: just as the grass and flower fade under
the burning sun, so one day will the rich be no more.[9] The only way they
can overcome the common destiny of fading away is by embracing lowliness,
by becoming joined to Christ through conversion and baptism in order to
enter the kingdom of God.

James teaches his listeners to value that which has enduring worth in
contrast to that which fades away.[10] The humble brother can rejoice because
he is not expending his energies on riches that will ultimately fade and bring
him nothing. Jesus also admonishes his listeners to store up enduring treasure in heaven (Matt 6:19; see Luke 12:16–21; 16:19–31) and teaches that
the poor are blessed (Luke 6:20). Many people seek riches for the sake of
security, comfort, or status, but James teaches us that it is the rich who are
really poor because the **beauty** of their life is only an **appearance** and will
soon fade away.

---

9. Sometimes the OT describes the rich as fleeting or passing: Job 24:24; 27:21; Ps 49:16–20; Wis 5:8–9.
10. Burton Scott Easton, "James," in *The Interpreter's Bible*, vol. 12, ed. George A. Buttrick (New
York: Abingdon, 1957), 25.

Reflection and Application (1:1–11)

The mystery of suffering is painful and troubling, and it can tempt us to conclude that God is not just, good, loving, and all-powerful. James does not entertain any such idea. Rather, he invites us to deeply trust in God's goodness, to place ourselves in God's loving hands, and to consider that trials are a step toward our becoming "perfect and complete" (1:4). Trust enables us to rejoice in the midst of suffering and difficulty, knowing that we are on the path to future glory (Rom 8:18; 1 Pet 4:13; 5:10).

This is difficult to accept, and I must confess that as I studied and wrote my comments on this passage, I repeatedly asked myself whether James's explanation is adequate. What helped me most was to consider the author of this letter, James the Just, who knew and loved Jesus and who died as a martyr (see introduction). This man of God believed and taught that trials can be considered all joy. His teaching echoes that of Jesus, who, shortly before he was tortured and put to death, prayed that his disciples might share his joy (John 17:13). The Acts of the Apostles and other New Testament books describe how the early Christians continually praised God in the midst of their persecutions, accepting martyrdom with serenity and even joy.[11] The same is true today. While many of us are learning to rejoice in the course of relatively minor troubles, some contemporary Christians have discovered this †grace in truly grave trials. Not long ago I heard a missionary priest tell of an African woman who converted to Christianity without her husband's knowledge. When he found out, he tortured her so terribly that she was left hideously disfigured. When horrified Christian missionaries rescued her, they asked how she had endured such torment and not renounced her faith. She replied that in the midst of her gruesome ordeal, amazingly, the joy of God came over her. In the midst of her suffering on earth, a foretaste of the resurrection and heaven had broken in.

And that is something James teaches us. James always has an eye on the next life, and he teaches us to determine the value of all things on the basis of their potential to bring us to eternal life. No doubt James himself tasted the joy of the coming kingdom during his earthly life, and he could thus exhort his readers so passionately to consider trials that prepare us for eternal life as "all joy" (1:2). May we trust James, the apostles, and the great martyrs who taught us by their afflictions that perseverance has its reward. May we accept the will of God even when we do not understand, and let perseverance be perfect in times of trial. May the peace and love of God, which surpasses all understanding, sustain us as we continue our journey to God (Phil 4:7).

11. Acts 5:41; Rom 5:3; 2 Cor 7:4; 8:2; Phil 2:7; Col 1:24; 1 Pet 1:6–8.

God's Desire for Our Life

James 1:12–27

Some years ago I heard a priest recount one of the greatest trials of his life. About five years after ordination, he began slowly to go blind. As he was less and less able to fulfill his ministry, his sorrow increased, and he interpreted his blindness as a penalty for his sins. Try as he might, he felt that he could never do enough to please God. In anger and despair, the priest turned to alcohol to ease his pain, but this led him further down the path of desolation. Eventually, however, through his intense struggles, he learned to ask for help, to be patient with himself and others, and to profoundly value kindness and gentleness. After some years like this, he was able to put away the alcohol and slowly accept his new life. He found new, creative ways to continue his priestly ministry. After many years, as this priest reflected on his life, he saw that his blindness was actually a gift from God because it had made him a better person, to the point that he was truly able to thank God for his trial.

If we reflect on this story, we see that the priest's suffering had two aspects. The first was the objective trial itself, his blindness. The second was subjective, the priest's *response* to the trial: anger and despair, leading to alcoholism. In the next section (1:12–15) James teaches about the inner conflicts and temptations that can influence our response to trials.

Life and Death (1:12–15)

¹²Blessed is the man who perseveres in temptation, for when he has been proved he will receive the crown of life that he promised to those

who love him. ¹³No one experiencing temptation should say, "I am being tempted by God"; for God is not subject to temptation to evil, and he himself tempts no one. ¹⁴Rather, each person is tempted when he is lured and enticed by his own desire. ¹⁵Then desire conceives and brings forth sin, and when sin reaches maturity it gives birth to death.

OT: Wis 1:13–16; 2:23–24; Sir 15:11–12
NT: Matt 4:3–11 // Luke 4:1–13; Rom 6:23; 7:5–25; Eph 2:1–3
Catechism: concupiscence, 1264, 2515–16; inclination to evil, 1707; disordered desires, 2535–40

Here James discusses the dynamics of temptation and its possible results. He speaks of the reward coming to a person who perseveres in temptation as the crown of life, but warns that if a person yields to evil desire and sin, the final outcome is death.

1:12   James begins by calling **blessed**, meaning fortunate or deserving of congratulation, the person who **perseveres in temptation**. The word for "temptation" is the same word that was used for "trials" in verse 2 (*peirasmos*). The word *peirasmos* can bear the nuance of either trial or temptation. A trial is an experience of suffering or trouble that tests a person's constancy or faith, while temptation refers to enticement to sin or to turn away from God. Only the context indicates which of the related meanings an author intends. Most commentators conclude that in verse 2 James meant "trials," but in verses 12–14 he means "temptation," since in verses 14–15 he discusses how a temptation can lead to sin. However, by using the same word in verse 12 as he did in verse 2, James links this discussion about temptation to his earlier teaching on trials. Temptations often arise in the midst of trials.

In verses 2–4 James spoke of the importance of perseverance in trials in order to become perfect or mature. The progression was: trials, perseverance, perfect person. In verse 12 James echoes his thoughts of verse 2, but instead of trials as suffering, now the term carries the nuance of temptation, and instead of becoming mature (perfect), the person will receive **the crown of life**. In the Greco-Roman world a crown of leaves was awarded to the victor at the end of a race; the New Testament often uses a crown as an image of final reward (1 Cor 9:25; 2 Tim 4:8; 1 Pet 5:4); here it refers to eternal life (see Rev 2:10). The progression in verse 12 is: temptation, perseverance, eternal life—adding a compelling motive to endure trial and resist temptation.

It is noteworthy that the crown of life is **promised to those who love him**. Ultimately, the decision to persevere is a decision to love God. A person who continues to trust in God and obey him even when it becomes hard to do so ultimately has chosen to love God. With God, everything can become bearable, for love "bears all things . . . hopes all things, endures all things. Love never fails" (1 Cor 13:7–8).

Next James gives a prohibition: one should not say that God tempts. He then gives two reasons: God is **not subject to temptation to evil**, and God **himself tempts no one**.

James calls God "not temptable" (*apeirastos*). That is, there is no inclination or tendency toward evil in God, nor does he engage in an interior battle against evil desires. Rather, God is holy and pure, and all that emanates from him is good, noble, and beautiful. Not only is he absolutely separated from anything evil, but also evil is unable to affect him or to tempt him.

The first affirmation about God naturally leads to the second. Because God is wholly separate from evil, he does not incite anyone to sin. Sin and evil are foreign to God, both in his own being and in his desire for human-kind (see 1:18). This idea was already present in the Old Testament: "Do not say: 'It was God's doing that I fell away,' / for what he hates he does not do. / Do not say: 'He himself has led me astray,' / for he has no need of the wicked" (Sir 15:11–12).[1]

Now that James has shown that God is not a source of temptation, he explains what *is* the source. As he did in verses 5–8, James explains that God is not the problem—we are! Temptation arises from our **own desire**. The Greek word translated as "desire" (*epithymia*) is a neutral term that can indicate either a good or an evil desire and is sometimes translated as "passion." James does not denounce all desires, only those that are disordered, that attract us to what is wrong or evil. The person who yields to temptation is a victim of seduction, **lured and enticed** by personal desires. The nuance of the Greek words is illuminating: "lure" (*exelkō*) means "to draw or drag out," while "entice" (*deleazō*) means "to lure with bait." Since these terms usually are used to describe the process of catching fish or animals with nets or bait, the metaphor is that of an angler or hunter who lures prey from a safe hiding place and entices it into being caught.[2] The passive form of these verbs here indicates an action done to the person: one is lured and enticed by one's own evil desires, becoming a victim of the force that wells up from deep within to trap and ensnare.

1:13

1:14

1. The †Septuagint version of Gen 22:1 says that "God tested [*peirazō*] Abraham," which may seem to contradict what James has just said: God "himself tempts [*peirazō*] no one." Bearing in mind the different nuances of the Greek word *peirazō* ("to test, tempt") in different contexts, we can say that God may indeed test us, as he did Abraham, or allow trials to beset us, as he did Job, but he never entices or lures anyone to sin.

2. Dan G. McCartney, *James*, BECNT (Grand Rapids: Baker Academic, 2009), 106; James Hardy Ropes, *A Critical and Exegetical Commentary on the Epistle of St. James*, ICC (1916; repr., Edinburgh: T&T Clark, 1978), 156.

1:15   Unlike the person who perseveres during a period of temptation (v. 12), this person surrenders to evil desires and allows them to grow. When one allows these evil desires to flourish through impure, angry, greedy, or resentful thoughts, the natural result ensues: **desire conceives and brings forth sin**. The term for "bring forth" literally means "to give birth," and a few verses later James will contrast this birth from evil desires with birth from the word of truth (v. 18).[3] In short, evil desires that are allowed to flourish lead to evil actions.

The process then moves to the next phase. When **sin reaches maturity it gives birth to death**. The word for "maturity" is from the same root as "perfect" in verse 4 and recalls the result of perseverance, becoming perfect or mature in Christian life. Sin that continues to grow and become "perfect" will bring about its final end—death. This is an unusual image: giving birth to death! The fruit of sin is always death (see Rom 6:23), and our sins allow death to strengthen its hold on us. Death here refers to spiritual death, which is separation from God. Just as the person who perseveres becomes perfect and receives the crown of life, so the one who is ensnared by his or her own desires and allows sin to mature will be alienated from God, resulting in death, eternal separation from God.

Thus James has painted a neatly balanced picture of the end of every human being, which is either life or death. There is no middle road and no gray area. Only two possibilities exist:

temptation—perseverance—*life* (v. 12)

or

temptation—sin—*death* (vv. 14–15)

The stakes are high, and every person must choose.

James's teaching shows that the battle to overcome evil is fought deep within the human heart. But his reasoning seems to have left the person in a terrible quandary. In verses 5–7 James taught that one who lacks wisdom must make an internal decision and become open to receive wisdom. But at the same time, evil desires well up deep within the human heart to ensnare and entrap, and so one is continually lured and enticed by one's own desires (vv. 14–15). How can a person overcome his or her disordered desires and choose the path of wisdom, to love God and persevere?[4] James will now answer this question.

---

3. These two verbs for "conceive" and "bring forth" are used together literally (Gen 4:1, 17, 25) and figuratively (Ps 7:15) in the †LXX version of the OT.

4. J. A. Motyer, *The Message of James: The Tests of Faith*, BST (Downers Grove, IL: InterVarsity, 1985), 55.

God's Perfect Gift (1:16–18)

---

¹⁶**Do not be deceived, my beloved brothers:** ¹⁷**all good giving and every
perfect gift is from above, coming down from the Father of lights, with
whom there is no alteration or shadow caused by change.** ¹⁸**He willed to
give us birth by the word of truth that we may be a kind of firstfruits of his
creatures.**

OT: Gen 1:1–2:4; Pss 103; 136
NT: John 1:1–18; 1 Cor 15:20–23
Catechism: divine providence, 302–8

Having insisted that God does not tempt us to sin, James now explains more
about God's nature and purpose. God is generous and good, and gives birth—a
new beginning—by the word of truth. This is the solution to the interior drama
of our desires.

Addressing his readers affectionately as **my beloved brothers**, James draws   **1:16**
them close for an important message. James's solemn warning, **Do not be deceived**, is found also in Paul's writing (1 Cor 6:9; 15:33; Gal 6:7). The idea of
deception contrasts with the wisdom and knowledge that James weaves through
the first chapter. In verse 5 James invites his readers to pray for wisdom; in verse
19 he implores them to "know"; and in verses 22 and 26 he cautions against
self-deception. The knowledge that James communicates to his readers is not
mere intellectual or academic knowing. Rather, it is the understanding of God's
will in times of trial (v. 5), the nature and purpose of God (vv. 17–18), the
conduct befitting God's servants (vv. 19–21), and an accurate understanding
of ourselves (vv. 22b–24, 26). Truth of this kind is paramount, for without it
salvation is impossible.

Next James begins speaking of God by saying that God is the source of   **1:17**
all good giving and every perfect gift. In verse 5 James said that God gives
generously and ungrudgingly, and he now goes further. The fact that there is
nothing good that does not ultimately come from God's hand indicates that
God is benevolent and that his very nature is to give. Among God's gifts are
the crown of life (1:12), wisdom (1:5; 3:13–17), the word of truth (1:18, 21–23),
and being the firstfruits of his new creation (1:18). Ultimately, all these perfect
gifts pertain to eternal life and salvation; God wills our salvation and life, not
damnation and death. To think otherwise is to be deceived.

James calls God **the Father of lights**, a description over which scholars have
puzzled. It is not found in the Old Testament. Some commentators suggest that

the title refers to God as the creator of the lights of the heavens—the sun, moon, and stars.[5] While it is certainly true that God created light and the heavenly luminaries, it seems that here James is saying that God is the origin of all that is excellent and morally light, all that is pure, lovely, and holy. In both Testaments, darkness symbolizes sin and death while light symbolizes holiness, purity, and beauty.[6] God himself is light, and there is no darkness in him (1 John 1:5).

James says that within God there is **no alteration or shadow caused by change**. The first word, "alteration," simply means "change." The second part of the phrase is difficult and may refer to shadows caused by changes in the movement of heavenly bodies that marked the passing of time as well as festivals and seasons.[7] In any case, unlike the created lights, the Father of lights never changes. God has always been pure, always wants our good, always desires life for us, and will never deviate in his actions or desires. It is sometimes challenging to believe in God's goodness in moments of trials. It can also be hard to believe that God loves us after we have committed a sin, but James stresses that God's attitude toward us, his desire for our good, never diminishes or changes. God can be completely trusted.

1:18   Finally James arrives at his climactic description of what God has done and his purpose in doing it. Unlike sin, which "gives birth" (*apokyeō* [v. 15]) to death, God desired to **give us birth** (*apokyeō* [v. 18]) through the **word of truth**. By using the same verb in verses 15 and 18, James sets up a sharp contrast between sin's offspring and God's. "The word of truth" is a way of referring to the †gospel (Eph 1:13; Col 1:5), the good news of Jesus Christ. By means of this word, God reveals himself to us in Jesus Christ. Through his death and resurrection Jesus has given us the possibility of being freed from our slavery to sin and evil desires. Christ cleanses us from sin "by the bath of water with the word" (Eph 5:26), baptism, which the New Testament describes as a new birth (John 3:5; 1 Pet 1:3, 23). In this sacrament we are reborn and renewed by the Holy Spirit (Titus 3:4–6).

James then explains the reason God gave us birth through the word of truth: so that we might be **a kind of firstfruits of his creatures**. The firstfruits were the first part of the harvest or flock, the part that belonged to God. The †Torah mandated a yearly offering of the firstfruits to God to thank him, to remind the Israelites of God's fidelity, and to indicate that the whole harvest came from God (Exod 23:16, 19; Lev 23:10–14; Deut 18:4). When James says that **we** (the

5. See Gen 1:14, 16; Ps 136:7; Ezek 32:8.
6. Isa 10:17; 60:19–20; 1 Pet 2:9; Rev 21:23; 22:5.
7. BDAG, "*aposkiasma*," 120.

word is emphasized in Greek) become a kind of firstfruits of God's creatures, he means that Christians become God's special possession, holy and sacred. The word of truth, then, is what fundamentally changes our lives, allowing us to enter into an intimate relationship with God and giving us the strength to overcome our evil desires.

Thus, James has shown that God is not the source of temptation; he is the source of life, and this will never change. His kind generosity is evidenced in his free, unmerited gift of new life through the word of truth. But James also knows that God respects human freedom and will not save us against our will. God requires our cooperation. James now turns his attention to describing what this response entails.

Welcoming the Life-Giving Word (1:19–21)

> [19]Know this, my dear brothers: everyone should be quick to hear, slow to speak, slow to wrath, [20]for the wrath of a man does not accomplish the righteousness of God. [21]Therefore, put away all filth and evil excess and humbly welcome the word that has been planted in you and is able to save your souls.

OT: Deut 6:4–9; Ps 12; Prov 29:11, 20; Sir 1:26–29
NT: Matt 5:21–26; Col 3:12–17
Catechism: Christian holiness, 2012–16

Returning to his discussion of disordered desires in light of our birth through the word of truth, James does not merely exhort readers to overcome sinful impulses by their own effort. Rather, he advises Christians to quiet themselves, to listen, to put aside immoral ways, and to humbly welcome the word that has the power to save them. Self-salvation is impossible; we all need to accept help from on high.

James begins with a series of exhortations: **be quick to hear, slow to speak,**   1:19–20
slow to wrath. All three teachings are found in the wisdom literature of the Old Testament.[8] The first command, "to hear," is left without an object. It may be that James means that we should hear "the word" (see 1:22; Deut 6:4), but it could also be a general command to be ready to listen humbly to anyone. Failure to listen carefully to what the other person is saying often leads to misunderstanding.

---

8. E.g., listening before speaking: Prov 18:13; restraining speech: Prov 10:19; 17:27–28; 29:20; Eccles 5:2; governing anger: Prov 14:29; 15:18; 16:32; Eccles 7:9.

Listening

LIVING TRADITION

To listen to God's word is an ancient instruction, and Israel is constantly exhorted in the Old Testament to hear and obey God's word (Isa 28:14; Jer 7:2). One of Israel's most beloved Scripture passages, known as the Shema, is a command to listen: "Hear, O Israel!" (Deut 6:4).

Listening to the word of God, believing and obeying it, and allowing oneself to be penetrated and transformed by it brings holiness. The Second Vatican Council stressed the necessity of first listening to the word of God, and then of making a suitable response, in order to become holy:

> Indeed, in order that love, as good seed, may grow and bring forth fruit in the soul, each one of the faithful must willingly *hear the Word of God and accept His Will*, and must complete what God has begun by their own actions with the help of God's †grace. These actions consist in the use of the sacraments and in a special way the Eucharist, frequent participation in the sacred action of the Liturgy, application of oneself to prayer, self-abnegation, lively fraternal service and the constant exercise of all the virtues.[a]

a. *Lumen Gentium* (Dogmatic Constitution on the Church) 42 (italics added).

Even the simple act of being open to what the other is saying can bring healing and restoration. In combination with listening, James advocates restraint in speech, which indicates a willingness to learn and avoid rash judgment. Proverbs puts it nicely: "Those who spare their words are truly knowledgeable. . . . Even fools, keeping silent, are considered wise" (Prov 17:27–28). Then, in the third exhortation, James advocates that we not act in anger, since anger does not work **the righteousness**, or justice, **of God**. Although anger is sometimes appropriate (James does not completely reject anger but instead urges being slow to wrath), the Bible warns us about this emotion.[9] It is easy to think that our anger is justified and will serve to correct an unjust situation. But anger "is not a pure emotion; it is usually heavily impregnated with sin—self-importance, self-assertion, intolerance, stubbornness"—and consequently it usually does not bring about the kind of justice that God desires.[10] God brings about the righteousness he desires through those who humbly accept his word and follow his commandments. James will address how a doer of the word brings justice in 1:22–27.

9. Besides the verses mentioned in the earlier note, see Sir 27:30; 28:8; 30:24; Matt 5:22; Eph 4:26, 31.
10. Motyer, *Message of James*, 66.

James instructs us to **put away all filth and evil excess**. The Greek verb 1:21
translated as "put away" is often used to speak of removing a garment;[11] putting
away "filth" and "evil excess" means removing everything that is morally sordid
or squalid. Bede the Venerable says that this means to cleanse both the body
and mind from vice and immorality, for a person who does not first turn away
from evil cannot do good.[12] A degenerate lifestyle blocks the transformative
power of the word of truth.

The final instruction in this series is to **humbly welcome**, or "receive with
meekness" (RSV), the implanted **word**. Those who receive the word of God with
humility do not rely on their own resources for salvation but instead recognize
that their only hope lies in God's gracious gift. Because of this, they gratefully
and obediently open their hearts to the word of God. In the Sermon on the
Mount, Jesus says that the meek will inherit the earth (Matt 5:5). Jesus himself
is meek and humble of heart (Matt 11:29), and those who depend on God will
lack for nothing (James 1:4–5).

The imagery of a **word that has been planted** recalls Jesus' parable of the
sower. The seed of the word was "planted" in us when we heard the good news
but requires "rich soil" to produce abundant good fruit (Mark 4:20). What
makes the soil rich is eagerness to listen to the word and put its message into
practice. In both the liturgy and private prayer we can open our hearts to the
message of the word; then we obey it in every dimension of our lives. Then we
will see it produce good fruit. The fact that it is able to **save your souls**—that
is, our lives—is due to the word's divine power.

Thus, the overcoming of our disordered desires and the salvation of our souls
do not come by our own efforts. Anyone trying to live a virtuous life knows
that it cannot be done without the grace of God. But James has shown that our
cooperation is also necessary in order to conquer evil desire so that sin cannot
be born in us (1:15). God has provided all the necessary means, but we must
listen to his word, allow it to take root in us, and obey its message.

Obedience to the Word (1:22–27)

---

[22]**Be doers of the word and not hearers only, deluding yourselves.** [23]**For
if anyone is a hearer of the word and not a doer, he is like a man who looks
at his own face in a mirror.** [24]**He sees himself, then goes off and promptly**

11. BDAG, "*apotithēmi*," 123–24.
12. Bede the Venerable, *The Commentary on the Seven Catholic Epistles*, trans. David Hurst, CSS 82
(Kalamazoo, MI: Cistercian Publications, 1985), 19.

forgets what he looked like. [25]But the one who peers into the perfect law
of freedom and perseveres, and is not a hearer who forgets but a doer who
acts, such a one shall be blessed in what he does.

[26]If anyone thinks he is religious and does not bridle his tongue but de-
ceives his heart, his religion is vain. [27]Religion that is pure and undefiled
before God and the Father is this: to care for orphans and widows in their
affliction and to keep oneself unstained by the world.

OT: Jer 31:31–34; Ezek 11:19–20; 33:30–33
NT: Matt 25:31–46; Mark 10:17–31; 12:28–34; Rom 12:2–3; Phil 1:8–11; 4:8–9
Catechism: imitation of Christ, 1693–96; human freedom, 1731–33; purity, 2520; conscience,
1776–77

Earlier in this chapter James painted a rather stark picture of what leads to
life and what leads to death (1:12–15). Then he spoke about the word of truth
that gave us new birth and is able to save our souls, but he urged us to conduct
ourselves appropriately (1:16–21). He now adds a warning to those who think
that they are listening to the word but who deceive themselves.

1:22–24 James first admonishes those who hear the word but do not do what it says.
He compares these to someone **who looks at his own face in a mirror** but
then goes away and **promptly forgets** what he saw. The Greek words for "own
face" are more literally translated as "natural face" or "face from birth." The
face represents the whole person. So this person looks at herself and sees who
she really is, but then leaves, ignoring what she has seen. She forgets about the
imperfections and deficiencies she has seen and continues on her path. In other
words, the person who looks and forgets has had the word implanted within but
does not respond in a manner that allows it to flourish and grow. As in Jesus'
parable of the sower, the seed has been sown, but it does not take root (Mark
4:14–19), leaving the person to deal with interior temptations on his or her own.

1:25 James contrasts the **hearer who forgets** with the **doer who acts**. First, continuing the comparison to someone who looks in a mirror, James provides an
intriguing description of the mirror: the doer is a person who **peers into the
perfect law of freedom**, a paradoxical reference to the word of God, since law
implies restriction, while freedom implies the absence of restriction. Of course,
James is referring to the †gospel, "the word of truth" (v. 18), the word "planted
in you" that "is able to save your souls" (v. 21). It is "perfect," or complete,
because Jesus fulfills the Scriptures in his person and ministry (Matt 5:17–20;
see Jer 31:31–34; Ezek 11:19–20). It is a message of freedom, since by it Jesus
frees us from slavery to sin and evil desires (John 8:31–32; Rom 6:17–18; 1 Pet
2:24), changing us from the inside out by the power of the Spirit (Rom 8:2–5;

Gal 5:16–25). Nevertheless, it can be called a "law" because it has ethical implications, a way of life modeled and taught by Jesus and summed up in the two great commandments.

In contrast to the one who looks at his own face and forgets, this person gazes into the law of freedom and discovers what sort of life she is to lead and what sort of person she should become.[13] This person **perseveres** in following the commands of Jesus, even in moments of trial and temptation (1:2–4, 12), and becomes Christlike. Everyone who perseveres in doing the word of God is **blessed**—that is, happy and fortunate—because, after enduring trials and temptation, that person will receive the crown of life, eternal life, that God has promised to those who love him (1:12).[14]

In short, there are two different hearers of the word. Both participate in liturgical celebrations and listen to preaching. But the first hearer, after considering the need to change, goes away and promptly forgets. The second hearer, by contrast, is a "doer" who looks deeply into the law of freedom, which is the gospel, and perseveres in believing and obeying it. James calls the latter blessed.

James continues to contrast those who are true followers of Jesus with those **1:26** who only think they are. He addresses a person who **thinks he is religious**, presumably someone who engages in religious activity such as liturgy, prayers, study, ministry, and so on. According to James, however, only adherence to the word of God indicates true devotion, and the person unable to **bridle his tongue** is not religious. It is interesting that James identifies speech as a measure of true religion. He has already urged his listeners to be "quick to hear, slow to speak" (1:19); he will return to this theme later in the letter (3:1–12). Those who can control their speech are the spiritually mature. They are the ones who have already listened; they have accepted the word with docility and humility and are experiencing its transforming effects in their lives (see 3:2). They do not give vent to their anger or let loose with inappropriate speech, gossip, or other sins of the tongue. Jesus said, "From the fullness of the heart the mouth speaks" (Matt 12:34): sinful speech reveals a sinful heart; a pure heart shows itself in pure speech. Those who control their speech have gone far on the path to freedom; they can govern their interior desires because they have persevered in following the "perfect law of freedom."

The Greek word translated as **religion** in verses 26–27 also means "wor- **1:27** ship" (e.g., Col 2:18). James contrasts empty ritual with true worship. He calls authentic religion **pure** and **undefiled**, two words that express the same thing

---

13. Dmitri Royster, *The Epistle of St. James: A Commentary* (Yonkers, NY: St. Vladimir's Seminary Press, 2010), 37.

14. See John Paul Heil, *The Letter of James: Worship to Live By* (Eugene, OR: Cascade, 2012), 60.

Pope John Paul II on Freedom and the Law

LIVING
TRADITION

Pope John Paul II reflected on the relationship between human freedom and God's law in his encyclical letter *Veritatis Splendor* (The Splendor of Truth):

> Human freedom and God's law are not in opposition; on the contrary, they appeal one to the other.... Saint Augustine, after speaking of the observance of the commandments as being a kind of incipient, imperfect freedom, goes on to say: "Why, someone will ask, is it not yet perfect? Because 'I see in my members another law at war with the law of my reason' (Rom 7:23).... In part freedom, in part slavery: not yet complete freedom, not yet pure, not yet whole, because we are not yet in eternity. In part we retain our weakness and in part we have attained freedom. All our sins were destroyed in Baptism, but does it follow that no weakness remained after iniquity was destroyed? Had none remained, we would live without sin in this life. But who would dare to say this except someone who is proud, someone unworthy of the mercy of our deliverer?... Therefore, since some weakness has remained in us, I dare to say that to the extent to which we serve God we are free, while to the extent that we follow the law of sin, we are still slaves."
>
> Those who live "by the †flesh" experience God's law as a burden, and indeed as a denial or at least a restriction of their own freedom. On the other hand, those who are impelled by love and "walk by the Spirit" (Gal 5:16), and who desire to serve others, find in God's Law the fundamental and necessary way in which to practice love as something freely chosen and freely lived out. Indeed, they feel an interior urge—a genuine "necessity" and no longer a form of coercion—not to stop at the minimum demands of the Law, but to live them in their "fullness." This is a still uncertain and fragile journey as long as we are on earth, but it is one made possible by †grace, which enables us to possess the full freedom of the children of God (cf. Rom 8:21) and thus to live our moral life in a way worthy of our sublime vocation as "sons in the Son."[a]

a. *Veritatis Splendor* 17–18.

and usually refer to the kind of worship that is acceptable to God. Here they describe conduct that is acceptable to God, agreeing with what the Old Testament says about what God truly desires: obedience to his word and mercy toward the needy (1 Sam 15:22; Isa 58; Hosea 6:6). The translation here, **God and the Father**, could seem to imply that God and the Father are two different entities. The Greek is clearer and is more helpfully translated as "the one who is God and Father" or "God, the Father" (NRSV).

True religion is **to care for orphans and widows in their affliction.** The law of the Old Testament commands that the widow and orphan receive special care (Deut 10:17–18; 26:13; 27:19), and the prophets railed against those who abused or neglected widows and orphans (Jer 7:5–6; 22:3; Zech 7:10). By taking care of the weakest, the truly religious person imitates God's justice and his nature as a life-giving father. True religion also means **to keep oneself unstained by the world**. To be unstained or unspotted means to be pure and without sin. Saint Peter's first letter describes Christ as a spotless, unblemished lamb (1 Pet 1:19), while 2 Pet 3:14 says that those who are awaiting Christ should be without spot or blemish. The word "†world" is variously used in the New Testament, but here, as in 4:4, it refers to human society insofar as it resists God and has a corrupting effect (see John 12:31; 1 John 2:15–17).[15] To be unstained by the world, therefore, means to avoid being influenced by its principles and standards (see 4:4). James has shown that God is pure (1:13), the Father of all that is good (1:17), and the one who gives birth to us by his saving word (1:18). Religion consists, then, in imitating God's pure, life-giving behavior both by being compassionate toward the vulnerable and by abstaining from what is corrupt in the surrounding society.

In this section (1:12–27) James has sketched the path to life and the path to death. Life comes through accepting the word of truth and persevering in it; death comes from being ensnared by one's own desires and the influence of the world. For James, life begins with knowing the truth. One must know the truth about God, who does not lead anyone to sin, and also welcome the "word of truth" (1:18, 21). We must grasp the truth about ourselves and whether we are really living God's word by peering into the law of freedom (1:25). James challenges us to be painfully honest with ourselves and measure ourselves against the only right norm, the word of God. This can be distressing at first; but once one accepts the truth in humility, one can repent and obey the word that leads to spiritual maturity and freedom.

Reflection and Application (1:12–27)

James is often regarded as the New Testament letter that concentrates on works, and that is true. James teaches that true religion consists of curbing the tongue and taking care of the poor and weak. But that is only part of the author's message. James also teaches that holy conduct results from allowing the word of truth, the gospel, to take root and flourish within us. Only then can we overcome our desires that lead to sin and death and learn to be obedient to God. In order to do this, we need to spend time in prayer and listen carefully to the gospel message. Prayer is a dimension of our lives where we discover that we

---

15. McCartney, *James*, 129.

are loved by God, learn that his commands are beautiful and good for us, and gain strength to put the precepts of the law into practice. Pope Benedict XVI says, "The Law of God, at the center of life, demands that the heart listen. It is a listening that does not consist of servile but rather of filial, trusting, and aware obedience. Listening to the word is a personal encounter with the Lord of life, an encounter that must be expressed in concrete decisions and become a journey."[16]

16. Pope Benedict XVI, General Audience, November 9, 2011.

Faith and Love

James 2:1–13

Pope Francis's apostolic exhortation *Evangelii Gaudium* (The Joy of the Gospel) echoes the teaching of James by placing care for the poor at the heart of the Christian life: "Each individual Christian and every community is called to be an instrument of God for the liberation and promotion of the poor, and for enabling them to be fully a part of society. This demands that we be docile and attentive to the cry of the poor and to come to their aid. . . . There is an inseparable bond between our faith and the poor."[1]

James begins this section by declaring that preferential treatment of the rich against the poor is incompatible with faith in Jesus Christ; this idea provides the fundamental theme of the section.[2] James then presents two reasons why faith in Jesus demands ethical behavior toward the poor: the poor are chosen by God (vv. 5–7), and the sin of partiality is tantamount to breaking the whole law (vv. 8–13).

Avoiding Partiality toward the Rich (2:1–4)

[1]**My brothers, show no partiality as you adhere to the faith in our glorious Lord Jesus Christ. [2]For if a man with gold rings on his fingers and in fine**

---

1. *Evangelii Gaudium* 48, 187.
2. Scripture teaches partiality to the poor in the sense of coming to their aid, since God himself looks out for the most vulnerable. It mandates various ways in which poorer members of the community are to be helped (Lev 19:9–10) and social structures are to protect and sustain them (Deut 15:1–11). In imitation of God, the Church exercises a preferential option for the poor, as is made clear in various documents of the Magisterium (Catechism 2448). In court, however, no partiality is to be exercised in the determination of guilt (Exod 23:3; Lev 19:15).

clothes comes into your assembly, and a poor person in shabby clothes also comes in, ³and you pay attention to the one wearing the fine clothes and say, "Sit here, please," while you say to the poor one, "Stand there," or "Sit at my feet," ⁴have you not made distinctions among yourselves and become judges with evil designs?

OT: Lev 19:9–10, 15, 33–34; Sir 35:15

NT: Rom 2:11; Eph 6:9; Col 3:25

Catechism: faith, 150–65; love for the poor, 2443–49, 2462–63; respect for the human person, 1929–33

Lectionary: 23rd Sunday in Ordinary Time, Year B (James 2:1–5)

2:1 James begins this section with a prohibition, **show no partiality**, followed by a long †conditional sentence: *if* the community pays attention to the rich and is dismissive to the poor, *then* it has **made distinctions** and **become judges**.

The Old Testament teaches that God does not discriminate (2 Chron 19:7), describing him as "a God of justice, / who shows no partiality" (Sir 35:15). Because he is just, he commands that the Israelites also render justice: "You shall not act dishonestly in rendering judgment. Show neither partiality to the weak nor deference to the mighty, but judge your neighbor justly" (Lev 19:15). Jesus himself was not influenced by a person's social status, wealth, or prestige, and even his enemies acknowledged that he did "not regard a person's status" (Mark 12:14). Since his message of salvation was for all, he received anyone who came to him and specially invited the burdened and oppressed (Matt 11:28; John 7:37; 12:32). Thus we see Jesus dining with tax collectors and sinners (Mark 2:15). Peter learned that "in every nation whoever fears him and acts uprightly is acceptable to him" (Acts 10:35), and Paul also taught that God has no favorites and does not judge on the basis of human social standing (Rom 2:11; Eph 6:9; Col 3:25). Thus, anyone who holds to **faith in our glorious Lord** ought not to make distinctions based on social status or wealth. James's persistent title for his listeners, "my brothers" (e.g., 1:2, 16, 19; 2:1), indicates his recognition that the bond created by a common faith in Jesus Christ establishes a fundamental equality.

The title **glorious Lord Jesus Christ** is used only here in the New Testament. The phrase in Greek is difficult to translate and could be rendered as "the Lord Jesus Christ of glory" or "Jesus Christ, the Lord of glory" (ESV). The word "glory" is used in the New Testament to refer to Jesus' state after his resurrection (see Luke 24:26; John 17:5). Thus the title "glorious Lord Jesus Christ" affirms that Jesus in his heavenly resurrected glory is the †Messiah and God (see explanation of "the Lord Jesus Christ," p. 16). By using this lofty title, James stresses the majesty of Jesus in order to spur his readers to reverence and right conduct.

Faith

BIBLICAL BACKGROUND

Faith describes the kind of relationship that God desires human beings to have with him. God created humankind and invites us into a relationship of †covenant love, a loyal love that he offers freely apart from anything we have done to deserve it. He calls us to respond to him with faith, and through baptism to enter into a relationship with the Father, Son, and Holy Spirit (Matt 28:19).ᵃ

In the Old Testament, among other Hebrew verbs for exercising faith, two verb roots are prominent. The first is *'mn*, from which we get the word "amen," and it means "to believe in, to be convinced, to regard something as firm and trustworthy." The second is *bth*, which means "to trust, to be confident, to feel secure."ᵇ Both describe how human beings should respond to God. We can and should be convinced of the truth of God's word; we can and should place great confidence and find security in God's promises, since his word is true and unchanging (Isa 40:8; Matt 5:18).

In the New Testament the word for "faith" (*pistis*) is related to the verb "persuade" (*peithō*), and an important dimension of faith is to accept that the †gospel is true and to entrust oneself to it. The content of the gospel centers on the life and teaching of Jesus Christ and the apostolic proclamation of who Jesus is and the significance of what he did. So Christian faith entails accepting that Jesus died for our sins, that God raised him from the dead, and that he is the Messiah, the Son of God, and Lord of the universe (Rom 10:9; 1 Cor 15:3–4; Phil 2:9–11). Another dimension of the Greek word for "faith" (*pistis*) is faithfulness—that is, keeping faith. Christian faith cannot be reduced to reciting or accepting various propositions; rather, it involves the whole person and entails surrendering oneself to Jesus as Lord and living in a way that reflects that belief.

a. Faith and baptism are inextricably related (see Mark 16:15–16). Through baptism we become united with Christ in his passion, death, and resurrection (Rom 6:3–6), and thus we can share in his trinitarian life.

b. Jean Duplacy, "Faith," in *Dictionary of Biblical Theology*, ed. Xavier Léon-Dufour, trans. P. Joseph Cahill (Gaithersburg, MD: The Word Among Us, 2000), 158.

James illustrates what partiality is and what is wrong with it by sketching **2:2–4** a scenario of what could take place in a Christian meeting. The setting is the **assembly** (Greek *synagōgē*, from which we derive "synagogue"), a word occasionally used in the early Church to refer also to Christian gatherings[3] and a natural word choice for Jewish Christians. Two men enter, and James describes how they are dressed. The first man wears **gold rings** and **fine clothes**, attractive

3. Dan G. McCartney, *James*, BECNT (Grand Rapids: Baker Academic, 2009), 138.

adornments that indicate his high economic and social status. The second is a **poor person** dressed in **shabby clothes**. The adjective "shabby" (*rhyparos*) is rare (used only here and in Rev 22:11) and means "filthy, squalid"; this man is dressed in grimy and perhaps smelly garments. If the congregation were to **pay attention** to the rich man and tell him, **"Sit here, please,"** but say to the poor man, **"Stand there"** or **"Sit at my feet,"** they would have acted wrongly. To sit at someone's feet indicates a subservient status, and the poor man may have been expected to render service or perhaps simply was not given a seat. James is concerned that the exterior appearance of the rich man will render him more valuable in the eyes of his readers than the poor man, and that the congregation will treat each man accordingly.

James finally draws a conclusion from his long conditional statement, in the form of a question: If you have acted this way, **have you not made distinctions among yourselves?** To make distinctions refers to discriminating or judging. In this case, the act of judgment is not good. To discriminate against the poor man in this way is to **become judges with** "evil thoughts" (NRSV, preferable to the NABRE's less literal **evil designs**). James implies that the community has established a ranking among its members based on exterior, worldly standards, not those of Christ. Christians are not to be people who sit in judgment, but instead be "hearers" and "doers" of the word (1:22), people who obey the law that God has revealed. There is only one judge, the God who gave the law and who has the power to save or condemn (4:11–12; 5:9).[4] Yet, James implies, members of the community are judging one another with evil thoughts instead of obeying God's law against partiality (see Lev 19:15; Deut 1:17). The evil thoughts are those that suppose that one person is worth cultivating, perhaps because of being able to bestow favors, and that another person, having no favors to bestow, is of little value and thus can be treated shabbily.[5]

Given the filthy clothes of the second man, the congregation may consider itself gracious in even allowing him to remain. But for James, mere toleration of the poor is not enough. Those who adhere to faith in Jesus must be perfect

---

4. James objects both to the "evil thoughts" of those who are partial to the wealthy and to their acting as judges, since God is the one who will judge. In doing so, he echoes Jesus' teaching against judging (Matt 7:1–5; Luke 6:37–38). However, these exhortations should not be interpreted as excluding all judging, since it is necessary for Christians to make judgments in light of the word of God and their consciences about whether a possible course of action is right or wrong and whether a teaching is true or false. In addition, Paul speaks of the importance of selecting judges to settle disputes between Christians (1 Cor 6:1–5) and the need for the Christian community to judge the grave misconduct of members of the community (1 Cor 5:9–13).

5. Greco-Roman society was built around relationships of patronage, which could induce people to ingratiate themselves with the rich and powerful in hopes of obtaining protection or other benefits.

as their Father in heaven is perfect (Matt 5:48), giving sunshine and rainfall to all people (Matt 5:45). James insists that the poor be welcomed with the same regard as the rich, for just as God shows no partiality, neither should the congregation. This is by no means an easy teaching, and once again, James asks his fellow Christians to reconsider their way of thinking and acting.

God's Choice of the Poor (2:5–7)

⁵Listen, my beloved brothers. Did not God choose those who are poor in the world to be rich in faith and heirs of the kingdom that he promised to those who love him? ⁶But you dishonored the poor person. Are not the rich oppressing you? And do they themselves not haul you off to court? ⁷Is it not they who blaspheme the noble name that was invoked over you?

OT: Exod 19:4–6; Deut 7:6–8
NT: Rom 7:4; Eph 2:1–13; 5:8–9; 1 Thess 1:4–6; 1 Pet 2:10–11
Catechism: God forms his people Israel, 62–64; the Church prepared for in the old covenant, 761–62; the Church instituted by Christ Jesus, 763–66

After indicating that disrespect for the poor and favoritism toward the rich are incompatible with faith in Jesus Christ (2:1–4), James now presents other arguments against such a practice. In this section he describes how the poor have been chosen by God (vv. 5–6a), while the rich cause trouble for the community in a variety of ways (vv. 6b–7). He uses a series of rhetorical questions that assume affirmative answers to make his point.

James begins with a command, **Listen**, a summons that the prophets often 2:5–6a used before making a weighty statement (Isa 1:10; Joel 1:2; Amos 3:1; Mic 6:1), followed by his usual affectionate term of address, **my beloved brothers**, stressing once again their familial relationship in Christ. What James teaches now is said in love but needs to be carefully considered. In the rhetorical question that follows, James gives four descriptions of the poor: they are chosen by God, they are rich in faith, they are heirs of the promised kingdom, and they love God.

In the first description, James focuses on divine election: **Did not God choose?** Our relationship with God owes everything to his initiative. One of the fundamental themes of the Old Testament is that God chose Israel from among all the people of the †world to be a people especially his own (Deut 7:6; 14:2). He brought the Israelites out of slavery, established a covenant with them (Exod 19:4–6), and gave them the land he had promised to them. "His love, moreover, is an elective love: among all the nations he chooses Israel and loves

45

her—but he does so precisely with a view to healing the whole human race."[6] God's healing plan comes to fruition in Jesus Christ, who shed his blood to redeem the whole world through faith in him. In the New Testament, Christians rejoice because they who were once "no people" are now also chosen by God to receive salvation and be his own.[7]

But what does James mean when he says God has chosen **those who are poor**? While the poor are not always virtuous, economic hardship and powerlessness often make people more open to God, since their suffering spurs them to seek his help, while prosperity sometimes has the opposite effect (Deut 8:11–17). In the Old Testament "the poor" often refers to the faithful poor who hope in God and are saved by him.[8] Jesus defined his Spirit-anointed mission as bringing good news to the poor (Luke 4:18), and he showed particular compassion for the poor and weak (Mark 1:41; 8:2; Luke 5:12–14). The church that James pastored in Jerusalem was especially poor and needed alms from Christians elsewhere on at least two occasions (Acts 11:28–30; 24:17; Rom 15:26). Paul writes to the church of Corinth, "Not many of you were wise by human standards, not many were powerful, not many were of noble birth" (1 Cor 1:26), because "God chose the lowly and despised of the world, those who count for nothing, to reduce to nothing those who are something" (1 Cor 1:28). In all these ways the Bible closely associates the poor with the people of God.

James further specifies whom he is speaking about by describing them as those who are poor **in the world**. "World" here may simply refer to the created order, but often in the New Testament it refers to human society insofar as it opposes God.[9] James said in 1:27 that pure and undefiled religion is to keep oneself unstained by the world, and in 4:4 he will teach that those who love the world are at enmity with God. So it is quite possible that in this text those who are "poor in the world" are not only economically poor but have remained pure by refusing to compromise themselves for the perks that the world offers. Matthew's and Luke's different versions of the Beatitudes refer to two kinds of poverty: in Luke's Gospel Jesus says, "Blessed are you who are *poor*" (Luke 6:20, emphasis added), addressing those of low economic status; however, in Matthew's Gospel he says, "Blessed are the *poor in spirit*" (Matt 5:3, emphasis added),

6. Pope Benedict XVI, *Deus Caritas Est* (God Is Love) 9.
7. See 1 Pet 2:10; Rom 8:3; Eph 1:11; 1 Thess 1:4.
8. See Pss 9:19; 37:14; Wis 2:10; Isa 41:17.
9. McCartney, *James*, 129. The Gospel of John often uses the term "world" to refer to society at enmity with God. The "world" in this sense cannot receive the Spirit (John 14:17); Jesus has revealed himself to his disciples but not to the world (14:22). The world, in the sense of society hostile to God, loves the unrighteous but does not love Jesus (7:7; 15:19). Further, those who follow Jesus do not belong to this world (17:14). Finally, †Satan is the prince of the world (12:31).

summoning everyone to the spiritual choice for humility and dependence on God that must characterize Jesus' disciples. In both Gospels, the reward that Christ promises the poor is God's kingdom.

In the second phrase describing those who are poor in the world, James says that they are **rich in faith**. By this he means that the poor have a rich relationship with God: they know, trust, and love him, and through their experience of his love they have come to realize that God knows and desires their good. This discovery of God's love renders his commandments a source of joy rather than a burden to be borne. The poorer a person is in terms of the "world," the richer can be his or her relationship with Christ.

Third, the poor are **heirs of the kingdom**. The kingdom of God, mentioned in James only here, will be fully established when God reigns over all and evil is finally abolished. In the meantime, the Church anticipates the kingdom insofar as it submits to Christ's reign so that God's will can be done and his purposes for humankind begin to find fulfillment. Christians look forward to the full realization of the kingdom in the new Jerusalem, where there will be no more pain and suffering (Rev 21:2–4). As "heirs," the poor receive the kingdom freely as a gift, both now and in the age to come (Luke 12:32; Rev 21:6; 22:17).

Finally, in the fourth phrase, God has promised the kingdom to **those who love him** (see Deut 6:3–5; Luke 10:25–27; James 1:12). By finishing his description with the word "love," James focuses on what the poor desire and choose. They have shown their love for God by rejecting the ideals and standards of the world that are opposed to him. In 4:4 James will teach that those who love the world are at enmity with God. There is no middle road.

James's description of the poor is clever: by calling the poor chosen, rich in faith, heirs of the kingdom, and those who love God, he actually describes what the Christian community is supposed to be. James shows the absurdity of disrespect toward the poor by his readers, for by rejecting the poor, they identify with the wealth and status of the world. If they place themselves on the side of the world, they are at enmity with God (4:4) and forfeit their standing as heirs of the kingdom.

James finishes his description of the poor with a solemn indictment: the congregation has **dishonored the poor person**. To shame the poor is an offense against God and a very serious sin (Prov 14:31; 17:5). Jesus identifies with the poor and makes it clear that treatment of the poor is treatment of him (Matt 25:40, 45). Those who adhere to faith in our Lord Jesus Christ must also identify with the poor and treat them well. By dishonoring the poor and thus offending God, James's readers have come dangerously close to rejecting their own special status as God's heirs and chosen ones.

2:6b–7   After explaining why the poor are to be honored, James now indicates why Christians should not give special treatment to people on account of their wealth. James levels three charges against the rich, and by saying "you" three times, he stresses the personal harm suffered by his readers at the hands of the rich.

The first charge is that the rich are **oppressing you**. The Greek verb translated as "oppress" is found in the prophets, who commonly denounce the rich for exploiting the poor.[10] The second charge is that they **haul you off to court**. The rich would commonly bring the poor into court to collect debts or rent, reducing them to slavery.

The third and most serious charge is that the rich **blaspheme the noble name**. "To blaspheme" means "to revile, slander." Rich people are abusing the name by which Christians are called. That noble name is "Jesus," which was pronounced over Christians at their baptism (Acts 8:16; 10:48);[11] having the name **invoked over** them means that they now belong to Christ. The phrase "to invoke the name upon" is used in Deut 28:10 to refer to Israel's choice by God, indicating that the people belong in a special way to the Lord. Thus Christians, who have had the noble name of Christ invoked upon them, have been specially chosen by Christ and belong to him.

James shows the foolishness of both welcoming the rich who harm the poor and rejecting the poor who are actually the ones God chooses. A person who seeks to become ingratiated with the rich renounces his or her standing as one of God's poor who have a privileged share in his kingdom. Later in the letter, James will again strongly castigate the rich for their oppression of the poor (5:1–6).

Reflection and Application (2:1–7)

Certainly there were well-to-do people within the early Church, and James is not excluding them from the Christian community; rather, he is correcting his readers' tendency to favor the rich. Those of us who are wealthy in comparison with the developing world can take comfort in the fact that we are not excluded, but we also need to pay close attention to James's teaching.

10. The word that James uses here (*katadynasteuō*) is used often in the †LXX translation of the prophets' condemnations of the mistreatment of the weak and needy: Jer 7:6; 22:3; Ezek 18:7; Amos 4:1; 8:4; Hab 1:4; Zech 7:10; Mal 3:5.

11. Patrick J. Hartin, *James*, SP 14 (Collegeville, MN: Liturgical Press, 2003), 121.

The Scriptures often warn of the lure of money and riches, but why is that so? Pope John Paul II says, "It is not wrong to want to live better; what is wrong is a style of life which is presumed to be better when it is directed towards 'having' rather than 'being,' and which wants to have more, not in order to be more but in order to spend life in enjoyment as an end in itself."[12] According to the pope, at the heart of an inordinate desire for money is a misunderstanding of one's identity. Since Jesus our king has identified with the poor, we must do the same. Our loyalty to Christ must surpass love of family, career, and material goods. He must be the center, and serving him must be the goal of our lives.

Goods must take a subordinate place in our lives. When money and possessions occupy the place that Christ should have in our hearts, we become their slaves. Thus we must ask ourselves these questions: Do we serve money, or does money serve us in our desire for holiness and to please God? Do we seek financial success to gratify our desires (4:3), or to fulfill the purpose for which we were created and redeemed? If we become slaves to money and belongings, we lose our freedom and mar our dignity as sons and daughters of God called to seek first his kingdom (Matt 6:33). We are in danger of the sin of idolatry, the love of possessions or pleasure (Eph 5:5; Col 3:5) more than God, our true joy.

I have been humbled and moved by many joyful Catholic families who live free from a disordered love of possessions, despite living in a wealthy country. I know of one family that skips dinner on Fridays and gives whatever they would have spent on the food to the Church. Another family, in which both husband and wife are lawyers, shops for clothes at thrift stores, not because they cannot afford new clothes, but so that they can give more money to those in need. These small sacrifices cannot save the world, but they can radically affect those who receive such generosity, as well as those who give. God does not ask us to save the world, but he does ask us to do our small part. To make such sacrifices requires love and trust in God. Our heavenly Father loves us: the one who brilliantly clothes the fields with flowers will provide everything we need (Luke 12:28; 2 Cor 9:8–11).

The Law of Freedom (2:8–13)

[8]However, if you fulfill the royal law according to the scripture, "You shall love your neighbor as yourself," you are doing well. [9]But if you show partiality, you commit sin, and are convicted by the law as transgressors.

12. *Centesimus Annus* (Centenary of the Encyclical *Rerum Novarum*) 36.

¹⁰**For whoever keeps the whole law, but falls short in one particular, has become guilty in respect to all of it. ¹¹For he who said, "You shall not commit adultery," also said, "You shall not kill." Even if you do not commit adultery but kill, you have become a transgressor of the law. ¹²So speak and so act as people who will be judged by the law of freedom. ¹³For the judgment is merciless to one who has not shown mercy; mercy triumphs over judgment.**

OT: Exod 20:1–17; Lev 19:18
NT: Matt 5:43–48; 9:13; 12:7; 22:36–40
Catechism: Twofold commandment to love, 2052–55

In this section James sets forth another reason that partiality is incompatible with faith in Jesus Christ: in committing the sin of partiality, the person has broken the law. James preemptively addresses his readers' response, the opinion that partiality is a small matter and certainly not a serious transgression. James argues that breaking even one part of the law means that the law has been transgressed.

2:8–9   James begins by contrasting partiality toward the rich with the law of love. In the first of two †conditional sentences, James says that **if you fulfill the royal law**, then **you are doing well**. When speaking of the law, James does not use more customary expressions such as "keeping" or "obeying" it, but rather says we are to "fulfill" the law, which suggests the idea of completing it, of perfect observance.¹³ The †Torah, or law, which is a perfect whole (1:25), is not to be obeyed only in part, since all of it comes from God (2:10–11). Instead, God's law is to be kept in its fullness.

The word "royal" literally means "belonging to a king." Our king Jesus—his title "Christ," meaning "†Messiah," is that of a king—taught that the commandments to love God with all our heart, mind, and strength (Deut 6:4–9) and to love our neighbor as ourselves (Lev 19:18) are the most important. The law and the prophets depend on these two (Matt 22:36–40 // Mark 12:28–31). On another occasion, Jesus told a young lawyer that if he kept these two commandments, he would have eternal life (Luke 10:25–28). Jesus himself fulfilled them perfectly, and those who follow him as his disciples are called to do the same. The "royal law" is thus the Torah fulfilled by Jesus. Saint Paul echoes this teaching of Jesus: "The commandments . . . are summed up in this saying, [namely] 'You shall love your neighbor as yourself'" (Rom 13:9). If a person fulfills this foundational commandment, he or she fulfills them all.

13. McCartney, *James*, 147.

James and Paul on the Law of Moses

When addressing Jews who wish to impose circumcision and the law of Moses on Gentile Christians, Paul teaches that Christ frees believers from the law of Moses (Rom 7:1–4; Gal 2:19–20). Gentile Christians do not need to become Jews by accepting circumcision and other Jewish identity markers prescribed by the law in order to belong to God's †covenant people. Justification—that is, right relationship with God—comes to both Jews and †Gentiles through faith in Jesus and union with his death and resurrection through baptism (Acts 15:9–11; Rom 6:3–10; Gal 2:15–16).

James, on the other hand, addressing Jewish Christians, stresses the unity between the †gospel and the law of Moses (especially as summarized in the two great commandments), referring to the whole as "the law of freedom" (1:25; 2:12). This positive estimation of the law of Moses is perfectly in keeping with that expressed by Christ in the Gospels (e.g., Mark 10:17–19) and was natural for Jews who accepted Jesus as the Messiah, since Jews were already accustomed to centering their lives on the †Torah.

The difference between Paul and James on this point should not be exaggerated, since Paul also sums up the requirements of the law as love of neighbor (Rom 13:10; Gal 5:14) and notes that the Holy Spirit enables Christians to fulfill "the righteous decree of the law" (Rom 8:4). Both James and Paul regard the law as revealed by God and stress its ethical dimensions. Neither requires Christians to observe its ritual elements, although it is likely that Jewish Christians in the first century, including Paul, observed at least some of these as well (see Acts 18:18; 21:20–27). According to Acts 15, Gentile Christians were required to observe only the parts of the ritual law that were required of Gentile resident aliens in Israel (Acts 15:19–20, 28–29; see Lev 17–18).

In the second conditional statement, James returns to the problem that he has been discussing: **if you show partiality**, then **you commit sin**. Showing partiality cannot be considered a small, insignificant fault, since those who do so will be **convicted by the law as transgressors**. To Jewish Christians, who had reverenced the Torah since childhood, the thought of being convicted of transgressing it was a serious matter. James grounds his teaching against partiality toward the rich not on personal opinion but on the basis of God's command revealed in the law of Moses (Lev 19:18) and confirmed by the Messiah.

The next two verses, each beginning with **For**, explain why being guilty of
2:10–11
partiality is so serious. James explains that anyone who **falls short in one particular** of the law will be held responsible for having broken the whole law: the

You Shall Love the Lord Your God

LIVING TRADITION

Saint Augustine explains the unity of the law as follows:

> No one loves his neighbor unless he loves God and tries his best to get that neighbor, whom he loves as himself, to love God too. If he does not love God, then he does not love himself, nor does he love his neighbor. That is why whoever would keep the whole law but fails in one point has become guilty of all of it, for he has acted against charity, on which the whole law depends. One becomes guilty of all the commandments when one sins against that virtue from which they all derive.[a]

a. *Letter* 167.5.16.

person has **become guilty in respect to all of it.** The phrase **he who said** is a circumlocution for "God." James directs his readers away from focusing on the gravity of a particular sin to focus instead on the lawgiver, God, thus offering a reason not to sin at all: love and respect for God. According to James, the law is not a series of individual commands that allow a passing grade if they are mostly fulfilled. Rather, the law is an indivisible whole that is either accepted and obeyed or disregarded and disobeyed.[14] He bases this teaching on the fact that God, who is one and indivisible, gave the whole law. Thus, to disobey or reject one of the commands—whether the sin is adultery, murder, or partiality—means to violate Christ's commandment to love God and neighbor.

2:12–13   In this section James brings his teaching on the gravity of partiality to its natural conclusion. Because breaking any part of the law makes a person a transgressor, we must examine all our actions because we will be held accountable. He gives a double exhortation to his listeners: **so speak and so act** as those who will be judged. The double "so" with these verbs stresses how each action is to be done with great care and concern. The first command, "speak," may seem like a small matter, but speech is important, as James will explain in the next chapter.

Our speech and actions must be carefully watched because we will be **judged by the law of freedom**. James spoke of the law of freedom earlier (1:25) in reference to the gospel, the word of truth that saves us (1:18, 21) and that requires a response of obedience—not just hearing, but doing (1:22–25). This "royal law" of the Messiah Jesus (2:8), whose fundamental precept is love of God and love of neighbor, is the standard by which our conduct will be measured. Although we are saved by †grace

14. The concept of the law as a unified whole and the violation of one commandment as tantamount to breaking the whole law was a principle recognized in early Judaism (*4 Maccabees* 5:20–21; *Testament of Asher* 2:5–10; Babylonian Talmud, *Shabbat* 70b).

through faith (Eph 2:8–9), the New Testament consistently teaches that we will be judged by our works (John 5:28–29; 2 Cor 5:10; Rev 20:13). Since **judgment is merciless to one who has not shown mercy**, we must be merciful if the gospel is to benefit us. Because **mercy triumphs over judgment**, we can avoid the just punishment due to our sins by showing mercy to others and loving our neighbors as ourselves (Lev 19:18; Mark 12:31).

Both the Old Testament and the New Testament teach the connection between showing mercy and receiving God's mercy. Ben Sira writes, "Forgive your neighbor the wrong done to you; / then when you pray, your own sins will be forgiven. . . . / Can one refuse mercy to a sinner like oneself, / yet seek pardon for one's own sins?" (Sir 28:2, 4). In the book of Daniel, the prophet advises the king, "Atone for your sins with righteousness, and your iniquities with mercy to the oppressed, so that your prosperity may be prolonged" (Dan 4:27 NRSV [4:24 NABRE]). Jesus also teaches on this topic: "Blessed are the

Figure 2. A sixteenth-century Dutch painting depicting a woman distributing bread to the poor, one of whom is Christ

merciful, / for they will be shown mercy" (Matt 5:7); "If you forgive others their transgressions, your heavenly Father will forgive you. But if you do not forgive others, neither will your Father forgive your transgressions" (Matt 6:14–15). The parable of the unforgiving servant underscores the necessity that those who have received mercy extend it to others (Matt 18:21–35; see 7:1–2). Jesus' apostles continue this theme. Peter writes, "Let your love for one another be intense, because love covers a multitude of sins" (1 Pet 4:8).[15]

Welcoming the poor who are clad in filthy clothing is a merciful act. When we act with mercy, God takes pity on us. Of course, the forgiveness of our sins is grounded in the sacrifice of Christ. Our love of neighbor and mercy to others

---

15. Many other texts, such as Rom 12:12–21 and Eph 4:31–5:2, summon Christians to generous and forgiving attitudes toward others in imitation of God and Christ.

Works of Mercy

Saint Augustine expresses how acts of mercy can vindicate us on the day of judgment:

> If we were in peril from fire, we would certainly run to water to extinguish the fire. . . . In the same way, if a spark of sin flares up from our straw, and we are troubled on that account, whenever we have an opportunity to perform a work of mercy, we should rejoice, as if a fountain opened before [us] so that the fire might be extinguished.[a]

It is not that our acts of mercy earn God's forgiveness, but rather that they express our faith and union with the one who has had mercy on us.

What are the works of mercy that plunge us into the fountain of God's mercy? According to the Catechism (2447), they are charitable actions by which we come to the aid of our neighbor in his or her spiritual and bodily necessities (Isa 58:6–7; Heb 13:3). Instructing, advising, consoling, and comforting are spiritual works of mercy, as are forgiving and bearing wrongs patiently. The corporal works of mercy consist especially in feeding the hungry, sheltering the homeless, clothing the naked, visiting the sick and imprisoned, and burying the dead (Matt 25:31–46). Among all these, giving alms to the poor is one of the chief witnesses to fraternal charity: it is also a work of justice pleasing to God (Tob 4:5–11; Sir 17:22; Matt 6:2–4).

a. *Catechizing the Uninstructed* 22 (quoted in Pope Francis, *Evangelii Gaudium* 193).

---

show that we are recipients of God's mercy in Christ and continue to depend on it, an expression of faith like that of the woman who was a sinner, whose "great love" showed she had been forgiven much (Luke 7:47–50). The fact that all of us have sinned greatly and will be judged ought to spur us on to seize opportunities to speak and to act with gracious kindness and generous compassion so that mercy will win out over judgment in our lives. Showing mercy is a way of expressing "faith in our glorious Lord Jesus Christ" (James 2:1).

To sum up, in this section (2:8–13) James continues his argument that favoritism toward the wealthy is incompatible with faith in Jesus Christ (2:1–4). He begins by saying that showing partiality is a sin, for it breaks the royal law of Christ, which commands love of neighbor (2:8–9), and to transgress any commandment is to "become guilty in respect to all of it" (2:10). This should motivate us to speak and act in accord with the gospel, the "law" that brings us freedom (2:12), for by showing mercy (and implicitly here James returns to the theme of welcoming the poor person in the congregation), we can obtain mercy (2:12–13).

Faith without Works

James 2:14-26

In this section James continues his teaching on faith and its implications for the Christian life. Faith that is not accompanied by concrete actions cannot bring salvation. To teach what saving faith is and is not, James uses four illustrations: the Christian who offers only consoling words to the hungry and ill-clad brother or sister (2:15–16); demons, who believe (2:19); Abraham, the friend of God (2:21–23); and Rahab, who welcomed Joshua's spies (2:25).[1] The first two are examples of faith that does not save, while the final two illustrate works that justify.

Faith without Works Is Dead (2:14–17)

> [14]**What good is it, my brothers, if someone says he has faith but does not have works? Can that faith save him? [15]If a brother or sister has nothing to wear and has no food for the day, [16]and one of you says to them, "Go in peace, keep warm, and eat well," but you do not give them the necessities of the body, what good is it? [17]So also faith of itself, if it does not have works, is dead.**

OT: Gen 15:1–6; Ps 15
NT: Matt 25:31–46; Luke 3:11
Catechism: works of mercy, 2447; almsgiving, 2462
Lectionary: 24th Sunday in Ordinary Time, Year B (James 2:14–18)

---

1. See J. A. Motyer, *The Message of James: The Tests of Faith*, BST (Downers Grove, IL: InterVarsity, 1985), 107.

According to the Catechism (142), "*By his Revelation*, 'The invisible God, from the fullness of his love, addresses men as his friends, and moves among them, in order to invite and receive them into his own company.' The adequate response to this invitation is faith" (quoting *Dei Verbum* 2). But what is faith? James does not offer a definition, but he does say something important about what it implies: the faith that saves must be expressed in practical charity.[2] Faith without love is dead.

2:14–17   In this first example, which deals with the hungry and ill-clad brother or sister, James begins with two rhetorical questions meant to prompt reflection on what saving faith is. The first asks, **What good is it**—literally, "what does it benefit"—**if someone says he has faith** but does not put it into action? James does not say that this person really has faith, but rather that this person *claims* to have it. A person may be mistaken in the belief that he or she is following Jesus Christ. James then asks, **Can that faith save him?** Clearly, the answer to this rhetorical question is no.

James answers this question with another hypothetical question that illustrates that this kind of faith does not save. It concerns a **brother or sister**—that is, a fellow Christian—who **has nothing to wear and has no food for the day**. This is the depths of misery, for food and clothing are necessities for human existence (see 1 Tim 6:8). That **one of you** fails to give vital necessities to someone in dire need indicates that the behavior that James condemns takes place where Christians know of the need and can do something about it. Rather than extend a hand, the person with resources bids the needy person, "**Go in peace**," a customary Jewish farewell greeting (Judg 18:6; 1 Sam 20:42; 2 Kings 5:19) used by Jesus (Luke 7:50; 8:48); the early Christians likewise said farewell with a greeting of peace (Eph 6:23; 1 Pet 5:14b; 3 John 1:15). This is followed by a wish that the hungry, naked person "**keep warm, and eat well.**" James drives the message home by repeating his initial question, **What good is it?** To have the means to help someone in grave need yet send that person away with mere good wishes is shocking and cruel.

Now James draws a conclusion from his example: **So also faith of itself, if it does not have works, is dead**—that is, ineffective, unable to save. Just as "Go in peace, keep warm, and eat well" is useless or worse if not accompanied by helping acts, so also confessing "our glorious Lord Jesus Christ" (2:1) is pointless if one does not do the merciful deeds that he commands in his royal law of love (2:8). If faith in Jesus does not bring us to conform to his way of life, then

---

2. The Catechism explains what faith is in paragraph 143 and elaborates helpfully on that explanation in paragraphs 144–59.

it is useful. Jesus himself made this point in the parable of the great judgment (Matt 25:31–46).[3] There Jesus taught that a person's salvation hinges on his or her care of the poor. The judge sends those on his left away with this explanation: "I was hungry and you gave me no food, I was thirsty and you gave me no drink, a stranger and you gave me no welcome, naked and you gave me no clothing, ill and in prison, and you did not care for me" (Matt 25:42–43). Thus, a person who has the kind of faith that does not issue in works of mercy has not been transformed by the love of God. His or her salvation is in jeopardy. Jesus' parable of judgment, quoted above, ends with the condemnation of those who have not obeyed: "Then he will say to those on his left, 'Depart from me, you accursed, into the eternal fire prepared for the devil and his angels'" (Matt 25:41).

The Old Testament teaches that care for the poor is a basic feature of life in †covenant relationship with God (Exod 22:25–27; 23:11; Deut 15:7–8). Giving alms to the poor was a central element of Jewish piety and the mark of a righteous person (Ps 37:21; Prov 21:26). The book of Tobit says that "almsgiving saves from death, and purges all sin. Those who give alms will enjoy a full life" (Tob 12:9), and Sirach teaches, "As water quenches a flaming fire, / so almsgiving atones for sins" (Sir 3:30). Serving the poor was so much at the heart of Jesus' ministry that he pointed to his preaching to the poor to demonstrate that he was fulfilling God's promises of salvation (Matt 11:5; see Luke 4:18). Jesus both teaches his followers to give alms (Luke 12:33) and, presupposing that they already give alms, instructs them how to do so properly (Matt 6:2).

In this section James refutes the claims of those who try to separate religion from ethics, faith from charity. God has a special tenderness and compassion for the poor (Sir 35:16–21), and he is not pleased if we have the means to help those suffering misery and despair but close our hearts and hands to them. Such actions are simply unacceptable to our good God, "who gives to all generously and ungrudgingly" (James 1:5) and whose blessings are given to be shared with those in need.

The Faith of Demons (2:18–19)

---

[18]**Indeed someone may say, "You have faith and I have works." Demonstrate your faith to me without works, and I will demonstrate my faith**

---

3. An alternative interpretation is that the parable depicts the judgment of non-Christians, "the nations," on the basis of how they treat Jesus' disciples, "these least brothers of mine" (Matt 25:32, 40). See Daniel Harrington, *The Gospel of Matthew*, SP 1 (Collegeville, MN: Liturgical Press, 1991), 358–60.

Universal Destination of Goods and Preferential Love for the Poor

LIVING TRADITION

Vatican Council II teaches that "God destined the earth and all it contains for all men and all peoples so that all created things would be shared fairly by all mankind under the guidance of justice tempered by charity."[a] This concept is known as the universal destination of goods, and it maintains that God gave the earth to humankind for sustenance, without excluding or favoring anyone.[b] Material goods are indispensable for persons to live a life of dignity and share in the development of society, and God intends that all should have access to them.

Despite enormous human progress, the evils of human misery and poverty exist. Such suffering and misery is incompatible with God's original design for humankind. The Catechism (2448) teaches,

> In its various forms—material deprivation, unjust oppression, physical and psychological illness and death—*human misery* is the obvious sign of the inherited condition of frailty and need for salvation in which man finds himself as a consequence of original sin. This misery elicited the compassion of Christ the Savior, who willingly took it upon himself and identified himself with the least of his brethren. Hence, those who are oppressed by poverty are the object of a *preferential love* on the part of the Church which, since her origin and in spite of the failings of many of her members, has not ceased to work for their relief, defense, and liberation through numerous works of charity which remain indispensable always and everywhere.[c]

The Church's teaching on the universal destination of goods and the preferential love for the poor indicates that the poor are not a burden or a problem to be solved but rather an opportunity to express our life in Christ. Those who are blessed with an abundance of material things should recognize that they have received much through God's generosity, so that they, in turn, can share with others (2 Cor 8:14; 9:8; Eph 4:28). Saint Gregory the Great taught, "When we attend to the needs of those in want, we give them what is theirs, not ours. More than performing works of mercy, we are paying a debt of justice" (Catechism 2446).[d] Likewise, Christians should work for the just ordering of society so that the poor may be able to satisfy their basic needs and have the opportunity to improve their material circumstances.

a. *Gaudium et Spes* (Pastoral Constitution on the Church in the Modern World) 69.
b. Pontifical Council for Justice and Peace, *Compendium on the Social Doctrine of the Church* 171.
c. CDF, instruction, *Libertatis conscientia*, 68.
d. *Regula Pastoralis* 3.21 (PL 77, 87). See also Pontifical Council for Justice and Peace, *Compendium on the Social Doctrine of the Church* 184.

to you from my works. [19]You believe that God is one. You do well. Even the
demons believe that and tremble.

OT: Deut 6:4–6
NT: Mark 1:21–24 // Luke 4:31–34; Mark 1:32–34
Catechism: fall of the angels, 391–95; exorcism, 1673; signs of the kingdom of God, 550
Lectionary: 24th Sunday in Ordinary Time, Year B (James 2:14–18)

In this section James offers his second teaching on true faith. Faith without works
cannot save, for even the demons have such faith. If orthodox belief without
love were enough, then even the demons would go to heaven.

James begins by saying, **Indeed someone may say**, followed by the words   2:18–19
of a hypothetical person. James is engaging in a style of argumentation known
as diatribe—a dialogue in which an imaginary opponent presents an objection
that the author refutes in order to develop his or her argument.[4] The hypothetical dialogue is found in 2:18–24, since in these verses James writes in the
second person singular, whereas in the prior verses and in those after verse 24
he returns to the second person plural. This is not apparent in contemporary
English translations since modern English does not distinguish between "you"
singular and "you" plural.

What follows seems a little bit odd. The reader would expect the imaginary
opponent to say, "*I* have faith and *you* have works," indicating that the other
side emphasizes faith while James emphasizes works. However, the opponent
says the opposite: **"You have faith and I have works."** Scholars have suggested
a variety of solutions to this problem, none of which is completely satisfactory.
What is clear, however, is that somehow the speaker separates faith and works,
as though the Christian life can be reduced to one or the other.

James rebuffs such thinking by saying that works demonstrate true faith.
Then in a series of terse statements he compares faith devoid of works to the
faith that devils have. His argument touches on one of the central teachings of
the Old Testament: **God is one**. This profession of faith is expressed in Deut
6:4: "Hear, O Israel: The †LORD our God, the LORD is one" (NIV). This teaching,
basic to Judaism, is that there is one God, and this God has an exclusive claim
on Israel. James acknowledges that his readers accept this fundamental tenet
of faith, observing wryly that they **do well**. However, he quickly proves that
belief in God's oneness is not enough, since even **the demons believe that and
tremble**. Correct belief about God, which the demons share, is not sufficient
for salvation. Faith in God must be lived out by obedience to God's commands.

4. Patrick J. Hartin, *James*, SP 14 (Collegeville, MN: Liturgical Press, 2003), 151.

Jesus taught the importance of acting on faith when he said, "Not everyone who says to me, 'Lord, Lord,' will enter the kingdom of heaven, but only the one who does the will of my Father in heaven" (Matt 7:21 [see Luke 6:46]). Faith that saves must be expressed in good works. Saint Thomas Aquinas said, "The truth of faith includes not only inner belief, but also outward profession, which is expressed not only by declaration of one's belief, but also by the actions by which a person shows that he has faith."[5]

Reflection and Application (2:18–19)

In this text James teaches that theological correctness is not enough. This ought to give Catholics pause when we reassure ourselves and proclaim to others that the fullness of the truth and the means of †grace are found in the Catholic Church. On its own, knowing the truth does not save; we must put it into practice. The importance of works that correspond to faith is part of that treasure of Catholic doctrine that we must hear and obey.

James's teaching should lead us not only to examine our practice as Catholics but also to respect other Christians, who may possess less of the truth but may be more faithful at practicing the truth that they know. For example, Catholics believe in the inspiration of Scripture and the urgency of preaching the †gospel as much as evangelical Protestants do. Yet often Protestants surpass us in their wholehearted response to these truths. It is fitting that we respect and learn from these brothers and sisters whenever they excel in practice of the faith that we share.

Works That Justify (2:20–26)

[20]Do you want proof, you ignoramus, that faith without works is useless? [21]Was not Abraham our father justified by works when he offered his son Isaac upon the altar? [22]You see that faith was active along with his works, and faith was completed by the works. [23]Thus the scripture was fulfilled that says, "Abraham believed God, and it was credited to him as righteousness," and he was called "the friend of God." [24]See how a person is justified by works and not by faith alone. [25]And in the same way, was not Rahab the harlot also justified by works when she welcomed the

5. *Summa theologiae* II-II, q. 5, a. 2.

**messengers and sent them out by a different route? ²⁶For just as a body
without a spirit is dead, so also faith without works is dead.**

OT: Gen 15:1–6; 22:1–19; Josh 2
NT: Rom 4; Gal 3:1–9
Catechism: obedience of faith, 144–47; God's promise and the prayer of faith, 2570–73

James continues his argument about the nature of real faith by drawing on
two examples of faith from the Scriptures: Abraham (vv. 21–23) and Rahab
(v. 25). He completes each example with a summary teaching statement (vv.
24, 26).

James addresses another rhetorical question to a hypothetical conversa-   2:20
tion partner who seems to insist that only faith is necessary. The Greek word
translated as **ignoramus** literally means "empty person," and it has overtones
of intellectual and moral error.⁶ Because the question deals with the meaning
of faith, the word probably means "ignorant."

Modern readers might be surprised by James's mode of addressing his imaginary opponent. We might be offended if a priest spoke like this in a Sunday
homily! But strong language was common in diatribe, and it was expected that
the person making this kind of argument would show strong emotion and speak
forcefully, as James does.

James's first example is **Abraham our father.** In Gen 12:1–3, God promised   2:21
Abraham that he would make of him a great nation, and the Old Testament depicts Abraham as the father of the Jewish nation (Isa 51:2; Sir 44:19–23). James
states that Abraham was **justified by works**—that is, judged to be righteous
on the basis of his conduct—**when he offered his son Isaac upon the altar.**
James is alluding to God's positive evaluation of Abraham's act of obedience
reported in Gen 22. At the moment Abraham lifts the knife to slay his son in
obedience to God's command, the angel of the Lord stops him and says on
the Lord's behalf, "Now I know that you fear God, since you did not withhold
from me your son" (Gen 22:12). A few verses later the Lord himself swears
an oath, "*Because you acted as you did . . .* , I will bless you," and confirms his
promises to Abraham (Gen 22:16–17 [italics added]). Both the angel's statement and the Lord's oath indicate that God sees Abraham as a righteous man
and will bless him.

Now James explains the relationship between faith and works in Abraham's   2:22
action. James explains that **faith was active along with his works** when Abraham

6. Peter H. Davids, *The Epistle of James: A Commentary on the Greek Text*, NIGTC (Grand Rapids:
Eerdmans, 1982), 126.

offered Isaac.[7] James clarifies the relationship still further: Abraham's **faith was completed by the works**, by his act of offering Isaac. Interestingly, the verb "completed" (*teleioō*) is related to the word "perfect" (*teleios*) used in 1:3–4 to describe a person who becomes mature through the testing of his or her faith.

2:23   This explanation of Gen 22 helps James's readers better understand an earlier passage in Genesis that made Abraham famous for his faith, since he is the first person the Bible describes as believing. James quotes Gen 15:6: **"Abraham believed God and it was credited to him as righteousness."** The patriarch believed God's promise that his offspring would be his heir and that his descendants would be as numerous as the stars (Gen 15:4–5). The fact that Abraham was credited with righteousness (NJB: "considered as . . . upright") indicates that this positive evaluation resulted not from his deeds but from his attitude of faith (a point that Paul emphasizes in Rom 4:3–12; Gal 3:6–9). According to James, **the scripture** of Gen 15:6 **was fulfilled** by Abraham's act of obedience when he was tested in Gen 22. Thus, James confirms the value of faith but shows that works are its necessary completion. Unlike the demons who believe but do not obey (2:19), Abraham believed and obeyed and is therefore described in Scripture as **"the friend** [or "the beloved"] **of God"** (see Isa 41:8).

2:24   The point is summed up in 2:24: **a person is justified by works and not by faith alone.** This statement preserves the role of faith but denies that belief is sufficient by itself. Rather, James insists that faith must be completed by corresponding works if a person is to be accepted as righteous by God—that is, justified by God.

2:25   The second example, Rahab, differs dramatically: Abraham was a man, the father of faith, and the father of the Israelites, while Rahab was a woman, a prostitute, and a foreigner. By

Wikimedia Commons

Figure 3. An angel saves Isaac from being sacrificed (Peter Paul Rubens, *The Sacrifice of Isaac*).

7. The Letter to the Hebrews confirms the role of faith in this event: "By faith Abraham, when put to the test, offered up Isaac. . . . He reasoned that God was able to raise even from the dead" (Heb 11:17–19).

Is James Responding to Paul?

BIBLICAL
BACKGROUND

James's stress on the necessity of works may seem to be at odds with Paul's teaching on the primacy of faith. Paul teaches that human beings are justified by faith in God, not by their works, whether "works of the law"—compliance with the law of Moses (Rom 3:28; 4:2; Gal 2:16)—or any good work (Eph 2:8–10; Titus 3:5). James does not claim that human deeds apart from faith in Jesus Christ bring us to salvation. But James complements and completes Paul's teaching by saying that faith must be expressed in actions, especially love for the poor. And, indeed, Paul himself accompanies his teaching about faith with a repeated summons to love (Rom 13:8–10; Gal 5:13–15; Eph 5:1–2; 1 Thess 1:3), and he speaks of "faith working through love" (Gal 5:6).

Some commentators have suggested that James is trying to correct Paul's teaching, but this seems unlikely. It is possible, however, that James is addressing a misunderstanding of Paul's teaching. It is important to note that the contexts of Paul's teaching and James's are different. Paul's message is directed against the teaching of some Jewish Christians who want to require Gentile Christians to follow the Mosaic law. In the face of that attempt, Paul teaches that only faith in Jesus Christ justifies—that is, places people in a right relationship with God. James's teaching is directed to Jewish Christians who lack charity toward one another. To them, James points out that simply believing in Jesus without acting is useless; rather, works are the manifestation of a life of genuine faith. Pope Benedict XVI explains, "Saint Paul is opposed to the pride of man who thinks he does not need the love of God that precedes us; he is opposed to the pride of self-justification without grace, simply given and undeserved. Saint James, instead, talks about works as the normal fruit of faith"[a] and as its necessary manifestation.

a. General Audience, June 28, 2006.

choosing these two very different examples, James illustrates that justification is available to anyone who follows the will of God.

The book of Joshua recounts the story of Rahab, a non-Israelite who recognized the power of the God of Israel and his intention to give the land to the Israelites (Josh 2:1–21). Because of that, she **welcomed the messengers** who were spying on the city of Jericho and hid them on her roof. During the night, she let the spies down on a rope on the other side of the city walls to escape the city authorities who were searching for them. Because she saved the spies, she and her family were spared when the Israelites returned to conquer the city.

It was her faith in the God of Israel expressed in action that saved her and her family from the demise of the city. In fact, her faith without action would have been useless. Like Abraham, Rahab first believed in God, and then her actions toward his messengers demonstrated her faith. As a result, she was saved from God's judgment on Jericho.

2:26   James finishes with a comparison. He likens a dead body, **a body without a spirit**, to **faith without works**. Without works, faith is no more alive than a corpse. It is works that give life to faith. The **spirit**, or "breath" (*pneuma*), is vital for a body to live. In the same way, faith cannot bring salvation if it is not accompanied by the works that give it life and vitality.

In this chapter James has emphasized that it is not enough simply to believe in God. Faith is useless unless it is accompanied by love of neighbor. Belief in God must lead into obedience and love if we are to be saved and enjoy God's company forever.

Reflection and Application (2:14–26)

Once when I presented a difficult topic in religion class, one of my students became exasperated and said, "Can't we just love one another? What's the point of all this?" While the student's impatience with learning was wrong, his concern was correct: being a Christian means to love.[8] And Jesus sets a very high standard for love. For example:

> "I say to you, whoever is angry with his brother will be liable to judgment, and whoever says to his brother, 'Raqa,' will be answerable to the Sanhedrin, and whoever says, 'You fool,' will be liable to fiery Gehenna." (Matt 5:22)

> "I say to you, offer no resistance to one who is evil. When someone strikes you on [your] right cheek, turn the other one to him as well." (Matt 5:39)

Jesus' words are so challenging that we are tempted to despair of ever keeping them, especially when we consider the motives of our hearts. Yet James teaches that works that correspond to our faith are necessary. What are we to do?

According to Pope Benedict XVI, it is precisely when we realize how difficult it is to love that faith begins.

---

8. See Pope Benedict XVI, "What It Means to Be a Christian," in *Credo for Today: What Christians Believe*, trans. Michael J. Miller et al. (San Francisco: Ignatius Press, 2006), 11.

For what faith basically means is just that this shortfall that we all have in our love is made up by the surplus of Jesus Christ's love, acting on our behalf. He simply tells us that God himself has poured out among us a superabundance of his love and has thus made good in advance all our deficiency. Ultimately, faith means nothing other than admitting that we have this kind of shortfall; it means opening our hand and accepting a gift.[9]

9. Ibid., 12–13.

The Destructive Power of the Tongue

James 3:1–18

The story is told that a certain nun often confessed to St. Philip Neri that she had gossiped. After one such confession, he gave her an unusual penance. He told her to take a feather pillow, go to the top of the church, rip open the pillow, and let the feathers blow away in the breeze. She did as instructed, and when she returned at her next confession, he told her to go and gather all the feathers now strewn throughout the city. Aghast, she replied that that would be impossible. "So it is," he said, "with the words you have spoken. They spread far and wide, and can never be gathered together again."

James, like St. Philip Neri, recognizes that words are powerful. With them we can console and comfort, but we can also inflict terrible wounds. In chapter 3, James speaks of the importance of controlling the tongue, and he employs a structure similar to that of chapter 2. There he began with a particular situation—a rich man and a poor man in the Christian assembly—and branched out to teach about related topics: judgment and mercy (2:13); faith and works (2:14–26). In this chapter also, James begins with a particular situation, that of teachers (3:1), then branches out to teach about the destructive power of the tongue (3:2–12) and about earthly versus heavenly wisdom (3:13–18).

The Tongue (3:1–12)

[1]Not many of you should become teachers, my brothers, for you realize that we will be judged more strictly, [2]for we all fall short in many respects.

66

If anyone does not fall short in speech, he is a perfect man, able to bridle his whole body also. [3]If we put bits into the mouths of horses to make them obey us, we also guide their whole bodies. [4]It is the same with ships: even though they are so large and driven by fierce winds, they are steered by a very small rudder wherever the pilot's inclination wishes. [5]In the same way the tongue is a small member and yet has great pretensions.

Consider how small a fire can set a huge forest ablaze. [6]The tongue is also a fire. It exists among our members as a world of malice, defiling the whole body and setting the entire course of our lives on fire, itself set on fire by Gehenna. [7]For every kind of beast and bird, of reptile and sea creature, can be tamed and has been tamed by the human species, [8]but no human being can tame the tongue. It is a restless evil, full of deadly poison. [9]With it we bless the Lord and Father, and with it we curse human beings who are made in the likeness of God. [10]From the same mouth come blessing and cursing. This need not be so, my brothers. [11]Does a spring gush forth from the same opening both pure and brackish water? [12]Can a fig tree, my brothers, produce olives, or a grapevine figs? Neither can salt water yield fresh.

OT: Pss 17:3–4; 19:15; 141:1–4; Prov 15:28; 18:6–8; 21:23; Sir 27:5–6; 28:13–23
NT: Matt 15:10–20; 12:34–37 // Luke 6:45; Col 4:6
Catechism: blasphemy, 2148

James first cautions his listeners not to become teachers without considering the risks (v. 1) and then launches into a reflection on the power of speech. First he says that a person who can bridle the tongue can control his or her whole body (v. 2). He then uses the metaphors of a bit and a rudder to illustrate how the tongue guides the whole person (vv. 3–5). Next he speaks of the effects of the tongue, comparing it to fire (vv. 5–6). After declaring that no one is able to tame the tongue (vv. 7–9), he concludes that one's speech reveals one's inner intentions (vv. 10–12).

James begins, as often, with an imperative followed by an explanation. The command could also be translated, "Let not many of you become teachers." Jews had a great esteem for teachers; the Hebrew word for "teacher" that James may have had in mind was "rabbi," which literally meant "my great one."[1] Jesus is often addressed as "teacher" or "rabbi" in the Gospels (Matt 8:19; Mark 4:38; John 1:38). In the early Church, teachers fulfilled a recognized ministry, and the ability to teach was a recognized charism of the Holy Spirit (Rom 12:7;

3:1

---

1. James Hardy Ropes, *A Critical and Exegetical Commentary on the Epistle of St. James*, ICC (1916; repr., Edinburgh: T&T Clark, 1978), 226.

The Teacher and the Wise Person

In this chapter James speaks of the teacher and of the person who is wise (3:1, 13). In the Old Testament it was a task of the wise to lead the young and inexperienced to true wisdom, which was grounded in the fear of the Lord and entailed upright conduct. The sages, such as the authors of Proverbs, Sirach, and Wisdom, were able to impart wisdom because they were imbued with the word of God, the ⁺Torah, which Ben Sira identifies with wisdom itself (Sir 24, especially v. 23). They had meditated deeply on it, and it had become part of their very being. They drew on their own experience and creativity to give expression to the word of God in their teaching, so that God's word remained dynamic through them. They communicated to their students not simply rational knowledge but an entire way of life that was reasonable and coherent because it was based on the word of God.

Jesus, who was often addressed as "teacher" or "rabbi" (Matt 8:19; 12:38; 19:16), continues the tradition of the sages in the Old Testament, but he differs from them in one dramatic respect: he speaks on his own authority and emphasizes a relationship with himself (Matt 5:21–45; 7:29; 10:37–39). Jesus calls his disciples to himself—that is, to listen and to imbibe *his* words, to emulate *his* actions, and to follow *him* even to his death on the cross. Jesus reveals God the Father (John 1:18; 14:9) and presents himself as the only way to the Father (John 14:6). Essentially, what Jesus teaches is how to have a relationship with him and, through him, with the Father. According to the New Testament, Jesus is not merely a teacher of wisdom, but is himself the embodiment of divine wisdom (Luke 7:35; 1 Cor 1:24, 30).

The apostles and James faithfully taught the Lord's message and followed him in his manner of life and death. The role of a Christian teacher cannot be reduced to that of simply imparting knowledge, as might be the case in other disciplines. A teacher of the faith must first listen to Jesus' words and be formed by them, entering into an intimate relationship with wisdom incarnate. A Christian teacher must live and act as Jesus did, even to the point of embracing the cross.

1 Cor 12:28; Eph 4:11). James considers himself a teacher, for he says "we who teach" (NRSV).

Such a respected role would naturally appeal to many people, but James cautions those who wish to become teachers that they will be **judged more strictly**. They will be held to a higher standard and be liable to a greater punishment if they fail to meet it (see Luke 12:47–48).[2] James's concern seems to be twofold.

2. Dan G. McCartney, *James*, BECNT (Grand Rapids: Baker Academic, 2009), 179.

First, since the teaching profession requires one to speak more, teachers may more easily fall into sin. Second, the tongue, though small, has wide-reaching potential. Words can be terribly effective, and so the teacher, who must speak frequently, has a greater potential to harm others.

James now turns the discourse to a treatise on speech and the tongue. He **3:2** states that all **fall short in many respects**. The Greek verb translated as "fall short" literally means "to stumble," and earlier in James it refers to not measuring up to the precepts of the law (2:10). James says that all fall short in various ways. But the one who makes no mistakes in speaking **is a perfect man, able to bridle his whole body also**. By "perfect" James does not mean the person is blameless or has achieved complete moral perfection. That would contradict the previous clause, "we all fall short," as well as being demonstrably untrue. The term "perfect" describes the one who is spiritually mature, having become what God wants him or her to be (see 1:4). Such a person controls the tongue, and having mastery over speech is an outward manifestation of inner self-mastery.

The teaching of James about speech echoes that of Jesus. Jesus also taught that there is a relationship between speech and the interior life: "From the fullness of the heart the mouth speaks" (Luke 6:45 [see Matt 12:34–35]). Jesus also links speech to future judgment: "I tell you, on the day of judgment people will render an account for every careless word they speak. By your words you will be acquitted, and by your words you will be condemned" (Matt 12:36–37). Since words will bring acquittal or condemnation, and only "perfect" or mature people are able to control their speech, these are the Christians who should be teachers of the faith.

James now compares the tongue to two small instruments. In the first ex- **3:3–5a** ample, people **put bits into the mouths of horses**, and this small bit guides the large body of a horse. James's point is that the tongue, small in size, directs the life of the person. In the second example, a **very small rudder** directs a large ship driven by powerful winds. This makes essentially the same point as the first example, but James adds that the rudder goes **wherever the pilot's inclination wishes**. This addition contributes something important: the ship's movement reveals the desire and wish of the one guiding it. James's point is that the person ought to control the tongue, not be controlled by it. James already indicated that someone who is perfect, meaning the mature person, is able to bridle the tongue and thus the whole body (v. 2). But if we do not control our tongue, as James will now explain, we fall subject to a terrible power.

James next compares the tongue to a small **fire that can set a huge forest** **3:5b–6** **ablaze**; in the same way the tongue can defile the whole person and bring great destruction.

The Destructive Power of the Tongue

BIBLICAL BACKGROUND

James's warnings about the destructive potential of the tongue belong to a venerable biblical tradition. Here, for instance, is a comparable passage from Sirach:

> Cursed be gossips and the double-tongued,
>   for they destroy the peace of many.
> A meddlesome tongue subverts many,
>   and makes them refugees among peoples.
> It destroys strong cities,
>   and overthrows the houses of the great.
> A meddlesome tongue drives virtuous women from their homes,
>   and robs them of the fruit of their toil.
> Whoever heed it will find no rest,
>   nor will they dwell in peace.
>
> A blow from a whip raises a welt,
>   but a blow from the tongue will break bones.
> Many have fallen by the edge of the sword,
>   but not as many as by the tongue.
> Happy the one who is sheltered from it,
>   and has not endured its wrath;
> Who has not borne its yoke
>   nor been bound with its chains.
> For its yoke is a yoke of iron,
>   and its chains are chains of bronze;
> The death it inflicts is an evil death,
>   even Sheol is preferable to it.
> It will have no power over the godly,
>   nor will they be burned in its flame.
> But those who forsake the Lord will fall victim to it,
>   as it burns among them unquenchably;
> It will hurl itself against them like a lion,
>   and like a leopard, it will tear them to pieces. (Sir 28:13–23)

James states that the tongue is placed among **our members as a world of malice**. "Members" refers to the parts of the human body, such as eyes, arms, or legs. James is describing the effect that this one organ has on the entire person. "The †world" ("the" is present in the Greek) refers to human society insofar as it is resists God (see 2:5), while "malice" (literally, "unrighteousness") refers to evildoing. James is saying that the tongue is like a colony of the world's rebellion within the body, a center of sin within a person.

James now describes the effects of this organ that he links with the unrighteous world. Words that the tongue utters are capable of **defiling the whole**

body. The verb "defile" (*spiloō*) means "to stain, pollute." This is a form of the word used in 1:27 to describe pure and undefiled religion as keeping oneself "unstained" (*aspilos*) from the world. The tongue is capable of staining the whole body.

Not only does evil speech defile us, but also the tongue is capable of **setting the entire course of our lives on fire**. The Greek is difficult here, and it literally reads "setting on fire the wheel of being." Scholars debate the meaning, but most think that it refers to the span of one's life. Thus, just as a small fire sets an entire forest ablaze, so too words can have far-reaching consequences. "The tongue's potential for damage, like that of a wildfire, extends well beyond its point of origin, spreading outward in an ever-widening circle."[3] Bede the Venerable applies the text to life: "Just as from a small spark a spreading fire often ignites a great forest, so an unrestrained tongue, feeding on its own trivialities, destroys the great stuff of good works, many fruits of the spiritual life, after it has spoiled them, but it also often devours countless leaves of speech which appeared excellent."[4] Even good speech and actions can be overshadowed and destroyed by evil talk. James does not specify the sins of the tongue, but if we take account of the biblical tradition in which he stands, we may conclude that he is warning against gossip, slander, complaining, boasting, rash words spoken in anger, and disrespectful or abusive speech.[5]

Finally, James explains why the tongue has this deadly capacity: it is **itself set on fire by Gehenna**. Gehenna was a valley south of Jerusalem that smelled of smoke and refuse because it was the city's garbage dump. It was a sinister place, since child sacrifices occurred there in Old Testament times (2 Kings 23:10; Jer 7:31; 19:5–6). It came to symbolize the place of God's judgment (Jer 19:6). Jesus used Gehenna as an image for divine retribution; thus most New Testament translations render the Greek word *geenna* as "hell" (Matt 5:22, 29–30). The tongue, then, is inflamed by hell and is an instrument of evil. James refers to the sinful tendency of human speech after the fall, a specific manifestation of what Paul refers to as "the †flesh" and Christian tradition calls "concupiscence." To sum up James's message: the tongue, because it is propelled by evil, has the capacity to defile one's whole being as well as the entire course of one's existence.

Next James makes the point that nobody is able to **tame the tongue** and   3:7–9
indicates how contrary this is to God's original plan by two allusions to the story of creation in Genesis. The first allusion—**every kind of beast and bird,**

---

3. McCartney, *James*, 190.

4. Bede the Venerable, *Commentary on the Seven Catholic Epistles*, trans. David Hurst, CSS 82 (Kalamazoo, MI: Cistercian Publications, 1985), 39.

5. See Exod 20:16; Lev 19:16; Prov 17:20; 20:19; Sir 22:20–22; Matt 12:36; 1 Pet 3:10.

of reptile and sea creature—recalls God's command to the human race: "Have dominion over the fish of the sea, the birds of the air, and all the living things that crawl on the earth" (Gen 1:28).[6] James indicates that humankind has indeed fulfilled this command of God because these animals **can be tamed**, and in fact every kind **has been tamed by the human species**—an indication of human dominion. But tellingly, humankind has been unable to exercise the same dominion over the tongue.

Why is taming the tongue so difficult? James says that the tongue is **a restless evil, full of deadly poison**. "Restless" (*akatastatos*) is the same word used in 1:8 to describe the unstable person who lacks wisdom and has not submitted to God. James's statement that the tongue is evil and full of poison, coupled with his previous saying that the tongue burns with the fire of Gehenna, indicates that the power that inflames the tongue and renders it hostile to God is sin.[7] The tongue is the means by which sin and evil are able to advance their purposes in a person.

James illustrates the cosmic disorder at work through the tongue by pointing out a terrible contradiction. With our tongue **we bless the Lord**, whom we can now approach and call **Father** as a result of the reconciliation Christ obtained for us (Eph 2:16–18). To praise and bless God, and especially to call him "Father," is the highest and truest function of the tongue.

In a second allusion to Genesis, James recalls that **human beings** are **made in the likeness of God**. James uses the same rare word for "likeness" (*homoiōsis*, found only here in the New Testament) that the †Septuagint employs in Gen 1:26, where God says, "Let us make human beings in our image, after our likeness." In Genesis "likeness" indicates that human beings bear a filial resemblance to God, since in Hebrew the same expression is used of the relationship of Adam to his son: Adam begot Seth "in his likeness" (Gen 5:3). By using this word, James underscores the inconsistency of blessing God and cursing people; to **curse** one who is a son or daughter of God is akin to cursing God himself.

By alluding to Genesis and recalling the fundamental dignity of the human person, James places speech in the context of God's original plan for creation and the human race. The animals were to be tamed, and human beings were to master themselves, but instead, since the fall the tongue can control a person's life. Also, since humans are made in the likeness of God and have an inherent

---

6. The list of tamed creatures that James provides—beast and bird, reptile and sea creature—reflects the Bible's classification of the entire animal world (Gen 1:26–30; 9:2). See Patrick J. Hartin, *James*, SP 14 (Collegeville, MN: Liturgical Press, 2003), 186.

7. Ibid., 187.

dignity, they should be blessed, not cursed. James implies that cursing another person is like cursing God! Thus God's original intention goes awry in the ways we speak to one another and about one another.

This need not be so, or better, "this ought not to be so." James raises the question of whether it is even possible to sincerely bless God and also curse a neighbor. Can someone who curses another person truly give heartfelt blessing to God? James employs two rhetorical questions whose implied answer is no. No, **a spring** cannot give forth **both pure and brackish water**, nor can **a fig tree . . . produce olives, or a grapevine figs**. Neither can a person truly bless God while cursing another. A person who curses a neighbor reveals a lack of honor and obedience to God, since the "royal law" directs us to love God and our neighbor (2:8–13). As was mentioned earlier, Jesus taught that our speech reveals our hearts: "From the fullness of the heart the mouth speaks" (Luke 6:45). Two centuries earlier Ben Sira wrote, "The furnace tests the potter's vessels; / the test of a person is in conversation. / The fruit of a tree shows the care it has had; / so speech discloses the bent of a person's heart" (Sir 27:5–6). Like Sirach, James understands that one's speech is a measure of one's interior life. An individual who is "perfect" or mature (3:2; see 1:4) will bless God and tame the tongue. But if a person's heart is filled with self-love, bitterness, or anger, this will be revealed in his or her speech. The First Letter of John teaches something similar: it is impossible to love God and hate one's brother or sister (1 John 4:20).

Thus our words are a measure of our inner spiritual life. "A fig must have a fig tree as its source, a grape can come only from a vine, an olive from an olive tree; salt water has a salt water source; sweet water a sweet source; bitter words a bitter heart; critical words a critical spirit; defamatory, unloving speech issues from a heart where the love of Jesus is a stranger."[8]

Reflection and Application (3:1–12)

Two of the Ten Commandments deal with speech. Among the first three, which instruct us in our relationship with God, is the second: "You shall not invoke the name of the LORD, your God, in vain" (Exod 20:7). Among the last seven, which inform us of God's intent for human relationships, is the eighth: "You shall not bear false witness against your neighbor" (Exod 20:16). Thus,

8. J. A. Motyer, *The Message of James: The Tests of Faith*, BST (Downers Grove, IL: InterVarsity, 1985), 127.

God's law commands the honoring of God's name in our speech and complete truthfulness in human exchange.[9]

Saint John Chrysostom, like James before him, sees these two commandments as related:

> Let nothing bitter proceed from the mouth that has been graced with such holy Mysteries. Let not the tongue that has touched the Lord's Body utter anything offensive. May we guard its purity, may we not utter curses with it! For if "slanderers shall not inherit the kingdom of God" (1 Cor 6:10), how much more will those who curse not inherit it. For the one who curses always does injury, and injury and prayer are in conflict; cursing and praying are utterly in contrast. . . . Do you implore mercy from God, and then curse another?[10]

The Wise Person (3:13–18)

¹³Who among you is wise and understanding? Let him show his works by a good life in the humility that comes from wisdom. ¹⁴But if you have bitter jealousy and selfish ambition in your hearts, do not boast and be false to the truth. ¹⁵Wisdom of this kind does not come down from above but is earthly, unspiritual, demonic. ¹⁶For where jealousy and selfish ambition exist, there is disorder and every foul practice. ¹⁷But the wisdom from above is first of all pure, then peaceable, gentle, compliant, full of mercy and good fruits, without inconstancy or insincerity. ¹⁸And the fruit of righteousness is sown in peace for those who cultivate peace.

OT: Prov 8:1–21; 22:8–10; Wis 7:7–14
NT: 1 Cor 1:18–24; Gal 5:17–26; 2 Pet 1:3–8
Catechism: definition of sin, 1851; different kinds of sins, 1852–53
Lectionary: 25th Sunday in Ordinary Time, Year B (James 3:16–4:3)

James implicitly returns to considering the kind of person suited to be a teacher in the Christian community by reflecting on wisdom. James indicates that wisdom from God is evidenced not in intellectual feats but in works done in humility. He compares two types of wisdom, one from above and one from below, and describes the results of each.

3:13   James begins with a rhetorical summons to those who are **wise and understanding** to identify themselves. This is the only time this Greek word for

9. Dmitri Royster, *The Epistle of Saint James: A Commentary* (Yonkers, NY: St. Vladimir's Seminary Press, 2010), 129.
10. *Homily* 6 on 1 Timothy (author's translation).

"understanding" appears in the New Testament, but in the †Septuagint it occurs in the phrase "wise and understanding" in reference to those whom God commands Moses to appoint as leaders and to Israel when it is obedient to God's law (Deut 1:13, 15; 4:6). James is addressing those who consider themselves wise in the ways of God and able to function as teachers of his people. James then uses an imperative to challenge teachers, leaders, and anyone who might aspire to such a role: **show . . . by a good life** that you are truly wise. In other words, do not just tell people how much you know, but demonstrate your wisdom by your life.

A concrete indication of a person's wisdom is a **good life** and **humility**. The Greek word translated as "good" indicates what is noble and praiseworthy; thus it points to a person who conducts herself in an upright, decent manner. The second characteristic, "humility" (*prautēs*), was mentioned in 1:21, where James exhorted Christians to humbly welcome the word within them. Other translations render this word as "meekness" or "gentleness"; it is the opposite of being aggressive, angry, or violent. Such gentleness is a fruit of wisdom; it cannot be attained through self-discipline or study alone but is a gift of God. In Gal 5:22–23 St. Paul identifies it as a fruit of the Spirit ("gentleness" in the NABRE). Jesus uses the adjective form of this word in the Beatitudes, saying that the "meek" will inherit the earth (Matt 5:5).

But if indicates a strong contrast between verse 13 and verse 14. In verse 13, James identified two qualities, goodness and humility, that mark a person's life with wisdom. Now he points to two qualities that indicate a lack of true wisdom: **bitter jealousy** and **selfish ambition**. **3:14**

"Bitter jealousy" is an intensely negative attitude toward another person's achievement or success;[11] "selfish ambition" is a disordered and excessive desire to get ahead in life. A person who uses every available means to attain a position above others is the opposite of one who is meek and trusts in God to advance or defend his or her position. James instructs his listeners to probe themselves to see if **in your hearts** there exists envy and selfish ambition. If so, James urges that they **not boast and be false to the truth**. A person who claims to be wise—that is, ready for a position of leadership—but whose heart harbors jealousy, bitterness, or strife is engaged in self-deception. James calls for a deep purity of heart and a profound, uncompromising cleansing of anything that is not from God.

James explains the root of **wisdom of this** jealous and selfish **kind** using **3:15–16** three increasingly negative adjectives. The first, **earthly**, contrasts with what is

11. BDAG, "*zēlos*," 427.

The Wise Person and the Fool

BIBLICAL BACKGROUND

In the Old Testament, especially the wisdom literature, two paths of life are marked out: the way of the righteous and wise person, and the way of the wicked and foolish person (e.g., Ps 1). The wise person is not necessarily the one who is the best educated or most cultured, but the one who wholly submits to God and who lives by the precepts of his law (Ps 19:8; Prov 9:10; Sir 19:17). As a result, the wise person can expect blessing, long life, and lasting memory (Pss 1:1–3; 37:27; 112:1–9). When read in the fuller light of Christ, this refers to eternal life in God's presence.

The fool, on the other hand, knows on some level what is good but rejects the ways of God and seeks to live by his or her own depraved ideas. In short, this person is one who refuses to obey, and whose folly is synonymous with sin. The life of the wicked person is fleeting and will eventually disappear and be forgotten (Pss 37:1–2, 20; 68:3); the New Testament reveals the ultimate fate of those who make such a choice (Mark 9:45–48; Rev 21:8).

heavenly; such earthbound wisdom stems from a realm other than God's. The second, **unspiritual** (*psychikos*), comes from the noun *psychē*, which means "life" or "soul." In the New Testament *psychikos* is contrasted to what is spiritual—that is, of the Holy Spirit (*pneumatikos* [1 Cor 2:14; 15:44–46])—hence the translation "unspiritual." In James, the word indicates one who is self-absorbed, thus indicating that "**wisdom of this kind**" reflects self-love and is about self-promotion.[12] The third, **demonic**, indicates that such wisdom is similar to that of the demons or derives from them. The devil was motivated by envy and selfish ambition (Wis 2:24). Thus, those who make prestige and worldly success their highest priority behave with the wisdom of the devil. In short, such wisdom serves "the world, the flesh and the devil."[13]

James identifies two outcomes of such wisdom: first, **disorder** (*akatastasia*). On two occasions James has used the adjectival form of this word: in 1:8, where he spoke of the double-minded person as "unstable" and vacillating, and again in 3:8, where he described the tongue as a "restless" evil. Now he uses the noun form "disorder," which is the opposite of stability, harmony, and peace. In 1 Cor 14:33 St. Paul says that God "is not the God of disorder but of peace." The second fruit of earthly wisdom is **every foul practice**, or wickedness. Thus, the kind of

12. McCartney, *James*, 201.
13. Douglas Moo, *The Letter of James*, PNTC (Grand Rapids: Eerdmans, 2000), 173.

wisdom that shows the way to worldly success, prestige, and coveted positions only serves to produce instability and evil.

Having shown the effects of earthly wisdom to be vices, James now describes **3:17** the wisdom from God (see 1:5, 17) with a series of adjectives and speaks about the virtues of those guided by it. The first adjective, **pure**, provides a lens for reading the rest of the list. Purity is not simply a passive lack of defilement but rather involves actively remaining "unstained by the world" (1:27).[14] The †world—society insofar as it is opposed to God—is characterized by those who are double-minded, having restless tongues; it is a realm where disorder and every kind of wickedness abound. To be pure means to be wholly and completely aligned with God, seeking to imitate him and live according to his commandments and laws. Those who are pure have decided to reject sin and choose God. Jesus says that the clean of heart will see God (Matt 5:8).

After noting purity, James constructs a list divided into three parts. The first, **peaceable, gentle, compliant**, describes the disposition of the wise person and provides a contrast with the one who is selfishly ambitious. These virtues describe a conciliatory person who is open to others and who is even ready to yield to the preferences of others. Such gentleness creates peace and goodwill. Saint Francis de Sales recognized that such behavior is true strength when he said, "Nothing is so strong as gentleness, nothing so gentle as real strength."[15]

The second part of the list of true wisdom's virtues, **full of mercy and good fruits**, deals with attitudes and actions to which wisdom leads. Mercy is a readiness to show compassion or to forgive. Good fruits are the concrete demonstration of this compassion.

The third part, **without inconstancy or insincerity**, describes the character of truly wise persons: they are honest and upright. Such people are like a rock—stable, constant, trustworthy. They are the opposite of those who are double-minded (1:8; 4:8) and lack perseverance (1:3–4, 12), whose hearts are not fully with God.

This final sentence, a proverb, speaks of the rewards for those who seek to be **3:18** peacemakers. Those who plant and cultivate **peace** will reap for themselves the **fruit of righteousness**—that is, a right relationship with God and, ultimately, salvation. Jesus said nearly the same thing in one of the Beatitudes: "Blessed are the peacemakers, / for they will be called children of God" (Matt 5:9).

14. Hartin, *James*, 210.
15. Adapted from C. F. Kelley, ed., *The Spiritual Maxims of Saint François de Sales* (New York: Harper, 1951), 124.

To sum up, in chapter 3 James began his argument by cautioning those who would be teachers, those who are considered wise within the community (3:1–2). Since teachers must necessarily use many words, they are in greater danger of sinning, for the tongue is a potent instrument that tends toward evil and is capable of causing enormous harm. The truly wise person is not necessarily the great scholar, but someone whose life is marked by humility, peace, and mercy; that person will receive the reward of righteousness, which is eternal life. Those whose lives are marked by ambition and rivalry are not wise, because they have embraced the wisdom from below that characterizes the devil. Thus, James sees one's life as either being motivated by God and his wisdom, which will produce fruits of peace, or influenced by the devil and his wisdom, which brings bitter jealousy and rivalry. One's decision to follow God or the world is evidenced by the fruits of one's life.

But what is a person to do who desires to tame the tongue? And how should one live so as to attain the wisdom of God? James will address these questions in the next chapter.

Lover of the World or Lover of God

James 4:1–10

In contrast to the last chapter, where James taught that peace is sown and cultivated by people who are wise and understanding (3:13, 18), he now speaks of wars and conflicts, and he focuses once again on the interior source of the problem. This section is divided into three parts. In the first part, James introduces his topic (vv. 1–3). Next, he focuses on the human heart that has committed "adultery" against God by loving the †world (vv. 4–6). Finally, James lays out the solution: those who have turned away from God need to humbly return to him (vv. 7–10).

Passion Is the Source of Conflict (4:1–3)

---

¹Where do the wars and where do the conflicts among you come from? Is it not from your passions that make war within your members? ²You covet but do not possess. You kill and envy but you cannot obtain; you fight and wage war. You do not possess because you do not ask. ³You ask but do not receive, because you ask wrongly, to spend it on your passions.

OT: Ps 66:17–20
NT: Rom 7:5–6; Gal 5:19–26
Catechism: passions, 1763–75; prayer of petition, 2629–33
Lectionary: 25th Sunday in Ordinary Time, Year B (James 3:16–4:3)

James begins with two rhetorical questions regarding the source of human **conflicts** and concludes that the culprit is **your passions**. The Greek word

4:1

rendered as "passion" in 4:1, 3, *hēdonē* (from which the English word "hedonism" is derived), means "pleasure, enjoyment"; here it refers to a disordered desire for pleasure and may also refer to desires for power and honor.[1] These passions **make war within your members**. While this phrase perhaps refers to conflict within a person, here it probably also refers to the "conflicts" that verse 2 describes among the members of the Christian community, the body of Christ. James is saying that the tensions and discord that exist in the church arise from unrestrained passions within the individual members.

4:2   James describes the interior and exterior behaviors to which these warring passions give rise. Verse 2 can be variously translated depending on where one inserts punctuation marks in the Greek text. The NABRE breaks the text into three statements: **You covet but do not possess. You kill and envy but you cannot obtain; you fight and wage war.** The NRSV (also the NJB and ESV) more plausibly translates the Greek with two statements, each one containing a cause and effect: "You want something and do not have it; so you commit murder. And you covet something and cannot obtain it; so you engage in disputes and conflicts."[2]

The first behavior that James condemns is an act of the will, to "covet." In the ninth and tenth commandments God commands the Israelites not to covet their neighbor's goods or wife (Exod 20:17). What exactly James's audience is coveting is not stated, but they do not obtain what they seek, and this leads to further evil acts. "To kill," like "wars" in 4:1, is not to be taken literally, but it serves as a powerful metaphor for the terrible harm that can result when unrestrained passions blind one person to the dignity of another. "Envy" refers to the jealous behavior mentioned in 3:14.[3] However, when those Christians caught by their desires still do not obtain what they are looking for, the next activity is worse: they "fight and wage war," figurative language suggesting that their actions now affect an even greater number of people. Those who indulge their passions have no peace; they live in turmoil within themselves and with hostility toward others.

After delineating these disordered emotions and the violent acts they produce, James explains why the desires are not being met: **You do not possess because you do not ask**. They have been going about it all wrong! Instead of attempting to obtain what they want through aggressive conduct, they should turn to prayer.

1. Dan G. McCartney, *James*, BECNT (Grand Rapids: Baker Academic, 2009), 207.
2. Since the early Greek manuscripts lack punctuation marks, there is no sure way to decide between the two translations.
3. At 3:14 James uses the noun form (*zēlos*) of the verb used here (*zēloō*).

James counters their anticipated reply ("But we have asked and received **4:3**
nothing!") by explaining, **you ask wrongly**. In 1:5–6 James taught his audience that if they lacked understanding in their trials, they should ask God
for wisdom in simple faith, and their prayer would be granted. However, this
promise presupposed that the person wants what God desires, and asks for the
†grace to know what to do and the strength to do it. Now James again teaches
about prayer, and here also he views it as a means of seeking God's will rather
than our own. This time he says that prayers that seek only to gratify one's own
desires will not be answered. God, our good Father, will not answer prayers
that would enslave us further to self-centered **passions**. Insofar as a person
aggressively pursues personal desires without regard to God's will, he or she
ceases to love God and neighbor.

Reflection and Application (4:1–3)

The book of Wisdom presents the wise and rich King Solomon recounting
how he obtained all that he had. He longed for God's wisdom, preferred it above
every other good, and prayed for it persistently, and God gave it to him (Wis
7:7–10). Wisdom, in turn, brought him riches and happiness and made him a
friend of God (7:11, 27).

Unlike Solomon, who understood that God could fulfill all his desires
through wisdom, the rich young man in the Gospel of Mark wanted to follow
Jesus but could not part with his possessions (Mark 10:17–22). Paradoxi-
cally, according to Jesus, if the man had been willing to give up these things
as Jesus' disciples had done, he could have received a hundred times more in
this present age (with persecutions!) and eternal life as well (Mark 10:29–30).
Our desires for good things are not condemned, but our relationship with
Jesus, "the wisdom of God" (1 Cor 1:24), must come first. He is the only one
who can truly satisfy us. It is not wrong to ask God for what we desire, but
if we seek material goods, honor, or pleasure without keeping Christ in the
center, we will experience the inner frustration and warring factions in our
communities that James describes.

The Lover of the World Is at Enmity with God (4:4–6)

**⁴Adulterers! Do you not know that to be a lover of the world means
enmity with God? Therefore, whoever wants to be a lover of the world**

makes himself an enemy of God. ⁵Or do you suppose that the scripture speaks without meaning when it says, "The spirit that he has made to dwell in us tends toward jealousy"? ⁶But he bestows a greater grace; therefore, it says:

> "God resists the proud,
>   but gives grace to the humble."

OT: Exod 20:5–6; 2 Chron 7:14; Ps 18:28; Ezek 23:37–39; Hosea 2

NT: 2 Cor 11:1–4; Phil 3:17–21; Rev 19:6–9

Catechism: desire for God, 27–30; purification of the heart, 2517–19; the battle for purity, 2520–27

4:4   Loving things more than we love Christ harms our relationship with God. James does not hold back in his criticism of such mistaken love, saying to his readers, **Adulterers!** The use of this term for unfaithfulness to God has a long history in the Old Testament. God called Israel into a special relationship of love with himself. In the exodus, God showed that he was both able and willing to save the nation; in return, he called Israel to trust and obey him (Exod 19:4–6). Yet time and again Israel fell into idolatry, preferring other gods to God, or, as Paul says, worshiping the creature instead of the creator (Rom 1:25). The prophets Hosea, Jeremiah, and Ezekiel liken Israel's penchant for other gods to adultery and thus call Israel an adulteress or prostitute. The New Testament identifies the Church as the bride of Christ (John 3:29; Eph 5:22–32; Rev 21:2), equating love of the †world with adultery. By calling those who are in friendship with the world "adulterers," James draws attention to God's nuptial †covenant relationship with his people. The Christian's deepest passion should be for God, not for things (see 4:1–3).

Once again, James takes aim at the center of the problem: the human heart. A person can love either God or the world but not both, and James presents the classic choice between the two ways. The Greek word rendered as **to be a lover** (*philia*) usually means "friendship" or "affection." The one who deserves our love and longing is God. As mentioned above (see commentary on 1:27), when Scripture speaks negatively of the world, it refers to human society insofar as it is opposed to God. To be a **lover of the world**, literally, "friend of the world" (NRSV), is to adopt the values and ideas of society that run contrary to God's teaching. The consequence is that a person **makes himself an enemy of God**.

James's teaching about the incompatibility of friendship with God and friendship with the world recalls Jesus' teaching about wealth: "No one can serve two

God's Exclusive Love for Israel and the Church

BIBLICAL BACKGROUND

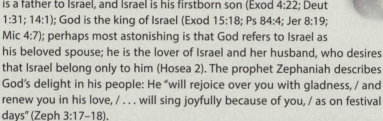

The Old Testament teaches that there is only one God and that he has an exclusive claim on Israel: "You are a people holy to the †LORD, your God; the LORD, your God, has chosen you from all the peoples on the face of the earth to be a people specially his own" (Deut 7:6). This relationship is described in a variety of ways: God is a father to Israel, and Israel is his firstborn son (Exod 4:22; Deut 1:31; 14:1); God is the king of Israel (Exod 15:18; Ps 84:4; Jer 8:19; Mic 4:7); perhaps most astonishing is that God refers to Israel as his beloved spouse; he is the lover of Israel and her husband, who desires that Israel belong only to him (Hosea 2). The prophet Zephaniah describes God's delight in his people: He "will rejoice over you with gladness, / and renew you in his love, / . . . will sing joyfully because of you, / as on festival days" (Zeph 3:17–18).

The New Testament often employs marital imagery to describe the relationship between Christ and his people. Ephesians describes the sacrificial love Christ has shown the Church: "Christ loved the church and handed himself over for her to sanctify her, cleansing her by the bath of water with the word" (Eph 5:25–26). He did so "that he might present to himself the church in splendor, without spot or wrinkle or any such thing, that she might be holy and without blemish" (Eph 5:27). As the bridegroom, Christ saves, nourishes, and cherishes his Church with a love beyond words. The Church, as his bride, belongs exclusively to him, and she is invited to respond to his gift of love with her own gift of love, expressed in devotion, trust, and obedience.

masters. He will either hate one and love the other, or be devoted to one and despise the other. You cannot serve God and mammon" (Matt 6:24 [see Luke 16:13]). James, like Jesus, teaches that one must choose.

4:5   Verse 5 is regarded by scholars as the most difficult in James for a number of reasons. First, with the words **scripture speaks**, James introduces a sentence that cannot be found in any biblical manuscripts: **"The spirit that he has made to dwell in us tends toward jealousy."** James is either misquoting a passage or quoting a text that has been lost that he regarded as inspired but was not received into the †canon. Second, the sentence is difficult to translate. Should the word "spirit" be capitalized to indicate the Holy Spirit? Fortunately, however, James's use of the word "jealousy" (*phthonos*) clarifies the meaning. This Greek word, unlike the word translated as "jealousy" in

3:14 (*zēlos*), has only a negative connotation in Scripture.[4] It is never used to describe God, but refers only to sinful envy and appears in lists of vices (see Rom 1:29; Gal 5:21).[5] This helps us see that "the spirit" cannot refer to the Holy Spirit, since James would not ascribe sin to the Spirit of God. Nor can God be the subject of the sentence, as the RSV and NRSV render it,[6] since God does not yearn enviously. Therefore, the NABRE translation remains the best one, which says that the spirit within us tends toward envy. Although God created the human spirit, ever since the fall it is inclined to sin. Thus, when this spirit within us yearns for possessions and pleasures of the world, the outcome is envy and fighting.

4:6   Using another quotation, this time from the †Septuagint of Prov 3:34, James indicates that the remedy for this spirit of envy comes from God (see 1:5, 21; 3:17–18). Wicked desires arise within human beings, but God does not abandon us to them. God comes to our aid and **bestows a greater grace**. But why is it that **"God resists the proud, / but gives grace to the humble"**? The proud are those who refuse to acknowledge their need of God and so do not accept his mercy and †grace. The proud person stands alone and self-sufficient, but the humble person acknowledges being in need of God and recognizes the inability to overcome envious desires without his grace. In other words, the humble person, with an open heart, begs God for his help. We need to humbly stand as beggars before God because, as Bede the Venerable observed, "They who in the midst of the wounds of their vices humbly put themselves in the hands of the true physician rightly receive the gift of the hoped-for cure."[7] Saint Augustine saw his sins as wounds that only God could heal: "I do not hide my wounds from you. I am sick, and you are the physician. You are merciful: I have need of your mercy."[8]

James sees the human heart torn between the world and God. Disorderly passions and "wars" with others are indications that we are choosing the world instead of God, that we have become "adulterers" in our relationship with God. The prerequisite for our healing is that we humble ourselves before God in order to receive his grace.

---

4. See 1 Macc 8:16; Wis 2:24; 6:23; Matt 27:18 // Mark 15:10; Rom 1:29; Gal 5:21; Phil 1:15; 1 Tim 6:4; Titus 3:3; 1 Pet 2:1; see also *3 Maccabees* 6:7.

5. E.g., in Exod 20:5, where God speaks of himself as "a jealous God," the word is not a form of *phthonos* but of *zēlos*; similarly at 2 Cor 11:2.

6. NRSV translation: "Or do you suppose that it is for nothing that the scripture says, 'God yearns jealously for the spirit that he has made to dwell in us'?"

7. *Commentary on the Seven Catholic Epistles*, trans. David Hurst, CSS 82 (Kalamazoo, MI: Cistercian Publications, 1985), 50.

8. *The Confessions*, trans. R. S. Pine-Coffin (London: Penguin, 1961), 232.

Reflection and Application (4:4–6)

James says that to love the world is to make oneself God's enemy. However, if we are honest, most of us find love of the world in ourselves. Whether it be a desire for the world's recognition and approval or for wealth or the pleasures of sin, there is a part of us powerfully drawn to the world. Does that make us God's enemy?

First, we must distinguish between being attracted to the world, tempted by its allurements, which is to some degree unavoidable, and the sin of loving the world, the consent of the will to desire what is wrong. If we find this sin in ourselves, all is not lost. James does not intend his teaching to condemn his readers, but rather to move them to repentance. He wants to wake us up to the radical incompatibility between loving God and loving the world.

Humbly Submit to God (4:7–10)

[7]**So submit yourselves to God. Resist the devil, and he will flee from you.**
[8]**Draw near to God, and he will draw near to you. Cleanse your hands,**
you sinners, and purify your hearts, you of two minds. [9]**Begin to lament,**
to mourn, to weep. Let your laughter be turned into mourning and your
joy into dejection. [10]**Humble yourselves before the Lord and he will exalt**
you.

OT: Ezek 36:25–29; Sir 3:18–19; 38:10–11
NT: Matt 5:3–11; 1 Pet 5:5–7; 1 John 1:9–10
Catechism: Jesus teaches us how to pray, 2607–15

This section, a string of ten imperatives pertaining to humility and repentance, provides instruction for how the "adulterous" person (see 4:4) can be reconciled with God. In essence, James exhorts his readers to a program of conversion.

The first command, **submit yourselves to God**, means to voluntarily become   4:7a
subject to God and to follow his commands. It is therefore an exhortation to return to the †covenant relationship with God.[9] Since God respects our freedom and does not force himself on us, we must willingly open our hearts to his teaching.

The next two commands can be read together: **Resist the devil, and he**   4:7b–8a
will flee from you is paired with **Draw near to God, and he will draw near**

---

9. Patrick J. Hartin, *James*, SP 14 (Collegeville, MN: Liturgical Press, 2003), 201.

to you. Each of us must decide deep within whom we want to be near: the devil or God. Resisting the devil means consciously turning away from his incitements to envy, jealousy, and discord, which wreak havoc on one's interior life and the community. One has to battle these deep sources of passion and not give in to them. Since this is impossible without grace, one must submit to God.

To "draw near" in relationship to God is a phrase used for priests (Exod 19:22; 40:32; Lev 21:21–23) and Israelites who "draw near" to God in public worship. By using this expression, James may be inviting his readers to return to God in the liturgical life of the community as well as in private prayer. God is eager for us to come to him, but we must approach him with the appropriate attitudes. Using a few more imperatives, James tells us what these are.

4:8b–10   The next imperative, **cleanse your hands**, means to make one's outward conduct pure. In the temple, priests practiced a ritual washing of hands before beginning their sacred duties (Exod 30:19–21); later the expression "clean hands" was used in a moral sense to refer to upright conduct (2 Sam 22:21; Ps 24:4). Like a fiery preacher, James addresses his readers as **you sinners**, people whose behavior deviates from God's standards. His next command is to **purify your hearts**, which means to renounce wrong motives, and he addresses it to those **of two minds**. Earlier James contrasted the double-minded person whose heart was divided with the "perfect" or mature person (see 1:4, 8; 3:2). This command means to turn to God, renouncing both the interior and the exterior dimensions of sin.

James instructs his audience **to lament, to mourn, to weep**,[10] and to let their **laughter be turned into mourning** and their **joy into dejection**. For a person who truly repents, often the awareness of God's holiness and love brings the ability to perceive the depths of his or her sinfulness, evoking sorrow and contrition. James encourages the external signs of lamenting and weeping not as a show or pretense but as the outward expression of a heart that is truly sorry. James has just reproved his readers for being "adulterers" and "of two minds," chastising them for divisions, envy, and loving the †world. These are serious sins, and the appropriate response to becoming aware of them is deep repentance characterized by sincere sorrow and a commitment to change one's behavior (Matt 3:8). Repentance is fundamental to becoming a Christian (Mark 1:15; Matt 3:2; Luke 24:47; Acts 2:38), and as long as we continue to sin, we have need of it (James 5:16; 1 John 1:9).

10. By inserting "Begin to," the NABRE translation obscures the parallel form of these imperatives (lament, mourn, weep) with those in the previous two verses (submit, resist, draw near, cleanse, purify).

Tears of Remorse

Saint Paul writes about how sorrow can lead to repentance: "I rejoice now, not because you were saddened, but because you were saddened into repentance.... For godly sorrow produces a salutary repentance without regret, but worldly sorrow produces death" (2 Cor 7:9–10). The desert fathers—hermits and ascetics who lived in the Egyptian desert beginning in the third century—regarded tears of repentance as a gift from God to be sought in prayer. They taught that a sustained and prolonged encounter with the word of God purifies the heart and leads to feeling interiorly pierced with remorse. This mourning results in tears of sorrow for offending God, an earnest plea for forgiveness, and genuine conversion of heart.

The Liturgy also recognizes that such tears are a gift. The Mass for the Forgiveness of Sins includes the following prayers, which implore the gift of tears:

> *Collect*: Almighty and most gentle God, who brought forth from the rock a fountain of living water for your thirsty people, bring forth, we pray, from the hardness of our hearts, tears of sorrow, that we may lament our sins and merit forgiveness from your mercy.
>
> *Prayer over the Offerings*: Look mercifully, O Lord, upon this oblation, which we offer to your majesty for our sins, and grant, we pray, that the sacrifice from which forgiveness springs forth for the human race may bestow on us the grace of the Holy Spirit to shed tears for our offenses.
>
> *Prayer after Communion*: May the reverent reception of your Sacrament, O Lord, lead us to wash away the stains of our sins with sighs and tears, and in your generosity grant that the pardon we seek may have its effect on us.[a]

a. *The Roman Missal: English Translation according to the Third Typical Edition* (Rome: Magnificat-Desclée, 2011), 1308.

James's final command is to **humble yourselves** before the Lord (see 3:13). God will not spurn a broken, humbled heart (Ps 51:19). In our state of lowliness, bowed down in grief and sorrow for sins, God will reach out to us, raise us to our feet, and **exalt** us, as Jesus taught in the parable of the Pharisee and the tax collector (Luke 18:9–14).

Reflection and Application (4:7–10)

I once had a professor of morality who lamented that most of his students compared mortal sin to a cliff. They wanted to know how near the edge they could walk without falling off, how much they could sin without losing their soul for eternity. Doubtless James would consider these students as sinners with two minds. There are only two roads, the way of the world and that of God, and we can choose only one. To attempt to sidle up to the edge of the cliff is to still love the world and, to that degree, to have rejected God. God desires to be loved completely and unreservedly, and anything short of that is spiritual "adultery."

Sometimes we think we can excuse our sins because they seem small, or because we know God is merciful, but every sin wounds our relationship with God and may cause conflict in human relationships as well. Acknowledging our selfishness and lack of love and imploring God for forgiveness can heal the brokenness and suffering caused by sin.

Exhortations against Pride

James 4:11–5:6

The book of Psalms tells us that the arrogant will not stand before the Lord (Ps 5:6), for God cannot endure haughty eyes and an arrogant heart (Ps 101:5). James, having just urged his listeners to humble themselves before the Lord (4:10), now warns them to avoid three kinds of behavior that demonstrate arrogance toward God. The first is speaking evil of a brother or sister (4:11–12); the second is attending to one's business as if God did not exist (4:13–17); the third is the enjoyment of wealth gained by injustice at the expense of those who are less fortunate (5:1–6). Each successive admonition is more severe. The third carries a condemnation and leaves the impression that punishment is imminent. James's powerful words are meant to bring his audience to repentance while there is still time (see 2 Pet 3:9).

Avoidance of Defamation (4:11–12)

> [11]Do not speak evil of one another, brothers. Whoever speaks evil of a brother or judges his brother speaks evil of the law and judges the law. If you judge the law, you are not a doer of the law but a judge. [12]There is one lawgiver and judge who is able to save or to destroy. Who then are you to judge your neighbor?

OT: Exod 20:16; Lev 19:16; Ps 101:5
NT: Matt 5:22; 7:1–5
Catechism: offenses against truth, 2475–87

4:11   In this first exhortation James weaves together themes that he has already discussed: proper speech (1:19–20, 26; 3:1–12), the law (1:22–25; 2:8–12), and judgment (2:13).[1] James addresses his listeners as **brothers** to underscore their equality and family relationship with one another in Christ, which entails the responsibility to love one another. He begins with a command: **Do not speak evil of one another**. To "speak evil" refers to both slander, which is to speak falsely against someone, and detraction, which is to defame the good name of another by a report that may be true but is disclosed without sufficient reason. Slander is a direct violation of the eighth commandment, "You shall not bear false witness against your neighbor" (Exod 20:16), and is also explicitly prohibited elsewhere in the Old Testament: "You shall not go about spreading slander among your people" (Lev 19:16). Obviously, speaking evil of another person violates the command to love one's neighbor as oneself (Lev 19:18; Matt 22:39).

James reinforces his condemnation of speech that denigrates another by pointing out that the person who **speaks evil of a brother or judges his brother** wrongs someone who is close and fundamentally an equal (which the repeated use of "brother" underscores). Such a person also **speaks evil of the law and judges the law** rather than humbly following the law. To speak against another means to ignore the law that forbids such behavior; the person who does so has determined which laws to keep and which to ignore.[2] Such a person assumes a position above both the brother and the law, thus becoming **not a doer of the law but a judge**, a role that belongs to God.

4:12   James indicates why setting oneself up as a judge is terribly wrong: by judging, one usurps the place of God, the **one lawgiver and judge**. By stressing that God is *one*, James recalls the first and greatest commandment: "Hear, O Israel! The †Lᴏʀᴅ is our God, the Lᴏʀᴅ alone! Therefore, you shall love the Lᴏʀᴅ, your God, with your whole heart, and with your whole being, and with your whole strength" (Deut 6:4–5 [see Matt 22:36–38]).[3] Once again, James shows that the two foundational commandments—to love God and to love one's neighbor—are closely connected. James pointed to this connection also in his discussion on partiality, where he urged the importance of following all the commandments because God gave them all (see James 2, especially vv. 10–11). Faith in God must determine how we treat our neighbor. Since God is the lawgiver, his word is the norm that enables us to discern what is good and what is not. Further, only God is the judge who has the power **to save or to destroy**: only "the Lᴏʀᴅ puts to death and gives life, / casts

1. C. Freeman Sleeper, *James*, ANTC (Nashville: Abingdon, 1998), 114.
2. Luke Timothy Johnson, *The Letter of James: A New Translation with Introduction and Commentary*, AB 37A (New York: Doubleday, 1995), 293.
3. Ibid., 294.

Avoiding Judging or Speaking Evil of Others

LIVING
TRADITION

Catholic tradition strongly reinforces the teaching of Scripture about speaking against or judging others. The Catechism (2477–78), like James, condemns unjust defamation of one's neighbor, even if what is spoken is the truth:

> *Respect for the reputation* of persons forbids every attitude and word likely to cause them unjust injury [see Code of Canon Law 220]. He becomes guilty:
>
> - of *rash judgment* who, even tacitly, assumes as true, without sufficient foundation, the moral fault of a neighbor;
> - of *detraction* who, without objectively valid reason, discloses another's faults and failings to persons who did not know them [see Sir 21:28];
> - of *calumny* who, by remarks contrary to the truth, harms the reputation of others and gives occasion for false judgments concerning them.
>
> To avoid rash judgment, everyone should be careful to interpret insofar as possible his neighbor's thoughts, words, and deeds in a favorable way.

Likewise, St. Francis de Sales warns against the sin of slander:

> Slander is a form of murder. . . . I earnestly exhort you, dearest Philothea, never to slander anyone either directly or indirectly. Beware of falsely imputing crimes and sins to your neighbor, revealing his secret sins, exaggerating those that are manifest, putting an evil interpretation on his good works, denying the good that you know belongs to someone, maliciously concealing it or lessening it by words. You would offend God in all these ways but most of all by false accusations and denying the truth to your neighbor's harm. It is a double sin to lie and harm your neighbor at the same time.[a]

a. *Introduction to the Devout Life* 29 (*Introduction to the Devout Life*, trans. John K. Ryan [New York: Doubleday, 1989], 201–2).

down to Sheol and brings up again" (1 Sam 2:6 [see Wis 16:13]). James finishes with a question that reminds his listeners of their true status before God: **Who then are you to judge your neighbor?** Since no human being is the lawgiver or judge, no one has the right to disregard the divine law and judge a brother or sister.

Reflection and Application (4:11–12)

Biblical wisdom teaching like that of James needs to be applied differently from moral absolutes like the Ten Commandments. While it is never permissible to worship other gods, commit adultery, or to murder, there are occasions when we can and even must "speak evil" of someone—for instance, to confidentially seek counsel about how to handle the misconduct of another, to protect someone from harm, or to report serious wrongdoing to legitimate authority. Some misdeeds are done in public, and there is no risk of talebearing in discussing them (although there may be a risk of making ourselves judges). Sometimes wrongdoing that is not publicly known should be made public, as when a corporation is doing harm and failing in its duties to the public good, and when public officials are mishandling their responsibilities to those who have elected them.

However, it must be said that our motives for speaking against someone are usually not so well founded. When we hear a juicy bit of gossip, we desire to repeat it, knowing that others would enjoy hearing what we have to say. When we are angry because of what we regard as an injustice toward ourselves or others, we are tempted to think that our telling anyone is justified. When we are envious of the ability, achievement, or social standing of another person, we imagine that informing people about their faults is legitimate. It is for ordinary circumstances like these that James reminds us not to place ourselves above God's law.

Living in God's Will (4:13–17)

---

¹³Come now, you who say, "Today or tomorrow we shall go into such and such a town, spend a year there doing business, and make a profit"— ¹⁴you have no idea what your life will be like tomorrow. You are a puff of smoke that appears briefly and then disappears. ¹⁵Instead you should say, "If the Lord wills it, we shall live to do this or that." ¹⁶But now you are boasting in your arrogance. All such boasting is evil. ¹⁷So for one who knows the right thing to do and does not do it, it is a sin.

OT: Ps 94
NT: Rom 1:18–22
Catechism: atheism, 2123–26, 2134, 2140; agnosticism, 2127–28

In this second exhortation (for the structure of the three exhortations in 4:11– 5:6, see this chapter's introductory paragraph above). James denounces what is sometimes called practical atheism—that is, living as though God does not exist. The problem arises when people exaggerate human ability to the point of ignoring their dependence on God. James first contrasts two ways in which

Christians speak about the future (vv. 13–15), then condemns the attitude of those who ignore God (v. 16), and finishes with a concluding proverb (v. 17).

The summons **Come now, you** introduces a new topic. The exhortation is 4:13–14 addressed to members of the Christian community who make plans to relocate for the sake of **doing business** in order to **make a profit**. James does not teach against engaging in business or selling at a profit. Rather, he reproves people for planning and acting without reference to God. They do not pray, seek his will, or acknowledge their dependence on him. In this way they fail to recognize God's sovereignty. This is the ordinary outlook of secular society in our own day, which we can easily absorb, worshiping God on Sunday yet failing to take his lordship into account the rest of the week. Those who act this way trust in their own abilities and talents and do not recognize that God is the source of every good gift (1:17). James shows the absurdity of relying only on oneself by recalling the transient nature of human existence, comparing it to a **puff of smoke** or a "mist" (NJB, RSV) that soon passes (see 1:9–11), a common theme of the Old Testament.[4]

The Christian should recognize God's governance of everything and place 4:15 his or her life and plans in the hands of God, who controls the future. Thus the Christian should say, **"If the Lord wills,"** as St. Paul is recorded as doing on several occasions.[5] What matters most, of course, is not saying the words but recognizing that all depends on God and letting God guide one's future. Such docility expresses trust in God's will rather than in one's own transient, fragile self and acknowledges that we are not in control of the circumstances of our lives. Saint John Chrysostom says, "James is not trying to take away our freedom to decide, but he is showing us that it is not just what we want that matters. We need God's †grace to complement our efforts and ought to rely not on them, but on God's love for us."[6]

The person who announces plans for the future without acknowledging God's 4:16 sovereignty is **boasting in . . . arrogance**. Ignoring God in this way manifests the willful, proud spirit of a person who subtly usurps the place of God; such an attitude is rightly called **evil**.

Boasting is fitting in the life of a believer when it is boasting in God—for example, when one recognizes the transforming power of God in one's life and glorifies the Lord (see Rom 5:2). When the Blessed Mother was miraculously with child, she magnified and glorified God for the work he had done for her (Luke 1:46–47). Never did Mary give herself honors, even though she received

4. E.g., Job 7:1–10; Pss 89:48; 90:10; 103:15–16; Isa 40:7.
5. See Acts 18:21; Rom 1:9–10; 1 Cor 4:19; 16:7.
6. *Catena in Epistolas Catholicas* 32 (ACCS 11:52).

extraordinary grace from God (Luke 1:28). Saint Paul boasts only in the cross (Gal 6:14) and instructs those who boast to boast in the Lord (1 Cor 1:31; 2 Cor 10:17).

4:17 As he does elsewhere (see 2:13; 3:18), James completes this section with a maxim. Placing this specific proverb at the end indicates that James has not been addressing his teaching to the uncatechized, but rather to one who **knows the right thing to do and does not do it**, either by doing what is wrong or by omitting what should have been done. Jesus taught in one of his parables, "That servant who knew his master's will but did not make preparations nor act in accord with his will shall be beaten severely; and the servant who was ignorant of his master's will but acted in a way deserving of a severe beating shall be beaten only lightly" (Luke 12:47–48). Knowing the truth and ignoring it is serious, for it means that we have placed ourselves and our wills above the will of God, who only wants our good (see Catechism 1849, 1855).

Reflection and Application (4:13–17)

Saint Thomas Aquinas teaches that inordinate self-love, which is pride, is the cause of all sins.[7] The first sin that Eve committed was the sin of pride. The serpent tempted Eve to eat the forbidden fruit of the tree of the knowledge of good and evil by saying, "God knows well that when you eat of it your eyes will be opened and you will be like gods, who know good and evil" (Gen 3:5). The serpent depicts God as fearful that human beings would become equal to him. Therefore, according to the serpent, God has falsely threatened human beings with death to deter them from eating the fruit in order to maintain his unique status as God. Eve succumbs to this argument; therefore, at the heart of her sin is pride, the desire to become equal to God, mistrusting his goodness. Too often we consider God's commands, which are a reflection of his love, to be an imposition or a burden. In doubting God's love for us, deciding that we know better than God what is right and wrong for us, and rejecting his commands, we commit the sin of pride.[8]

Catholic tradition identifies pride as one of the seven capital sins, the others being greed, envy, wrath, lust, gluttony, and sloth. Capital sins are those that engender other sins and vices. The Catechism (2094) says that pride is "contrary to love of God, whose goodness it denies," and can actually lead to hatred for God and cursing him.

7. *Summa theologiae* I-II, q. 77, a. 4.
8. Joseph Ratzinger (Pope Benedict XVI), *In the Beginning: A Catholic Understanding of the Story of the Creation and the Fall*, trans. Boniface Ramsey (Huntington, IN: Our Sunday Visitor, 1990), 87–88.

Boasting

LIVING TRADITION

Saint Augustine describes astronomers who study the skies without reference to God. Like James, he attributes this attitude to arrogance:

> The reason and understanding by which they investigate these things are gifts they have from you. . . . They lapse into pride without respect for you, my God, and fall into shadow away from your light. Although they can predict an eclipse of the sun so far ahead, they cannot see that they themselves are already in the shadow of eclipse. This is because they ignore you and do not inquire how they came to possess the intelligence to make these researches. Even when they discover that it was you who made them, they do not submit to you so that you may preserve what you have made, nor, such as their own efforts have made them, do they offer themselves to you in sacrifice. Their conceit soars like a bird; their curiosity probes the deepest secrets of nature like a fish that swims in the sea; and their lust grows fat like a beast at pasture. . . . Yet if they make this sacrifice to you, O God, you are the consuming fire that can burn away their love for these things and re-create them in immortal life.[a]

Saint Basil the Great explains the folly of human boasting: "Humanity, there is nothing left for you to boast of, for your boasting and hope lie in putting to death all that is your own and seeking the future life that is in Christ. Since we have its first fruits we are already in its midst, living entirely in the grace and gift of God."[b]

a. *The Confessions*, trans. R. S. Pine-Coffin (London: Penguin, 1961), 93.
b. *Homily* 20.3 (quoted in *The Liturgy of the Hours: Lenten Season / Easter Season* [New York: Catholic Book Publishing Company, 1976], 2:223–24).

The virtue opposite to pride is humility, by which we recognize our complete dependence on God and surrender to his will. Humility restores the proper relationship between us and God, for we see that we can do nothing without God and that God has created us in love and desires our salvation. This brings about trust in God's tenderness and goodness, and enables us to love him in return.

Condemnation of the Rich (5:1–6)

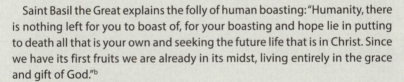

¹**Come now, you rich, weep and wail over your impending miseries. ²Your wealth has rotted away, your clothes have become moth-eaten, ³your gold and silver have corroded, and that corrosion will be a testimony against**

you; it will devour your flesh like a fire. You have stored up treasure for the last days. ⁴Behold, the wages you withheld from the workers who harvested your fields are crying aloud, and the cries of the harvesters have reached the ears of the Lord of hosts. ⁵You have lived on earth in luxury and pleasure; you have fattened your hearts for the day of slaughter. ⁶You have condemned; you have murdered the righteous one; he offers you no resistance.

OT: Ps 49:17–21; Prov 11:28
NT: Matt 6:19–21; Luke 16:19–31
Catechism: unjust wages, 2409–10
Lectionary: 26th Sunday in Ordinary Time, Year B (James 5:1–6)

This final exhortation (for the structure of the three exhortations in 4:11–5:6, see this chapter's introductory paragraph above), which like the previous one begins with "Come now, you," is addressed to the "rich." This reproof is the most severe of the three. In a series of increasingly scathing accusations, James excoriates the rich on four counts: hoarding wealth (vv. 2–3), withholding wages (v. 4), living in luxury and pleasure (v. 5), and condemning and murdering the righteous (v. 6). The text does not indicate whether the "rich" are pagans who are oppressing economically disadvantaged Christians or are wealthy members of the Christian community who behave like pagans. The aim of this preaching is both to warn of the danger of riches and pride, which lead to violating God's law and incurring his judgment, and to comfort those who suffer under the heavy hand of the rich and powerful.[9]

5:1   James begins with imperatives: **weep and wail**. In 4:9 he called upon the "lovers of the †world" to weep and mourn as a means of repentance; now the **rich** are to weep and wail over their **impending miseries**. This is the only time the Greek verb *ololyzō* ("to wail") is used in the New Testament, but in the †Septuagint it often describes the appropriate response to approaching judgment or calamity (see Isa 13:6; Ezek 21:17). The verb *ololyzō* is onomatopoetic and vividly portrays howling in terror, which is the fate of the wicked at the time of judgment. James 1:9–11 depicted the rich as passing, but here James indicates that their fate is actually much worse than ceasing to exist: the command to wail indicates that the time of judgment is at hand. The miseries coming upon them will pay them back for the oppression that they have inflicted.

5:2–3   In the first accusation, that of hoarding wealth, James uses three images of decay to describe the future loss and punishment that await the rich who do not repent of their wrongdoing (specified in vv. 3d–6). The first image is that

---

9. See James Hardy Ropes, *A Critical and Exegetical Commentary on the Epistle of St. James*, ICC (1916; repr., Edinburgh: T&T Clark, 1978), 282.

Judgment

LIVING TRADITION

Catholic doctrine distinguishes between "particular judgment" and the last judgment. This distinction reflects the teaching of the New Testament, which "speaks of judgment primarily in its aspect of the final encounter with Christ in his second coming, but also repeatedly affirms that each will be rewarded immediately after death in accordance with his works and faith" (Catechism 1021). "Particular judgment" takes place at the moment of death when the soul separates from the body and is judged. Those who die in God's †grace and friendship and are perfectly purified immediately see God face to face in his heavenly glory, the "beatific vision." Those who die in God's grace and friendship but are still imperfectly purified, although their final salvation is assured, will go through a purification known as purgatory. Those who die in mortal sin without repenting and accepting God's merciful love will be separated from him forever by their own free choice. This state of definitive self-exclusion from communion with God is called hell (Catechism 1023–33).

The general judgment, or last judgment, will take place when Christ returns in glory. When he comes, the dead will rise through the power of his resurrection. Then Christ will judge all people: he will pronounce the final word on history and reveal the truth of each one's relationship with God. Finally, all will see that God's justice triumphs over all injustices and that his love is stronger than death (Catechism 997, 1038–41).

their **wealth has rotted away**. "Wealth" means an abundance of earthly goods, and here it refers to the totality of what the rich possess. James foretells the day when their wealth, perhaps like rotten fruit, will spoil and its value completely disappear. The next two images repeat the same idea but focus on typical signs of wealth in the ancient world. Their **clothes have become moth-eaten**. In the first-century Mediterranean world even more than today, wealth and status were expressed by wearing expensive and beautiful garments (Luke 16:19). James warns that someday their fancy robes will be ruined, worthless. Finally, their **gold and silver have corroded** or rusted. The verb for "corroded" is in an intensive form and gives the sense that the metal is completely rusted and nothing of the original remains. Gold and silver do not literally rust, but through these images James conveys that every treasure of the world will fail, and "even the most precious and apparently most indestructible things are doomed to decay."[10]

10. William Barclay, *The Letters of James and Peter*, DSBS (Philadelphia: Westminster, 1976), 116.

Wealth and Almsgiving

BIBLICAL
BACKGROUND

The Scriptures teach that wealth can be a blessing from God.[a] Nevertheless, an abundance of material resources cannot compare to God's greatest gift, eternal life, and everything in our lives should be directed to this goal (Mark 8:36). Though material possessions are given to benefit us and those in need during our earthly pilgrimage (Acts 20:33–35; Eph 4:28), Scripture often warns against wealth. Money is dangerous because we too easily can come to love it, leading to the neglect of things that are far more important. Saint Paul writes,

> Those who want to be rich are falling into temptation and into a trap and into many foolish and harmful desires, which plunge them into ruin and destruction. For the love of money is the root of all evils, and some people in their desire for it have strayed from the faith and have pierced themselves with many pains. (1 Tim 6:9–10)

Moreover, with wealth comes a certain status in society and independence that undermine awareness of one's dependence on God. The wealthy person can easily become arrogant. So St. Paul advises Timothy, "Tell the rich in the present age not to be proud and not to rely on so uncertain a thing as wealth but rather on God" (1 Tim 6:17). A person does not have to be rich for money to become the center of his or her life. Jesus warns that we cannot serve both God and mammon (Matt 6:24; Luke 16:13).

continued on next page

But worse than losing their wealth is the judgment that the rich will face. The **corrosion will be a testimony** against them, meaning that their rusted, rotted wealth will serve as evidence to indict them of excessive and wasteful accumulation (saving rather than sharing). This same corrosion will devour their **flesh like a fire**. Fire often symbolizes final judgment (Isa 66:24; Matt 10:28; 18:9; Rev 20:9), and James is saying in metaphorical language that the same divine judgment that will someday render their wealth worthless will destroy them as well. Finally, James explains the reason for such a gruesome end: they have **stored up treasure for the last days**.[11] James is being sarcastic, for by storing up worldly and corruptible wealth, they have

11. The phrase translated as "for the last days" can be more literally rendered "in the last days," which yields a somewhat different meaning. In keeping with the NT perspective that since the coming of Christ we live in the last days (1 Cor 10:11; 1 John 2:18), this translation emphasizes the irony: how pointless to store up earthly wealth when history is nearing its end and God's kingdom is at hand.

So if wealth presents such a danger for us, can it be harnessed for our spiritual good? The Old Testament teaches that sharing our wealth, almsgiving, saves from death and purges sins (Tob 4:10; 12:8–9; Sir 29:12–13). Few Christians realize that the Gospels record more teaching by Jesus about wealth and money than about most other topics. In some texts Jesus indicates that our wealth is not really our own, but rather is a resource entrusted to us for which we must someday give an account.[b] In other texts Jesus offers investment advice that is truly radical: "Sell your belongings and give alms. Provide money bags for yourselves that do not wear out, an inexhaustible treasure in heaven that no thief can reach nor moth destroy. For where your treasure is, there also will your heart be" (Luke 12:33–34 [see Matt 19:21]). Wealth is fleeting, whereas "treasure in heaven" lasts forever and can never be taken away. While wealth in this world distracts from what is important, heavenly treasure draws us onward. Saint Paul echoes Jesus' emphasis on almsgiving and his metaphor of storing up treasure for our ultimate future: he instructs the wealthy "to do good, to be rich in good works, to be generous, ready to share, thus accumulating as treasure a good foundation for the future, so as to win the life that is true life" (1 Tim 6:18–19). According to Jesus and Paul, wise financial planning prioritizes almsgiving. Besides, generous giving can be an excellent medicine for an unhealthy attachment to wealth and possessions (Mark 10:21–27).

a. Gen 13:2; 2 Chron 1:11–12; Job 1:1–3, 10; 42:12; 1 Tim 6:17.
b. See, for instance, Matt 25:14–30; Luke 12:15–21 (especially v. 20); 16:1–13 (especially vv. 10–11), 19–25.

actually stored up a "treasure" of judgment for themselves. In 2:13 James indicated that "the judgment is merciless to one who has not shown mercy," and the rich have not shared their treasure and shown mercy. Instead of merciful acts, they hoarded rotting wealth, and so they will meet a merciless judgment.

James's warning echoes the words of Jesus: "Do not store up for yourselves treasures on earth, where moth and decay destroy, and thieves break in and steal. But store up treasures in heaven, where neither moth nor decay destroys, nor thieves break in and steal" (Matt 6:19–20). Jesus explains how to accumulate this lasting treasure: "Sell your belongings and give alms. Provide money bags for yourselves that do not wear out, an inexhaustible treasure in heaven that no thief can reach nor moth destroy" (Luke 12:33).

5:4 The second accusation leveled against the rich is that they cheat their workers. Deuteronomy taught that failing to pay one's workers is a serious sin for which there will be a reckoning:

> You shall not exploit a poor and needy hired servant, whether one of your own kindred or one of the resident aliens who live in your land, within your gates. On each day you shall pay the servant's wages before the sun goes down, since the servant is poor and is counting on them. Otherwise the servant will cry to the †Lord against you, and you will be held guilty. (Deut 24:14–15 [see Lev 19:13; Mal 3:5])

Because the day laborer lived at subsistence level, withholding his wages likely meant that he could not feed his family; the book of Sirach compares it to murder: "To deny a laborer wages is to shed blood" (Sir 34:27). But God hears the cry of the poor, and James indicates that the **cries of the harvesters** in hunger and misery have reached the Lord. James is referring to circumstances of injustice that particularly rouse God to take action.[12] By calling God the **Lord of hosts**, a title used in the Old Testament to show God as a warrior and master of the armies of heaven (Ps 46:12; Isa 13:13; 14:27), James emphasizes God's power to avenge the poor who have been defrauded.

5:5   The third charge accuses the rich of living in **luxury and pleasure**, meaning a decadent lifestyle. Their self-indulgence, although enjoyable for a time, has the unintended result of preparing their **hearts for the day of slaughter**. This metaphor is that of calves being **fattened** for slaughter. For the calf, the abundance of food and luxurious living is undoubtedly pleasant in the short run, but it is only preparation for its death. So it is with the rich who live in comfort and luxury and do not think either of their poor neighbors who are suffering or of their own eternal destiny. Their egos are "fattened"; they are arrogant and naively confident, when in reality they are destined for slaughter.

The teaching of James echoes Jesus' parable of the rich fool. The fool lives a self-centered life, storing up treasures, but then he dies and leaves his wealth behind, losing all that he had saved (Luke 12:16–21). Likewise, Jesus' story about Lazarus and a rich man who lived luxuriously draws a stark contrast between their two present lifestyles and the future when their fortunes will be reversed (Luke 16:19–31). Jesus teaches explicitly about the future reversal coming to those who think only of satisfaction in this life: "But woe to you who are rich, / for you have received your consolation. / But woe to you who are filled now, / for you will be hungry" (Luke 6:24–25).

5:6   The fourth and final charge against the rich is that they have **condemned**, even **murdered, the righteous one**. The verb "condemn" suggests a court setting and can indicate the imposition of a death sentence. The rich are able to use

---

12. In the OT, cries of the powerless that moved God to action were the cries of the oppressed in Egypt (Exod 3:7–10) and those of widows and orphans against those who wrong them (Exod 22:21–22).

their influence in courts of law to file charges and obtain the verdicts that they desire, while the righteous poor seem to have no recourse to the legal system. This recalls James's statement that the wealthy drag believers into court (2:6).[13]

The identity of "the righteous one" has been debated. Several biblical texts refer to Jesus as "the righteous one," so it is possible that James is speaking of the death of Jesus.[14] Since the wealthy high priests and elders of the people had a key role in the death of Jesus, James and other Jews in Jerusalem probably would have considered Jesus as having been killed by the rich. Besides, Christ is the embodiment of the righteous poor whom the wicked kill (see Wis 2:7–20). They, like Jesus, offer **no resistance**. But God will vindicate them. James seems to be echoing Jesus' teaching that whatever is done to "the least of these" is done to him (Matt 25:40).

To sum up, in this section James condemns three arrogant behaviors: speaking evil of our brothers and sisters (4:11–12), living our lives without acknowledging our dependence on God (4:13–17), and using wealth selfishly and unjustly (5:1–6).

Reflection and Application (5:1–6)

James's condemnation of the rich is difficult to hear and even scary for those of us who live in the West and are rich in comparison to the rest of the world. We need to examine whether our lifestyle contributes to the impoverishment or oppression of others (for example, buying goods that were produced unjustly) and consider what we can do to help those who are poorer than we. A modest lifestyle, almsgiving, and charitable works are fundamental to Christian living, and injustice to the poor must be radically excluded. It is equally necessary to do whatever is in our power to bring about a just social order.

Acknowledging the world's poverty and the suffering of hundreds of millions of people can be overwhelming, and it is tempting to close our eyes to problems that seem insoluble. But Christ, who is our savior and teacher, did not hesitate to dirty his hands in the messiness of human life. He embraced our suffering all the way to the cross, and on the cross he transformed suffering into love. We too are called to deny ourselves and take up our cross daily (Luke 9:23), to embrace the suffering of others, relieving their misery as we are able

---

13. Murdering the righteous one may allude to the teaching in Sir 34:27 that withholding wages is tantamount to murder.

14. Acts 3:14; 7:52; 22:14; 1 Pet 3:18; 1 John 2:1, 29, 3:7.

and pursuing justice, as we offer up our suffering and prayers, extending the transformative suffering of the cross.

At times it can feel as though our acts of charity are barely a drop in comparison to the ocean of suffering and poverty in the world. But we can pray fervently for the coming of Christ's kingdom, which the poor will inherit, where the hungry will be filled, where those who weep now will laugh, and where the persecuted will be vindicated (Luke 6:20–22); and in the meantime we must do all we can to shape society more into what God intends it to be. Ultimately, our hope is in God, who has promised to wipe away tears and put an end to death, mourning, and pain (Rev 21:4).

Patient Perseverance

James 5:7–11

In the previous chapter James chastised those who were arrogant, and he condemned with particular ferocity the rich who oppress the poor (5:1–6). Now he turns his attention to the community, using the familiar "brothers," and his tone is warm and encouraging. In the face of oppression at the hands of the rich and powerful, James counsels his listeners to persevere with patient endurance.

Be Patient Until the Lord Comes (5:7–11)

---

[7]Be patient, therefore, brothers, until the coming of the Lord. See how the farmer waits for the precious fruit of the earth, being patient with it until it receives the early and the late rains. [8]You too must be patient. Make your hearts firm, because the coming of the Lord is at hand. [9]Do not complain, brothers, about one another, that you may not be judged. Behold, the Judge is standing before the gates. [10]Take as an example of hardship and patience, brothers, the prophets who spoke in the name of the Lord. [11]Indeed we call blessed those who have persevered. You have heard of the perseverance of Job, and you have seen the purpose of the Lord, because "the Lord is compassionate and merciful."

OT: Exod 34:6
NT: Rom 1:11–12; 5:3–5; 12:9–18; Col 1:9–12; 1 Thess 3:10–13; 2 Thess 2:16–17
Catechism: last judgment, 1038–41
Lectionary: 3rd Sunday of Advent, Year A (James 5:7–10)

In these verses James again summons his readers to trust in God during their various trials. At the beginning of the letter he urged perseverance through trials in order to become mature in character, "perfect" (1:2–4); now he counsels it because the coming of the Lord is near (5:8). James gives a series of three exhortations—be patient, be firm, do not complain about one another—intended to help his readers to keep trusting in God, and he encourages them to draw strength from the example of faithful people who lived before them.

5:7 James's first instruction, **Be patient**, establishes the main theme of this section. He uses some form of the word "patient" four times in these verses (vv. 7 [2x], 8, 10). His use of **therefore** makes plain that patience is a necessary response to the abuses described in the preceding verses. In the previous section James portrayed the ultimate end of the rich as a day of slaughter (5:5). But now when he describes the future of the faithful, **the coming of the Lord**, he obviously regards it as a positive event. James encourages the members of the church to wait patiently for the merciful Lord to return and take his faithful disciples to himself, where they will receive the fruit of their patience, and their persecutors will be deprived of their power to persecute.[1]

James offers the example of the **farmer** who receives the fruits of the earth because of **the early and the late rains**. In Palestine, rain comes in October and November, which provides for the spring harvest, and then again in April and May, which secures a good summer harvest. The farmer trusts in God to send these rains and provide for the farmer's well-being. "The farmer needs patience to wait until nature does her work; and the Christian needs patience to wait until Christ comes."[2]

5:8 After once again stressing that they **must be patient**, James gives his second instruction: **Make your hearts firm**. The New Testament often commends strengthening one's heart. The model of this activity is Jesus, who resolutely turned to Jerusalem to face his death. The Greek literally says that Jesus "made his face firm" (Luke 9:51), and the verb is the same one that James uses here. Saints Paul and Peter also write about the importance of God strengthening our hearts so we can persevere through trial (1 Thess 3:13; 2 Thess 2:17; 1 Pet 5:10). The person who makes his or her heart firm is single-minded, the opposite of the double-minded person, whose commitment to the Lord vacillates (James 1:6–8).

1. Bede the Venerable, *Commentary on the Seven Catholic Epistles*, trans. David Hurst, CSS 82 (Kalamazoo, MI: Cistercian Publications, 1985), 58.
2. William Barclay, *The Letters of James and Peter*, DSBS (Philadelphia: Westminster, 1976), 121.

The reason to be firm is that **the coming of the Lord is at hand**. Just as John the Baptist and Jesus and preached that "the kingdom of God is at hand" (Matt 3:2; 4:17; Mark 1:15), so James and other New Testament authors declare that the return of Jesus is near (the literal meaning of "at hand"). How are we to interpret this statement twenty centuries later? It helps to realize that the Old Testament prophets also speak of God's final judgment and salvation as "near" or soon (Jer 51:33; Bar 4:22, 24; Zeph 1:14). God's perspective on time is obviously different from ours. Also, regardless of how the human authors understood what they were saying, the Holy Spirit's goal is always to rouse human beings to make ready for God's salvation and judgment, which might come upon them sooner than they expect.

James's next instruction, **Do not complain**, is addressed to them as **broth-** 5:9
ers. The Greek word rendered as "complain" means "to sigh, groan, express discontent."[3] It is acceptable to grieve over the difficulties of life,[4] but not to grumble or protest against God's designs. James adds the phrase **about one another**, indicating that his readers are not to grumble about one another. Situations of great pain and suffering can cause people to turn on one another. But James calls them "brothers," reminding them of the familial relationship that exists among them by virtue of their calling in Jesus.

According to James, they should avoid complaining so that they **may not be judged**. In 4:11 he exhorted the members of the community not to speak ill of one another, because by doing so they make themselves judges. James sees complaining about and speaking evil of one another as closely related, and now he warns against such behavior by implicitly applying Jesus' words in the Sermon on the Mount: "Stop judging, that you may not be judged" (Matt 7:1 [see Luke 6:37]). This danger is real, since Jesus Christ the **Judge is standing before the gates**; his coming is imminent. Instead of leading us to complain about our brothers or sisters in the faith, hardships ought to increase our longing for redemption, which will be finally accomplished when Christ returns. Knowing that judgment is near, we should keep our eyes fixed on Jesus' coming and patiently persevere.

But how are we to do this? In verses 10–11, James points to the example 5:10–11
of ancestors in the faith who were severely tried yet remained faithful, trusting that God, who is merciful and compassionate, desired their good. Often in the Old Testament, God's saving actions in the past become the basis for his people's hope in the present. In Ps 22 the psalmist is tormented and

3. BDAG, "*stenazō*," 942.
4. See Isa 59:10; Lam 1:21–22; Mark 7:34; 2 Cor 5:2, 4.

near death, yet he finds hope and consolation in considering those who came before him: "In you our fathers trusted; / they trusted and you rescued them. / To you they cried out and they escaped; / in you they trusted and were not disappointed" (Ps 22:5–6 [see Sir 2:10]). By recalling the lives of the faithful who endured great trials and were saved by God, James strengthens his readers in their moments of trial. He presents two models of such fidelity, the prophets and Job.

The **prophets** are those **who spoke in the name of the Lord**. They fearlessly addressed kings, powerful elites, and angry crowds

Figure 4. *Job on the Dunghill* by Gonzalo Carrasco

bent on their destruction. Proclaiming the truth is a risky business, and the prophets often risked their lives to proclaim God's word. But God never abandoned them, and by his †grace they were able to speak God's message, despite being threatened, mocked, and imprisoned.[5] Because of their perseverance, James calls them **blessed**, a word that indicates that a person has been the recipient of divine favor.[6] Like the prophets before them, James's readers will be blessed if they continue to proclaim the word of the Lord and do not lose faith when they suffer severe tests and trials.

The second example is **Job**, whose **perseverance** is pointed out.[7] The book of Job recounts the story of a just man whom God allowed †Satan to torment. Job's belongings and children were taken, and then his body was attacked by sickness (Job 1:1–2:8). When Job was near death and in great pain, his wife advised him to curse God and die (Job 2:9), while his friends accused him of wrongdoing. Job, despite being alone in the world, sick, and cast as a sinner, remained firm, completely convinced that somehow God would vindicate him, though his circumstances indicated otherwise. In the

---

5. E.g., see Jer 11:18–23; 18:18; 36:11–38:6.
6. BDAG, "*makarios*," 611.
7. In 5:11 James uses the verb "persevere" (*hypomenō*) and the noun "perseverance" (*hypomenē*) (see 1:3–4, 12), and he calls those who persevere "blessed," as in 1:12.

Compassionate and Merciful God

BIBLICAL BACKGROUND

In the Old Testament, God passed by Moses and called out, "The †LORD, the LORD, a God gracious and merciful, slow to anger and abounding in love and fidelity" (Exod 34:6). This formula, which describes God's character, is repeated eight times in the Old Testament and is alluded to at least another twenty times.[a] The first attribute, "merciful," expresses tender love between those who have a deep bond, or a person who is concerned about another's sufferings. It is especially used of a superior toward an inferior. Thus God looks upon his own as a merciful father looks upon his child.[b] The second attribute, "gracious," indicates God's willingness to bestow grace and favor upon his people, even though his people can neither earn nor deserve it. God is also "slow to anger," meaning that he is not hasty in punishment, and when we sin, he gives us time to repent. Finally, God is "abounding in love and fidelity." The term for "love" (Hebrew *hesed*) is difficult to translate, and its meaning includes "mercy, loyalty, loving-kindness." The term for "fidelity" (Hebrew *emet*), which derives from the same Hebrew root as "truth," indicates firmness and dependability. God can be trusted because he is true to his word and always does what he promises to do.

a. Num 14:18; Neh 9:17b; Pss 86:15; 103:8; 145:8; Joel 2:13; Jon 4:2; Nah 1:3.
b. TWOT, "*raham*," 841–42.

end, God did vindicate him, and God even commanded Job to make intercession for his friends, who had not spoken correctly about God (Job 42:8). The example of Job summons Christians to look beyond their present sufferings and to continue to trust in God. It is easy during bad times to doubt that God is love (1 John 4:8) or to think that following Jesus is a mistake. James offers the example of Job to encourage his readers to be steadfast as he was, because they have **seen the purpose of the Lord**; that is, they have seen the good outcome that came to Job (Job 42:10–17). Job's end serves to encourage James's readers to hope for the same good outcome for themselves. Although it is sometimes difficult to ascertain God's purpose in the midst of persecution, James assures his readers that it is always the salvation of his people (see Rom 8:28; 1 Tim 2:4).

The stories of the prophets and of Job bear out that God's plan is always one of love, for he is **compassionate and merciful**. The Old Testament often notes that God is merciful and gracious (Exod 34:6; Pss 103:8; 111:4); the Greek word for "compassionate" used here emphasizes tenderness and deep feeling.

Reflection and Application (5:7–11)

Saint John, who had a deep understanding of God's nature, goes so far as to say that "God is love" (1 John 4:8). A few verses later he says that when we come to love God and know his love for us, fear of punishment is expelled from our hearts (1 John 4:18). Through prayer and the reading of Scripture, we too can come to grasp the depth of God's love for us, and our fear can be replaced with love and trust. When we allow ourselves to be loved by God and entrust our hearts to him, he can guide us to eternal life with himself, which is what he desires for all of us (1 Tim 2:3–4).

Saints throughout the centuries have stood for truth in times of great trial, and they can aid us both by their intercessory prayer and by their example. At the present moment, men and women throughout the world are suffering persecution and martyrdom for their faith in Jesus, and their example can strengthen us in patient perseverance.

While I was studying in Rome, I met a priest from Iraq who was also studying there, and we became friends. During that time, Iraqi Christians began to be tortured and murdered by Islamic extremists, and he would tell me about family members, friends, and fellow priests who were being kidnapped or killed. He was especially anguished when a brother priest, Fr. Ragheed Ganni, was murdered on the steps of his church. Shortly after the death of Fr. Ragheed, Faraj Rahho, the bishop of Mosul, was also murdered.

After my friend finished his studies, he was directed by his bishop to return to Iraq as a pastor of a parish. Knowing well the situation to which he was returning, he told me that he was going to Iraq to die. When I asked him why he would ever go, he responded, "I am a priest. And as long as there are Christians in Iraq, I must go to serve them." He responded as Jesus did, accepting the cross that he would have to bear in service of his people and his witness to the truth, knowing that he could be killed or kidnapped at any moment. As of this writing, he is still alive, patiently persevering in his ministry each day despite the dangers and distresses that he shares with his people.

The doctrine of the communion of saints teaches us that we are never alone, but we belong to a great body of believers, both past and present, who advance the kingdom of God by overcoming hatred with prayer, love, and sacrifice. If we live our own trials well, perhaps generations to come will be able to look to us for hope and inspiration in their times of difficulty.

Final Instructions

James 5:12–20

Throughout this letter James has spoken of the unbreakable bond between love of God and love of neighbor. He has largely concentrated on the second of these—how we ought to conduct ourselves in human relationships—through his exhortations about helping the needy, controlling the tongue, and avoiding injustice to workers and attachment to wealth. Now, in this final section of the letter, James closes with exhortations about how the community should live its relationship with God. Christians should be careful to honor God's name (v. 12), to pray at all times (vv. 13–18), and to confess their sins (v. 16). James closes by warmly encouraging us to rescue sinners from the error of their ways (vv. 19–20). Jesus says that he came to seek and save the lost (Luke 19:10); to follow in his footsteps is proof that we have come to share his heart.

Avoidance of Swearing (5:12)

¹²**But above all, my brothers, do not swear, either by heaven or by earth or with any other oath, but let your "Yes" mean "Yes" and your "No" mean "No," that you may not incur condemnation.**

OT: Exod 20:7
NT: Matt 5:34–37; 2 Cor 1:17–20
Catechism: taking the name of the Lord in vain, 2150–55

5:12   James has indicated the importance of governing one's speech, explaining that
       controlling the tongue leads to perfection (3:2). Such control involves being
       slow to speak (1:19), bridling one's tongue (1:26), not cursing (3:9–10), not
       speaking evil of people (4:11), not boasting (4:16), and not complaining about
       others (5:9). Now he takes up the theme again, with a prohibition, **do not
       swear**, and a precept, **let your "Yes" mean "Yes."** Again, the motive is to avoid
       condemnation when God judges. James introduces this teaching by saying,
       But above all. All sins of the tongue are to be avoided, but respect for God's
       holy name has a special importance.

       To swear, or to take an oath, means to affirm the veracity of one's statement by
       explicitly or implicitly invoking divine punishment if one is not telling the truth.[1]
       In the past, oaths were commonly used to give credibility to statements. Given
       the human tendency to lie, listeners often discount the truth-value of speakers'
       statements. Invoking a deity, which raises the stakes if one is lying, adds weight
       to one's words. In the Old Testament, taking an oath is not prohibited and is
       occasionally required (e.g., Exod 22:10; Num 5:19–22). Deuteronomy 6:13 says,
       "The †Lord, your God, shall you fear; him shall you serve, and by his name shall
       you swear."[2] However, in first-century Judaism, oaths were sometimes abused as
       a means to avoid telling the truth (see Matt 23:16–22). Jesus fulfills and perfects
       the law (Matt 5:17) by summoning his disciples to tell the truth without swearing.

       > But I say to you, do not swear at all; not by heaven, for it is God's throne; nor by
       > the earth, for it is his footstool; nor by Jerusalem, for it is the city of the great
       > King. Do not swear by your head, for you cannot make a single hair white or
       > black. Let your "Yes" mean "Yes," and your "No" mean "No." Anything more is
       > from the evil one. (Matt 5:34–37)

       Jesus' teaching also guards against violations of the second commandment,
       "You shall not invoke the name of the Lord, your God, in vain" (Exod 20:7).
       Every oath involves invoking God's name. The Catechism (2153) comments,
       "Discretion in calling upon God is allied with a respectful awareness of his pres-
       ence, which all our assertions either witness to or mock." Jesus himself never
       swore, because his word itself is truth. He said, "Heaven and earth will pass
       away, but my words will not pass away" (Mark 13:31), indicating the veracity
       and reliability of what he says. Our words should be like his words.

       ---

       1. BDAG, "*omnyō*," 705.
       2. Another example is Ps 63:12: "All who swear by the Lord shall exult." Even God takes an oath
       based on his own veracity: "I swear by my very self—oracle of the Lord—that because you acted as you
       did in not withholding from me your son, your only one, I will bless you" (Gen 22:16–17).

Oaths

LIVING TRADITION

It is noteworthy that Jesus' teaching against taking oaths in the Sermon on the Mount (Matt 5:33–37), which James echoes here, is not interpreted by either St. Paul or most teachers in the Christian tradition as a literal prohibition, but rather as a forceful exhortation to avoid unnecessary oaths and to speak the simple truth, which is how Jesus' comments conclude (Matt 5:37).

In his letters Paul uses oaths to underscore the veracity of what he says; several times he calls on God as his witness.[a] On the assumption that Paul knew of Jesus' teaching against oaths in the Sermon on the Mount, we may infer that, rather than disregarding it (since Paul clearly treats Jesus' teaching as authoritative),[b] Paul understood it as a command to be completely truthful in speech rather than as a literal prohibition. Because he knows that he is telling the truth, Paul does not hesitate to swear to what he is saying.

Likewise, the Catholic Church has not interpreted the words of Jesus as a literal prohibition. According to the Catechism (2154),

> Following St. Paul [see 2 Cor 1:23; Gal 1:20], the tradition of the Church has understood Jesus' words as not excluding oaths made for grave and right reasons (for example, in court). "An oath, that is the invocation of the divine name as a witness to truth, cannot be taken unless in truth, in judgment, and in justice." [Code of Canon Law 1199 §1]

a. 2 Cor 1:23; 11:31; Gal 1:20; 1 Thess 2:5.
b. See Acts 20:35; 1 Cor 7:10, 25; 11:23–25; 1 Thess 4:15.

Constant Prayer (5:13–18)

¹³Is anyone among you suffering? He should pray. Is anyone in good spirits? He should sing praise. ¹⁴Is anyone among you sick? He should summon the presbyters of the church, and they should pray over him and anoint [him] with oil in the name of the Lord, ¹⁵and the prayer of faith will save the sick person, and the Lord will raise him up. If he has committed any sins, he will be forgiven.

¹⁶Therefore, confess your sins to one another and pray for one another, that you may be healed. The fervent prayer of a righteous person is very powerful. ¹⁷Elijah was a human being like us; yet he prayed earnestly that it might not rain, and for three years and six months it did not rain upon

the land. [18]Then he prayed again, and the sky gave rain and the earth produced its fruit.

OT: 1 Kings 17–18; Ps 38:6, 19; Sir 21:1; 28:2
NT: Matt 9:2 // Mark 2:5 // Luke 5:20; John 20:22–23; 1 John 1:8–9; 2:12
Catechism: persevering in prayer, 2738–45; anointing of the sick, 1499–1532
Lectionary: optional reading in the Mass for the Sick (James 5:13–16)

After emphasizing truthful speech and the holiness of God's name, James issues an exhortation to pray in every circumstance. He employs questions that
enable readers to locate themselves in one of three categories that encompass
a range of human experience: those who suffer, those who are in good spirits,
and those who are sick. He then guides each person to the kind of prayer suited
to his or her circumstances.

5:13   James first addresses those who are **suffering**. The Greek word translated as
"suffering" means "undergoing hardship" or "experiencing sadness"; it encompasses a range of afflictions including misfortune, physical sickness, or sickness
of soul. James urges such a person to **pray**, presumably to cry out to God to be
delivered or to obtain strength to get through the difficulties.

James next addresses those who are **in good spirits**, who are content because
they are experiencing God's blessings, perhaps even spiritual joy, in contrast
to those who are suffering. The appropriate response to God in their positive
situation is again prayer, but of a specific kind: they should **sing praise**. The
Greek word for "sing praise" is *psallō*, from which we get the word "psalm."
Originally the word was used to indicate a song sung to the accompaniment
of a harp (see Ps 33:2). Over time, however, the connection with the musical
instrument diminished, and "to psalm" came to refer to singing to God with
voice and heart (see 1 Cor 14:15).[3]

5:14   James next turns his attention to a more specific category: those who are **sick**.
The appropriate response is prayer once again, but this time James does not advocate individual prayer; rather, the sick should **summon the presbyters of the
church**. The word "†presbyter" (Greek *presbyteros*, from which the English word
"priest" derives) can indicate someone of advanced age, an older man. However,
in Acts and the New Testament Epistles the word usually refers to someone who
holds the office of presbyter in the Church (Acts 14:23; 15:2; 1 Tim 5:17, 19).

James uses the term *ekklēsia* ("church"), whereas in 2:2 he called the Christian assembly a *synagōgē* ("synagogue"). The term *ekklēsia* means "gathering,

3. Patrick J. Hartin, *James*, SP 14 (Collegeville, MN: Liturgical Press, 2003), 266. See Eph 5:19–20,
where the same verb is used.

Figure 5. Farmers pausing for prayer (Jean-François Millet, *The Angelus*)

assembly"; in the †Septuagint it refers to the assembly of Israel. In the New Testament, the church is the people of God that Jesus gathers and unites to himself, the body of Christ.

The presbyters are summoned to do two things: to **pray over him and anoint [him] with oil**. To "pray over" indicates the laying on of hands. Anointing with oil for healing was common in both the Jewish and the Hellenistic cultures.[4] Jesus himself healed many, and he authorized his disciples to do the same (Matt 10:1, 8; Luke 9:2; 10:9). Mark reports that the disciples "drove out many demons, and they anointed with oil many who were sick and cured them" (Mark 6:13)—the only mention of the disciples using oil in healing. James's instruction shows that the practice of Jesus and his disciples continued. The Church today continues Jesus' healing mission; from the beginning the Church has called upon its priests to anoint with oil and pray over the sick and dying.

4. There are several references in ancient Jewish literature to the use of oil for healing. See James Hardy Ropes, *A Critical and Exegetical Commentary on the Epistle of St. James*, ICC (Edinburgh: T&T Clark, 1978), 305.

The prayer and anointing with oil are to be done **in the name of the Lord**. In the Old Testament, God revealed his name to Moses, "I AM" (Exod 3:14), meaning "I am the one who will always be present among my people." God made his name dwell among them in the temple (Deut 12:11), indicating his presence there and his desire to be approached by his people and to live in union with them. In the New Testament, Jesus says that he has made known God's name (John 17:6, 26), meaning that he has revealed and made God present to humankind in a new and enduring way. In Jesus, God gives himself entirely to humankind in order to transfer us from slavery to the status of adopted sons and daughters, forgiving our sins and bringing us into union with himself. Thus, the name of Jesus—his presence and power—overcomes evil, sickness, and death.

To "pray in the name of the Lord" means to ask something on Jesus' authority, in union with him, and according to his will (John 14:13–14; 15:16). To "anoint with oil in the name of the Lord," or to perform an action in the name of the Lord, such as healing or exorcism (Acts 3:6; 16:18), means to be authorized by and united to Jesus in the performance of this act. By praying and anointing in the name of the Lord, presbyters continue the mission of Jesus to overcome the forces of evil, sickness, and sin in the †world.

5:15   The prayer of the presbyters is called a **prayer of faith**. James has already taught that those asking for wisdom need to ask in faith (1:6–8), and that prayers for selfish desires are not answered (4:3). Putting these verses together, we are to believe in God and pray to do his will. In the Gospels, Jesus performed miracles for those who exercised faith—that is, those who asked him expectantly for what they needed and who believed and trusted in him.

The prayer will have three effects: it will save the sick person, the Lord will raise that person up, and his or her sins will be forgiven. In the first effect, the Greek verb for **save** (*sōzō*) has a twofold meaning. It refers to physical healing (e.g., Mark 5:23; Luke 17:19) but also to eternal salvation (Rom 5:9–10; James 1:21; 2:14). Thus, the prayer of faith can both heal **the sick person** and bring him or her to eternal salvation. The second effect is that **the Lord will raise him up**. The Greek verb translated as "raise" also has a twofold meaning: in healings performed by Jesus and his disciples it refers to the person standing up after healing (see Matt 9:5–7; Mark 1:31; Acts 3:7); it is also used to refer to resurrection from the dead (Matt 28:6; Mark 16:6; Luke 24:6, 34). Once again, there is both a physical and a spiritual dimension to the †grace received. Finally, **If he has committed any sins, he will be forgiven**. This last effect is in a conditional phrase, indicating that a person's sickness is not necessarily a consequence of personal sin, but if in fact he or she is in need of forgiveness,

The Sacrament of Anointing

The Church understands James's teaching about prayer over the sick and anointing with oil by a presbyter as the biblical basis of the sacrament of the anointing of the sick. The Council of Trent solemnly declared,

> This sacred anointing of the sick was instituted by Christ our Lord as a true and proper sacrament of the New Testament. It is alluded to indeed by Mark [Mark 6:13], but is recommended to the faithful and promulgated by James the apostle and brother of the Lord [James 5:14–15].[a]

The council indicated that James teaches all the elements of the sacrament: the matter (oil), the form (liturgical prayer over the sick person), the proper minister (presbyter), and the effect of the sacrament (healing and salvation).[b]

In the Western Church, over the course of the centuries the sacrament of the anointing of the sick came to be conferred almost exclusively on those who were at the point of death, and so it acquired the name "extreme unction"— that is, anointing at the end. The Second Vatican Council restored the original practice of the Church of administering the sacrament as a prayer for healing for those who are seriously ill but not necessarily near death.

The Catechism (1532) summarizes the many graces of the anointing of the sick by listing its effects:

- the uniting of the sick person to the passion of Christ, for his own good and that of the whole Church;
- the strengthening, peace, and courage to endure in a Christian manner the sufferings of illness or old age;
- the forgiveness of sins, if the sick person was not able to obtain it through the sacrament of penance;
- the restoration of health, if it is conducive to the salvation of his soul;
- the preparation for passing over to eternal life.

a. Council of Trent (1551), *Doctrine on the Sacrament of Extreme Unction* 1.1 (DS 1695).
b. Ibid. (DS 1696).

the Lord will give that grace as well. Jesus forgave a paralyzed man's sin prior to healing him (Matt 9:2; Mark 2:5; Luke 5:20); likewise, he cautioned a man healed after thirty-eight years of sickness not to sin again (John 5:14). Thus, the prayer and anointing of the presbyters is powerful indeed, offering the possibility of both physical and spiritual healing.

In every situation of life, then, whether suffering, joy, or sickness, a person should engage in individual or communal prayer. In the case of sickness, one

Confession in Catholic Tradition

The *Didache*, a Christian document dating from the late first or early second century AD, teaches, "Assemble on the Lord's day, and break bread and offer the Eucharist, but first make confession of your faults, so that your sacrifice may be a pure one" (14:1).[a]

Saint Augustine interpreted the words of James as referring to the efficacy of fraternal confession of sins and prayer for one another.

> Having confessed our sins to one another, we should pray for each other as Christ also intercedes for us [Rom 8:34]. Let us hear the Apostle James teaching very openly this very point and saying, "Confess your sins to one another, and pray for yourselves." For the Lord too gave us an example in regard to this. For if he who neither has, nor had, nor will have any sin prays for our sins, how much more ought we, one for the other, pray for our sins! And if he for whom we have nothing to forgive forgives us, how much more ought we to forgive one another who cannot live here without sin [Matt 6:12]![b]

As the Church grew, confession began to be made to the priest, who represented the Church. This was a natural development, since Jesus gave authority to the apostles to forgive or retain sins (Matt 18:18; John 20:23), and their authority passed on to the †bishops and priests.

Saint Thomas Aquinas applies the words of James to sacramental confession: "The precept about confession was not instituted by a man first of all, though it was promulgated by James: it was instituted by God."[c] James encourages the confession of sins in order to be healed, and our understanding of the sacrament of penance is based, at least in part, on what he said.

a. From *Early Christian Writings*, trans. Maxwell Staniforth (New York: Penguin, 1968), 234.
b. *Tractates on the Gospel of John 55–111*, trans. John W. Rettig, FC 90 (Washington, DC: Catholic University of America Press, 1994), 22–23, tractate 58.5.
c. *Summa theologiae* III Supplement, q. 6, a. 6.

should receive the sacrament of the anointing of the sick. Just as Jesus himself prayed constantly and taught his disciples to do likewise, now James teaches us to do the same.

5:16–18   James concludes his exhortation to the sick with one more recommendation: **Therefore, confess your sins to one another and pray for one another**. Confessing one's sins brings cleansing from sin and peace with God. The psalmist speaks of his sin as a festering wound in his soul that was healed only after he confessed it to God (Ps 32:3–5).

But what exactly does James mean by confessing sins to one another? Jesus

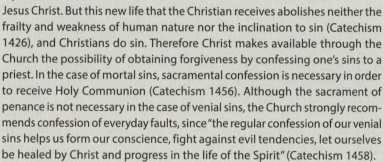

The Sacrament of Reconciliation

LIVING TRADITION

The Council of Trent associates James 5:16 with sacramental confession: "The whole Church has always understood that the complete confession of sins, like the sacrament of anointing, was also instituted by the Lord (James 5:16; 1 John 1:9; Luke 5:14; 17:14), and is by divine law necessary for all who have fallen after baptism."[a]

The sacrament of baptism is the primary sacrament of the forgiveness of sins; the sacrament of penance restores the grace of baptism that is lost through sin. Through the sacrament of baptism, a person is liberated from sin and enters into communion with Jesus Christ. But this new life that the Christian receives abolishes neither the frailty and weakness of human nature nor the inclination to sin (Catechism 1426), and Christians do sin. Therefore Christ makes available through the Church the possibility of obtaining forgiveness by confessing one's sins to a priest. In the case of mortal sins, sacramental confession is necessary in order to receive Holy Communion (Catechism 1456). Although the sacrament of penance is not necessary in the case of venial sins, the Church strongly recommends confession of everyday faults, since "the regular confession of our venial sins helps us form our conscience, fight against evil tendencies, let ourselves be healed by Christ and progress in the life of the Spirit" (Catechism 1458).

a. Council of Trent (1551), *Doctrine on the Sacrament of Penance* 5.1 (DS 1679).

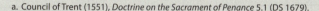

taught that we should be reconciled with one another before we bring an offering to God (Matt 5:23–24), which implies some sort of confession of fault to another. The First Letter of John also encourages confession of sin, although it is not clear whether confession to someone besides God is involved: "If we acknowledge our sins, he is faithful and just and will forgive our sins and cleanse us from every wrongdoing" (1 John 1:9).

In support of his recommendation that Christians pray for one another, James explains that the **fervent prayer of a righteous person is very powerful**. A righteous person is one who stands in good relationship with God. James assumes that the community is composed of righteous people and that, as a result, the members of the Christian community can and should aid one another through prayer. He provides an example of the power of the prayer of a righteous person. **Elijah** was renowned for his zeal for God and the †covenant; he suffered great hardships in his service to God and performed many miracles by God's power. But James describes Elijah as **a human being like us**. By underlining the commonality between Elijah and his readers, James teaches that our prayers can be just as effective as Elijah's.

The Powerful Prayer of the Righteous

The Church Father Tertullian (160–225) elaborates on the powerful prayer of the righteous:

> The prayer of the just turns aside the whole anger of God, keeps vigil for its enemies, pleads for persecutors.... Prayer is the one thing that can conquer God.... Its only art is to call back the souls of the dead from the very journey into death, to give strength to the weak, to heal the sick, to exorcise the possessed, to open prison cells, to free the innocent from their chains. Prayer cleanses from sin, drives away temptations, stamps out persecutions, comforts the fainthearted, gives new strength to the courageous, brings travelers safely home, calms the waves, confounds robbers, feeds the poor, overrules the rich, lifts up the fallen, supports those who are falling, sustains those who stand firm.[a]

a. *On Prayer* 28–29 (quoted in *The Liturgy of the Hours, Lenten Season / Easter Season* [New York: Catholic Book Publishing Company, 1976], 2:249).

James describes Elijah as one who **prayed earnestly that it might not rain**. Elijah, speaking the word of God, announced that there would be no rain (1 Kings 17:1), and the ensuing drought and famine lasted three years. When he prayed again, the drought ended (1 Kings 18:41–45) and the **earth produced its fruit**. The implication here is that just as Elijah's prayer was effective in bringing new life to the parched land, so too the prayer of the righteous person will be effective in bringing the fruit of healing.[5]

Reflection and Application (5:13–18)

In this section James advocates prayer at all times and points to the saving work of the sacraments of anointing and reconciliation.

Physical Healing

Some years ago a newly ordained priest serving in the cathedral of the diocese of Karaganda in Kazakhstan decided to invite parishioners who were seriously ill to come to a weekday Mass and remain afterward to receive the sacrament of anointing of the sick. As the priest tells the story, he had not succeeded at administering the sacrament to half the people before he was forced to stop

5. Hartin, *James*, 272.

and quiet the congregation, since many whom he had anointed and prayed for experienced immediate healing and were talking excitedly. He was as astounded and overcome at God's power as they were.

In another case, a priest of the diocese of Toledo, Ohio, was visiting a member of his parish in the hospital. He offered to anoint and pray for the patient in the bed next to his parishioner, since that man had throat cancer and was due to be operated upon the next day. The man welcomed the priest's ministry. A couple of days later the priest called to see how his parishioner was faring and asked also about the man in the next bed. The parishioner responded by immediately passing the phone to his neighbor. Surprised that the man was able to speak, the priest was amazed to learn that no surgery had been performed since no cancer was found. The man had been completely cured!

In both these cases the healing work of Christ exceeded everyone's expectations. These examples do not mean that all will be healed physically, but it is certain that all who approach this sacrament with sincerity and faith can expect to be saved and raised up by the Lord in one way or another.

Forgiveness

A friend of mine had an extremely difficult employer, and though he endured unnecessary humiliation and even cruelty, he could not leave his job because he had no alternative and he had dependent children. He stayed at this job for quite some time, until finally he found something else. After he left, he found himself struggling with great anger toward his former employer. Though he wanted to forgive, he found it almost impossible. But then he decided to go to confession. He poured out his heart to the priest, who patiently listened to him, counseled him, and gave him absolution. My friend recounted to me that almost immediately after his confession his anger went away, he was able to forgive everything, and he experienced great peace. He told me how beautiful it was to be freed from the shackles of his spiritual suffering and enjoy the freedom and peace of God that came to him through the sacrament of reconciliation.

Countless stories like this are told by people who have experienced God's mercy, grace, and freedom through the sacraments. Though we live in a †world marred by sin and are touched by it ourselves, God has given us the possibility of overcoming our sinful tendencies and truly living in the freedom of the children of God. God is a good father who generously and tenderly comes to meet us through these channels of grace. He reaches out to heal our broken hearts and stricken bodies, fills us with hope and peace, and gives us the strength to continue to combat the sin in our world.

Bringing Back Sinners (5:19–20)

---

¹⁹**My brothers, if anyone among you should stray from the truth and someone bring him back, ²⁰he should know that whoever brings back a sinner from the error of his way will save his soul from death and will cover a multitude of sins.**

NT: 1 Tim 4:16; 1 Pet 4:7–8
Catechism: to bear witness to the truth, 2471–74

Throughout the letter, James has been speaking of the "works" that should characterize a Christian (2:14–26; 3:13). These include caring for widows and orphans (1:27), showing mercy (2:13), avoiding partiality and evil speech (2:1–9; 3:1–12), persevering through trials (1:12), and praying in all circumstances of life (5:13–14). Now James ends his letter of exhortation by encouraging the greatest spiritual work of mercy a Christian can do: to bring someone back to the right path. It is a perfect finish because it concerns the salvation of others.

5:19–20   James speaks of people who belong, or once belonged, to the Christian community: those **among you** who **stray from the truth**. The verb "stray" (*planaō*) refers here to those who once followed Christ but then wandered away.⁶ James has previously spoken about the truth. In 1:18 he said that Christians are brought to birth through "the word of truth," meaning that believers are reborn in baptism through accepting the †gospel. In 3:14 he warned his readers not to boast and "be false to the truth," but rather to examine their hearts to ascertain the true motives for their actions. Here the truth encompasses both Christian teaching and the faithful practice that flows from a heart submitted to God. James's concern is for those who have wandered from this truth.

The Christian is called to be one who **brings back a sinner**. The Greek verb translated as "bring back" (*epistrephō*) refers to leading someone to conversion, the change of mentality and lifestyle that results from recognizing one's error and returning to the way of truth. Repentance and faith compose the essential human response that the gospel requires, and the call to both was part of Jesus' first public proclamation (Mark 1:15).

---

6. BDAG, "*planaō*," 822.

120

The result of bringing someone back to the right way is to **save his soul from death** and to **cover a multitude of sins**. Psalm 32:1 states, "Happy are those whose transgression is forgiven, whose sin is covered" (NRSV). The Greek verb for "cover" (*kalyptō*) means "to hide, conceal." To "cover sins" is an idiom for forgiveness, building on the image of God putting our sins out of his sight.

What is not clear from the text is whose soul gets saved. Does "his soul" refer to the sinner or the one who called the sinner back? The sentence is ambiguous. Since the possessive pronoun "his" is closer to the word "sinner," it more likely means that the sinner is saved. However, it cannot be ruled out that James is speaking about the salvation of the person who brings back the sinner. There is ample evidence that such an understanding was prevalent from the time of the prophet Ezekiel, who taught, "If . . . you warn the just to avoid sin, and they do not sin, they will surely live because of the warning, and you in turn shall save your own life" (Ezek 3:21 [see Dan 12:3]). Paul wrote to Timothy, "Attend to yourself and to your teaching; persevere in both tasks, for by doing so you will save both yourself and those who listen to you" (1 Tim 4:16). Two centuries later, Origen (184–253) listed the ways in which someone may gain forgiveness of sins: baptism, martyrdom, almsgiving, forgiveness of others, love, penance, and converting "a sinner from the error of his way."[7]

In any case, James's final sentence points to the reason he has written. He probably realized that his letter was not an easy read. He excoriated his readers for their uncharitable speech, lack of assistance toward the poor, and dalliance with the †world. In addition, he called them adulterers and suggested that bitter jealousy and selfish ambition might live in their hearts (3:14). But he ends the letter by indicating his reason for writing: the salvation of his readers and of those who have wandered from the truth. Like Christ before him, as a †bishop and defender of the truth, James the Just seeks to save his flock and cover a multitude of sins, continuing the saving activity of his Master (1:1). There is no greater work.

---

7. *Homily* 2.5. See Origen: *Homilies on Leviticus 1–16*, trans. Gary Wayne Barkley (Washington, DC: Catholic University of America Press, 1990), 47.

General Introduction to First, Second, and Third John

The New Testament contains three letters attributed by tradition to the apostle John. They are commonly known as the †Johannine Epistles. The first letter, 1 John, by far the most substantial of the three, offers a profound teaching on Christian faith and love. Second John (thirteen verses) is a brief letter of greeting from the author to a local church. Third John (fifteen verses) is a personal letter from the author to a certain Gaius, a leader in a local church.

Various questions perennially confront the reader of the three Letters of John. Are they all from the same author? How are the letters linked historically? Why is there no opening or closing greeting in 1 John?[1] And why were 2 John and 3 John preserved at all and included in the †canon of the New Testament?[2]

Most scholars believe that 2 John and 3 John were preserved because they were copied and circulated along with 1 John. Because 1 John and 2 John share language and themes, many scholars believe that they were written at about the same time, with 3 John coming later. Some commentators even suggest that 2 John may have been sent as a cover letter for 1 John, or that all three letters were written at the same time and sent together as one package.[3]

---

1. Rudolf Schnackenburg calls the lack of a true opening greeting in 1 John "an enigma" (*The Johannine Epistles*, trans. Reginald and Ilse Fuller [New York: Crossroad, 1992], 4). Apart from the Gospels and Acts, 1 John is the only writing in the NT that has neither an opening nor a closing greeting.

2. "It is a miracle that despite the enigmatic sender . . . and their insignificant contents these two letters were preserved at all" (Martin Hengel, *The Johannine Question* [London: SCM, 1989], 26).

3. Luke Timothy Johnson offers this as a plausible historical hypothesis (*The Writings of the New Testament: An Introduction*, rev. ed. [Minneapolis: Fortress, 1999], 561–62). The weakness of this hypothesis is the statement in both 2 John and 3 John that the author has much more to say, but rather than using "paper and ink," he hopes to come and speak to them in person. Why would he write this if he were also including a lengthy written letter (1 John) composed of "paper and ink"?

Although we cannot determine the exact historical relationships among the three letters, we can see that they are closely linked and mutually illuminate one another. Given the striking similarities in style and language, it is very likely that they come from the pen of the same author. Some scholars in the past century argued that the author of 2 John and 3 John is not the author of 1 John, but today there is a general consensus that the three letters come from the same hand (see the introduction to 1 John for a discussion of authorship). In this commentary I will assume that the same author wrote all three letters.

Given the brevity of 2 John and 3 John, there is no significant development of major themes to be found in them, but we can still discern various threads that connect the three letters, such as love for one another, walking in the truth, unity in the Church, and caution against deceivers. By reading each letter in light of the other two, we can gain insight into obscure or ambiguous passages and reach a better understanding of what John is saying in each letter.

Daniel Keating

Introduction to 1 John

Saint Augustine began his homilies on 1 John by telling his readers that in this letter John "said many things, and nearly everything was about charity."[1] Broadening this, the Venerable Bede opened his commentary on 1 John with this summation: "The blessed apostle John wrote this letter about the perfection of faith and charity, praising the faithfulness of those who were persevering in the unity of the Church."[2] At a much later date, the great preacher John Wesley praised 1 John as being "the deepest part of the Holy Scripture. . . . Here are sublimity and simplicity together, the strongest sense and the plainest language."[3]

The Aim of 1 John

The aim of 1 John is to declare, with clarity and simplicity, the qualities of those who truly belong to God the Father and have †fellowship with him and his Son Jesus Christ. In other words, John sets forth in this letter the basic criteria that distinguish those who truly belong to God from those who do not.

Against those who are denying essential truths about Jesus, John teaches that Jesus is the Son of God, who has truly taken on our †flesh and died for our sins on the cross. Against those who have failed to love their brothers and sisters

---

1. *Homilies on 1 John*, prologue (*Homilies on the First Epistle of John*, trans. Boniface Ramsey, ed. Daniel E. Doyle and Thomas Martin, WSA 3/14 [Hyde Park, NY: New City Press, 2008], 19). Augustine delivered this series of ten homilies during the Easter season in 407.

2. *Commentary on the Seven Catholic Epistles*, trans. David Hurst, CSS 82 (Kalamazoo, MI: Cistercian Publications, 1985), 159. Bede, a doctor of the Catholic Church, died in 735.

3. Cited in Peter Rhea Jones, *1, 2 & 3 John*, SHBC (Macon, GA: Smith & Helwys, 2009), 14. Wesley, a highly respected Protestant preacher and biblical commentator, died in 1791.

by providing for material needs, John declares what genuine love is by pointing to the example of Jesus and showing the origin of love in God himself. For John, no one can rightly claim to love God and be joined to Christ who does not show love to brothers and sisters. In short, the aim of 1 John is to declare the signs of true faith and genuine love.

But John writes this letter not only to clarify the marks of a true Christian. His ultimate goal is to bring his readers into deeper fellowship or communion with God and with one another. For John, this living communion with the Father and Son that we share *is* eternal life.

Authorship and Date

The First Letter of John itself gives no clue as to its author. It has no opening or closing greeting, and no names are named anywhere in the letter. Even if we look to 2 John and 3 John for help, the author identifies himself simply as "the †presbyter" (*presbyteros*), or "elder." This title could refer to his age or his position, or both, but it does not disclose his personal identity.

The Christian tradition dating from the late second and early third centuries identifies the author of 1 John as the apostle John, the son of Zebedee, who wrote this letter toward the close of the first century.[4] These early Christian authors, however, do not say why they attribute this letter to the apostle John. There may have been a record of John's authorship handed down by those who preserved the letter, but it is also possible that the early Church came to this conclusion because the language and literary style of 1 John are unmistakably similar to that of the Fourth Gospel, also attributed to the apostle John.

Scholars today generally agree with the tradition that 1 John should be dated to the end of the first century, but there is sharp disagreement about the identity of the author. Because 1 John is so similar in style and language to the Fourth Gospel, the question about the authorship of 1 John is closely tied to the authorship of the Fourth Gospel. We cannot go into the complex issues surrounding authorship of the Fourth Gospel here, but we can identify the main options by asking the following questions: Is the author of the Fourth Gospel

---

4. Rudolf Schnackenburg, *The Johannine Epistles*, trans. Reginald and Ilse Fuller (New York: Crossroad, 1992), 41. Irenaeus of Lyons, writing in the late second century, is the first Christian writer to identify "John the disciple of the Lord" as the author of these letters (*Against Heresies* 3.16.5, 8). But scholars debate whether Irenaeus is referring to John the son of Zebedee or John "the Elder," who was known as a distinct figure in the church in Asia. By the third century, Tertullian and Dionysius of Alexandria clearly identify the author of 1 John as John the apostle, the son of Zebedee.

John the son of Zebedee (the "†beloved disciple" [see John 13:23; 19:26])? Or, is the author, the beloved disciple, not one of the twelve apostles but another eyewitness disciple of Jesus who bore his own distinct testimony? Or, is the Fourth Gospel the product of a school of disciples of the beloved disciple who together compiled this Gospel after his death? From the testimony of John 21:24, it seems that the followers of the beloved disciple were responsible at least for publishing the Fourth Gospel and may have had a hand in its final editing, but they clearly attribute the testimony written in the Fourth Gospel to the beloved disciple himself.

Assuming that the Gospel of John comes from "the disciple Jesus loved," we can now pose the relevant questions concerning the authorship of 1 John:[5] Is the author of 1 John the beloved disciple himself, whether the apostle John or another eyewitness disciple of Jesus? Or, is the author one of the followers of the beloved disciple, a member of his school writing after his death? We cannot answer these questions with certainty, but I am inclined to the view that the author of 1 John is the beloved disciple himself and that the same hand wrote both the Gospel and the Letters. Not only do the clear and simple cadences of 1 John match those of the Fourth Gospel (especially chaps. 13–17), but also the authoritative tone of 1 John and the author's testimony that he saw, heard, and touched the "Word of life" (1:1–3) point not to a second-generation follower of the beloved disciple but rather to one who heard Jesus speak and who lay upon his breast (John 13:23).[6] Whether this beloved disciple is John the apostle, the son of Zebedee, is a further question that we cannot answer with certainty.

The Recipients of the Letter

The First Letter of John is addressed to a Christian community that had recently experienced an internal rupture in its life. On the basis of clues within the letter itself (especially 2:19), it appears that some portion of the local church had recently dropped out of the church and was following teaching that in some way denied the reality of Jesus' †incarnation. John is writing to

5. For a helpful summary of the complex issues surrounding the authorship of 1 John, see Raymond E. Brown, *The Epistles of John: Translated, with Introduction, Notes, and Commentary*, AB 30 (Garden City, NY: Doubleday, 1982), 14–35.

6. The view that the same author, the beloved disciple, wrote both the Gospel and the Letters has recent support from Martin Hengel (*The Johannine Question* [London: SCM, 1989], ix) and Richard Bauckham (*The Testimony of the Beloved Disciple: Narrative, History, and Theology in the Gospel of John* [Grand Rapids: Baker Academic, 2007], 9–91).

encourage those who have remained, in order to clarify the characteristics of Christian life and faith and to assure them that they are in a true and living relationship with God.

The letter itself, however, gives no precise indication of who the recipients are or where they are living. Nor does it clearly identify the views of those who have left the church. Because these questions remain open, there is room for a great deal of speculation about the history of this community, about the views of the opponents who seceded, and about what happened in the generation that followed. Raymond Brown's elaborate theory concerning the background to 1 John and its historical aftermath has strongly influenced scholarly interpretations of the letter.[7] Brown himself concedes, "My reconstruction claims at most probability; and if sixty percent of my detective work is accepted, I shall be happy indeed."[8] Recent commentators disagree with central pillars of Brown's reconstruction and are more cautious about what we can plausibly reconstruct of the historical background.[9]

The problem is not that scholars develop historical reconstructions for the setting of the letter, but that these reconstructions function as the lens through which we read and interpret the letter. They often play too large a part in how the letter is interpreted. In this commentary, while noting references to the division in the church and the influence of the false teachers, I will not rely on speculative historical reconstructions of the history of the community to which John wrote to interpret the text.

The Intended Audience

We can tell very little about the intended audience of the letter, except that they have been through a division in the church and are in need of an encouragement that both clarifies the truth and fortifies the heart. A majority of scholars conclude that the recipients of the letter probably are not Jewish believers in Jesus, but rather †Gentiles who have come to the faith. Why? Because there are no quotations of the Old Testament and only one fleeting reference (to Cain in 3:12). The reasoning goes like this: if the recipients of the letter were mainly Jews, the author certainly would have appealed to the Old Testament to undergird his teaching (as the Gospel of John does). Since he does not, he is most

---

7. See Raymond E. Brown, *The Community of the Beloved Disciple* (Mahwah, NJ: Paulist Press, 1979), and Brown's further statement of the theory in *Epistles of John*, 69–115. One or another variation of this hypothesis has become dominant in modern scholarship.

8. Brown, *Community of the Beloved Disciple*, 7.

9. See, e.g., Bauckham, *Testimony of the Beloved Disciple*, 9–14.

probably writing to a Gentile audience. This is a possible conclusion, but the lack of Old Testament references may also have to do with the circumstances that brought about the crisis and the nature of the disagreement that John has with those who departed.

Those Who Left the Church

In 2:19 John refers to people who left the church, saying, "They went out from us. . . . Their desertion shows that none of them was of our number." By examining the views that John rejects in the letter, we can gain a very basic idea of what they believed and taught. First, it appears that in some way they denied the incarnation of the Son, that he "came in the flesh." In other words, they were deficient in their understanding of the full humanity of Christ. Second, they seem to have made a claim to be without sin, or at least to be no longer capable of sinning. Third, John charges them with a failure to keep the commandments of the Lord; in John's eyes they were not living according to the truth. And finally, John accuses them of failing in fraternal love. Because those who left the church appear to have denied the real humanity of Christ and disdained the commandments, many scholars

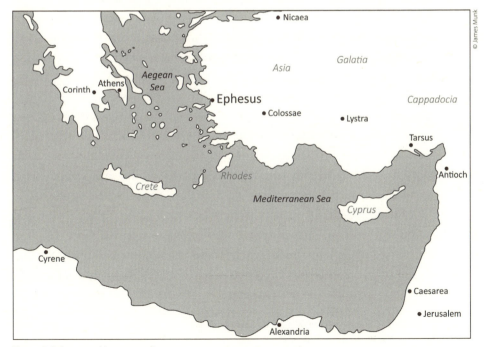

Figure 6. Ephesus and its surroundings

believe they represent an early form of †gnosticism, but we cannot identify them with any precision.[10]

Location

The letter itself does not divulge a location or give clues to where the community was situated, but many locate the church in or near the city of Ephesus in Asia Minor, because this is the traditional site for the later ministry of the apostle John, the presumed author of the letter.

Theological Themes

The first theme to emerge in 1 John is the *true and real incarnation of the Son of God* (1:1–3). He is the "Word of life" that John and others have heard, seen, and touched. Confession of Jesus Christ as the Son of God who has come "in the flesh" (4:2–3) is an essential characteristic of true Christian faith.

The second and perhaps predominant theme in the letter is *the call to love the brothers and sisters,* not just in word but in practice. John tells us that "God is love," and that "in this is love: not that we have loved God, but that he loved us" (4:8, 10). Time and again John calls us to love one another as God has loved us. Displaying genuine love for one another is a second essential mark of true Christians.

A third theme in 1 John is *a correct and balanced understanding of sin.* On the one hand, John says that those who say they have no sin are liars, and he calls the faithful to confess their sins (1:8–10). On the other hand, he says that he is writing so that we may not sin (2:1); he states that those who are begotten of God "cannot sin" (3:9); and he declares that the one who sins has neither seen nor known God (3:6). How can these two claims about sin be reconciled? Explaining the apparently conflicting claims that 1 John makes about sin is one of the most challenging tasks that face the interpreter of this letter.

A fourth theme that recurs throughout 1 John is *the distinction between God and "the world,"* between those who belong to God and those who love the †world. When John speaks of the "world," he is not talking about the created material world as such but is pointing to disordered appetites of the body, lust for possessions, and presumption that leads us into sin. The letter offers a

---

10. Early Church tradition often linked them to the heretic †Cerinthus, though in fact their views do not closely match what we know of him. For a summary of the historical evidence for Cerinthus and his possible link with the secessionists in 1 John, see Brown, *Epistles of John*, 766–71.

ringing call for Christians to separate themselves from worldliness while at the same time loving those who are in the world.

A fifth theme is *the role of the Spirit* in the Christian life. According to John, the Spirit is the "anointing" within us who grants us knowledge of the truth and leads us in a true confession of our faith. It is because we have the Spirit dwelling in us that we know we belong to the Father and the Son.

The role of the Spirit points to a final theme that underlies the whole letter: *true Christian life—eternal life—means fellowship with God himself.* "What we have seen and heard / we proclaim now to you, / so that you too may have fellowship with us; / for our fellowship is with the Father / and with his Son, Jesus Christ" (1:3). It is no accident that John speaks repeatedly in the letter about a mutual "abiding" with the Father, the Son, and the Spirit. For John, true and eternal life is a matter of relationship—a relationship with the Father and the Son through the Spirit, and relationships with one another through bonds of mutual love and common faith.

Language, Style, and Outline

Language

The language of 1 John is deceptively simple and basic. The author uses a relatively small number of words to express profound truths in language that Raymond Brown identifies as "quasi-poetry."[11] As in many kinds of poetry, including that of the psalms and the prophets, the grammar of 1 John is often unclear and difficult to untangle. Put simply, John's precise meaning is sometimes uncertain because the logical connections between parts of his sentences are ambiguous.[12] We will periodically need to judge between two or more possible interpretations, looking especially to other passages in the †Johannine writings for guidance. In addition, John often employs a kind of shorthand by which he moves from one idea to another without showing the intermediate steps that link them together. This requires unpacking so that John's thought and teaching may be clarified.

Style

The First Letter of John displays several stylistic features that we should be aware of as we read through the letter. The first and most striking feature is the use of †antithesis. John frequently contrasts one statement with its contrary to

---

11. Ibid., 128.
12. John Painter calls this the "tangled Greek" that occurs in the letter (*1, 2, and 3 John*, SP 18 [Collegeville, MN: Liturgical Press, 2002], 69).

sharpen his point. This oscillation between positive and negative statements strongly marks the whole letter. A second stylistic feature is repetition of key words and a return to key themes. John uses relatively few words but repeats them often and teaches by means of a periodic return to his main themes. But John almost never says the same thing in exactly the same words. Thus, a third feature of John's style is variation of his main themes.[13] Like a musical composer writing variations on a single theme, he expresses the same topic in new ways, enabling us to view a truth from diverse angles.[14]

Outline

The First Letter of John is notoriously difficult to outline in discrete, consecutive sections. F. F. Bruce sums up the views of many readers by concluding that "attempts to trace a consecutive argument throughout 1 John have never succeeded."[15] Instead of a linear progression, John provides a spiral ordering of topics whereby he states a theme and then circles back to it one or more times in the letter. To bring some shape to this spiral approach, I have divided the letter into three "movements" (based on the themes of light, righteousness, and love) that contain many of the same interwoven themes.[16] Rather than resisting John's circular approach by forcing the letter into a linear mold, it is best to allow John to lead us back and forth across his main themes, so that at letter's end we are able to understand his message more deeply and are moved to respond in faith and love.

1 John in the Lectionary

Strikingly, 1 John is never read during ordinary time in the Church's cycle of readings but is kept for the seasons of Easter and of Christmas and Epiphany. Large sections of the letter are read on Sundays in Easter (cycle B), reflecting John's teaching on the new and eternal life that we share in Christ Jesus. But

---

13. Brown refers to "the author's love for varying his formulas" (*Epistles of John*, 201).

14. Francis Martin shapes his treatment of 1 John explicitly on the model of symphonic variations in which a theme is stated and then developed through variations that distinguish and reunite the theme across several movements. See Francis Martin, "1 John," in *The International Bible Commentary*, ed. William R. Farmer (Collegeville, MN: Liturgical Press, 1998), 1825.

15. F. F. Bruce, *The Epistles of John: Introduction, Exposition and Notes* (London: Pickering & Inglis, 1970), 29. Hengel describes the letter as being "relatively unarranged" (*Johannine Question*, 47).

16. I am following Jones (*1, 2 & 3 John*, 6) in adopting a three-part movement structure to the letter. Painter (*1, 2, and 3 John*, 117–18) and Martin ("1 John," 1825–27) also divide the letter into these exact three sections. For a summary chart that catalogues the various ways scholars have structured 1 John, see Brown, *Epistles of John*, 764.

1 John is specially fitted for the Christmas season, when the entirety of the letter is read, beginning on December 27, the Feast of John the Apostle, and ending with the final day of the octave of Epiphany. In a marvelous way, 1 John unfolds the mystery of the Word made †flesh and reveals to us what we are to become as the children of God.

Interpreting and Applying 1 John for Today

The First Letter of John is deeply relevant to our times. In the first place, it reminds us how important it is to know and confess true faith. In an age when truth is relativized and when even Christians have a difficult time expressing the content of what they believe, John reminds us that Christians must believe and confess that Jesus Christ is the unique Son of God who has truly come "in the flesh" and has redeemed us by his sacrifice on the cross.

Second, 1 John shows us that genuine Christian life must be a life of love—love for God and for one another. It is not enough to confess that we love God; we must demonstrate this love through real and concrete action toward our brothers and sisters. This love, originating in God, is a sign of God's presence to an unbelieving world.

Third, 1 John obliges us to face up to our sin. In a world that denies or minimizes the reality of sin, we need to hear John's message that if we say "we are without sin," then "we deceive ourselves, and the truth is not in us" (1:8). At the same time, John tells us that the goal is not to commit sin (2:1). He calls us today to pursue a life of holiness, and he gives the expectation that by the †grace of God we can really change and begin to live a new life.

Finally, 1 John announces a message that is at the heart of the †New Evangelization: true and eternal life is found in fellowship and communion with the living God (Father, Son, and Spirit) and with one another (1:3). The Christian life cannot be reduced to simply believing certain truths, or avoiding sin, or even loving one another faithfully. All these find their place in a living relationship with God that we enter into even now and that will come to fullness in the life to come.

Outline of 1 John

Prologue: The Word of Life (1:1–4)

First Movement: Walk in the Light (1:5–2:27)

A. Walk in the Light and Do Not Sin (1:5–2:2)

    God Is Light; Walk in the Light (1:5–7)

    Acknowledge and Confess Sin (1:8–10)

    Christ Our Advocate and Atonement (2:1–2)

B. Keeping the Commandments and Loving the Brothers and Sisters (2:3–17)

    Walk the Way That Christ Walked (2:3–6)

    The New Commandment: Love Your Brother and Sister (2:7–11)

    Address to Children, Fathers, and Young Men (2:12–14)

    Do Not Love the World (2:15–17)

C. Antichrist and Denial of the Truth (2:18–27)

    The Coming of Antichrist and the Departure from the Church (2:18–19)

    Contrast: The Anointing Received versus the Lie of Antichrist (2:20–27)

Second Movement: Walk in Righteousness (2:28–4:6)

A. The Children of God (2:28–3:10)

    God's Righteous Children (2:28–3:2)

    Purity and Sin Contrasted (3:3–6)

    Children of God versus Children of the Devil (3:7–10)

B. Loving One Another in Truth (3:11–24)

    Genuine Love Contrasted with Murder (3:11–18)

Confidence before God (3:19–22)
Summary: Believe and Love (3:23–24)
C. Test the Spirits (4:1–6)
The Spirit of God versus the Spirit of Antichrist (4:1–3)
From God, Not from the World (4:4–6)
Third Movement: Walk in Love (4:7–5:12)
A. Walking in Love (4:7–21)
The Order of Love (4:7–10)
The Perfection of Love (4:11–18)
Summary on the Love of God (4:19–21)
B. Faith as the Foundation of Love (5:1–12)
Children of God Living in Faith and Love (5:1–5)
Threefold Testimony: Water, Blood, and Spirit (5:6–8)
The Testimony of God to His Son (5:9–12)
Summary and Conclusion (5:13–21)
Purpose of the Letter and Confidence in Prayer (5:13–15)
Praying for Fellow Christians (5:16–17)
Conclusion: What We Know in Jesus Christ (5:18–21)

Prologue: The Word of Life

1 John 1:1–4

The prologue to 1 John is both beautiful and challenging. We know implicitly that the Word it is speaking about is Jesus, but at the same time the sentence structure is awkward and the main verb ("proclaim") does not show up until verse 3! This probably is not accidental; John may have wanted his opening words to cause us to pause and reflect. As readers we simply cannot skim over these profound lines. We have to go back over them several times before we can begin to make sense of their meaning. As we do, we slowly begin to grasp John's subject—the Word of life—and our eyes are opened to see the deep truths unveiled.

The Word Made Flesh (1:1–4)

¹What was from the beginning,
    what we have heard,
    what we have seen with our eyes,
    what we looked upon
    and touched with our hands
    concerns the Word of life—
²for the life was made visible;
    we have seen it and testify to it
    and proclaim to you the eternal life
    that was with the Father and was made visible to us—
³what we have seen and heard
    we proclaim now to you,
    so that you too may have fellowship with us;

> for our fellowship is with the Father
> and with his Son, Jesus Christ.
> [4]We are writing this so that our joy may be complete.

NT: John 1:1–18; Phil 2:16; 2 John 1:12
Catechism: proclaiming Jesus Christ with joy, 425; communion with the Father and the Son, 2781

1:1   The opening verse presents us with four parallel clauses, each beginning with "what." Shortly we will learn that the subject of these four clauses is the "Word of life," but to start with, we are given four descriptions of a subject without knowing what the subject is.[1]

First, we are told that this subject **was from the beginning**. What "beginning" is John referring to here? The Gospel of John (1:1) opens with the words "In the beginning . . ." In that context "beginning" refers to the creation of the world in Gen 1. Here, however, "beginning" most likely points to the *eternal* origin of Jesus, the "eternal life that was with the Father" (v. 2) and was then made visible.

Second, John says that this subject is **what we have heard**. What group is represented by "we" here? These are the first disciples of Jesus who accompanied him in person and who heard him preach and teach. John then adds a third description: **what we have seen with our eyes**. Not only did they hear this subject, but also they were eyewitnesses to it. Fourth and finally, John adds, **what we have looked upon / and touched with our hands**. Is "looked upon" just a repetition of "seen"? Possibly, but many commentators believe that John is pointing to a deeper kind of seeing here, such that they not only saw with their physical eyes but also "beheld" with a deeper insight.[2] The sense of touch is now added: those who were "earwitnesses" and eyewitnesses also touched this subject with their very hands. There is something inescapably physical about this subject that was heard, seen, and touched.

Only now at the end of the verse does John reveal the identity of his subject, telling us that this **concerns the Word of life**.[3] This sheds some light but also keeps us to a degree in the dark. A word can be heard, but how can a word be seen or touched? Our subject is clearly much more than simply a message that conveys life. As John will disclose in verse 3, this "Word of life" is the person of Jesus Christ.

1:2   Verse 2 is an interjection, marked off from the main sentence by dashes, that gives us a further description of the "Word of life." John declares that **the life was made visible**, and then he more fully explains what he means by adding

1. In the Greek text the pronoun "what" is in the neuter. This leaves the reader at this point unclear about the identity of the subject, which John will declare only in v. 3.
2. "Looked upon" translates the same Greek verb found in John 1:14: "We *saw* his glory." This may point to a deeper kind of seeing that penetrates beyond the merely physical.
3. The NJB is more explicit: "The Word of life: this is our theme."

we have seen it and testify to it / and proclaim to you the eternal life / that was with the Father and was made visible to us. John has now identified his subject by three parallel titles: "the Word of life," "the life," and "the eternal life." As F. F. Bruce observes, "If the Gospel speaks of the incarnation of the Eternal Word, the Epistle speaks of the manifestation of the Eternal Life."[4]

What does John tell us about this "eternal life"? First, this life was "with the Father," a phrase that echoes John 1:1, which states that the Word "was with God." Second, this life was then "made visible" such that John and the other eyewitnesses "have seen it." This closely parallels the Gospel prologue: "And the Word became flesh . . . and we have beheld his glory" (John 1:14 RSV). Third, John says that he is testifying to and proclaiming what he has seen—he is truly fulfilling the role of an †evangelist.

John now completes his opening sentence and sums up in shorthand what **1:3** he has said thus far in verses 1–2: **what we have seen and heard / we proclaim now to you.** But then he adds the intended result of this proclamation: **so that you too may have fellowship with us; / for our fellowship is with the Father / and with his Son, Jesus Christ.** The logic here is not at all obvious. What exactly is John saying?

John often compresses a great deal of material in a few words—we can call this "†Johannine shorthand." We have to decompress and expand those words to get at his meaning. In this case, John is assuming that he and the other apostles, who were eyewitnesses of Jesus, have already come into living †fellowship with Jesus through hearing and believing his word. Is the "Word of life" a message or a person? It is both at the same time. The Word of life is Jesus Christ himself, but it is also the message about him that John is proclaiming in this letter. The †gospel is a message about a person who himself imparts eternal life.

And so John says that he is now proclaiming that same word to his hearers, so that they too may come into that living fellowship that John already shares "with the Father / and with his Son, Jesus Christ." The key word here, "fellowship" (*koinōnia*), can also be translated as "communion." The intended result of John's testimony, then, is nothing less than genuine communion with the Father and the Son, shared with all those who have already entered into this communion (see sidebar, "*Koinōnia*," p. 140).

Only now does John give the proper name of his subject, "Jesus Christ," the Father's Son. Now we know the personal identity of "the Word of life" and "the eternal life." Why does John delay in naming his subject? Because he wants his readers to peer more deeply into what he is saying about that subject. By

---

4. F. F. Bruce, *The Epistles of John: Introduction, Exposition and Notes* (London: Pickering & Inglis, 1970), 37.

Koinōnia

BIBLICAL BACKGROUND

In the New Testament the Greek word *koinōnia* is translated in a variety of ways: "sharing," "partnership," "contribution," "participation," "communion," and "fellowship." It can refer to the sharing of money and material resources within the Christian community (2 Cor 8:4; 9:13; Heb 13:16). It is used to designate the common life shared by the first Christians in Jerusalem after the outpouring of the Holy Spirit: "They devoted themselves to the teaching of the apostles and to the communal life [*koinōnia*], to the breaking of the bread and to the prayers" (Acts 2:42). *Koinōnia* also applies to our relationship with the persons of the Trinity: we are called into "fellowship" with Jesus Christ (1 Cor 1:9); we jointly share "fellowship" with the Father and the Son (1 John 1:3, 6); and Paul prays for an increase in "communion" with the Holy Spirit (2 Cor 13:13 NRSV). Paul also speaks of our *koinōnia* ("participation, communion") in the body and blood of Christ in the Eucharist (1 Cor 10:16). When we have *koinōnia* with God, we share in his life and power; when we have *koinōnia* with one another, we place our lives in common and share our resources as brothers and sisters. In 1 John, *koinōnia* describes both our fellowship with God and with one another—a rich communion of life and bonds of love that are meant to characterize the faithful.

referring to what was heard and seen and touched, and by speaking of "the eternal life / that was with the Father," John reveals a great deal about Jesus even before he names him,[5] and he anticipates one of the principal themes of the letter, the †incarnation of the Son.

1:4   To complete the prologue, John adds, **We are writing this so that our joy may be complete**. By "we" John is referring to himself, but he writes here on behalf of all those who heard, saw, and touched the Word of life.[6] The reference to "writing" shows that 1 John was not originally given orally and then later written down. John is intentionally composing a written message to his audience in order to testify about the Word of life.

Many early manuscripts have "so that *your* joy may be complete."[7] This well-attested reading would seem to make more sense: the joy of those who receive

5. The prologue to the Gospel of John (1:1–18) adopts the same strategy: the proper name "Jesus Christ" is not revealed until v. 17.
6. In the remainder of the letter, John uses only the first person singular ("I") when referring to himself as the writer of the letter (twelve times).
7. This exact wording is also found in John 16:24: "Ask and you will receive, so that your joy may be complete."

The Two Prologues

BIBLICAL BACKGROUND

The Christian tradition and most modern scholars are in general agreement that the Gospel of John was written before 1 John and so supplies important background for this letter. It is also evident that the prologue to 1 John has close affinities with the prologue to the Gospel (John 1:1–18) and that they share many themes and words in common. For example, both describe a "Word" in relation to "the beginning" that was with God the Father and was then made manifest to us; both speak of this Word in relation to "life"; and both conclude by identifying this Word as the Son of God, Jesus Christ. But there are also differences in phrasing and in emphasis; the two prologues are by no means identical. How should we understand the relationship between them? Some commentators believe that 1 John is simply an expansion and further explanation of the Gospel prologue, giving special attention to the eyewitnesses and to the proclamation of the message. Others believe that by underlining the historical manifestation of the Word to the eyewitnesses who heard, saw, and touched him, 1 John was written specifically to correct flawed interpretations of the Gospel prologue that denied the fully human reality of Christ. Whether the prologue of 1 John was written as an expansion of the Gospel prologue or a clarification of it, the two prologues should be read together for the complementary yet distinctive witness that they give to the Word, who has appeared for our salvation.

the testimony is brought to completion by coming into fellowship with God and with other Christians. But the reading "*our* joy," adopted by most modern translations, also rings true. For those who have already been brought into the communion of the Father and Son, it is a source of great joy to announce this word and to welcome others into that fellowship. Perfect joy comes not from hoarding the gospel and its riches but from sharing it and enabling others to come into the same life-giving fellowship.

Reflection and Application (1:1–4)

The prologue to 1 John shows us something important about the work of evangelization. John is proclaiming a word, and that word happens to be a person. He is proclaiming "a word about the Word" that he has personally encountered—heard, seen, and touched. And this proclamation does not convey just information or even inspiration; it actually imparts life and communion.

No merely human word can impart "eternal life" and "fellowship with God." But the word of the gospel can and does. It is a word that imparts life because when this word is received in faith, it brings about communion with the Word who is life. And the result of this is deep joy—joy both for the one who proclaims the word and for the one who receives it, because both now share in the life-giving fellowship of the Triune God. There are many facets to the broad work of evangelization, but the prologue reveals its heart and center: to proclaim the One we have personally encountered so that we may all joyfully share in the eternal life of God.

First Movement:
Walk in the Light

1 John 1:5–2:27

Walk in the Light and Do Not Sin

1 John 1:5–2:2

John began the letter with the theme of life. He now takes up the metaphor of light to address how we are to live. The proclamation of the †gospel results in communion with God, but this requires that we actually "walk" in a new way of life. It is to this new way of life and the problem of sin that John now turns.

God Is Light; Walk in the Light (1:5–7)

> **⁵Now this is the message that we have heard from him and proclaim to you: God is light, and in him there is no darkness at all. ⁶If we say, "We have fellowship with him," while we continue to walk in darkness, we lie and do not act in truth. ⁷But if we walk in the light as he is in the light, then we have fellowship with one another, and the blood of his Son Jesus cleanses us from all sin.**

NT: John 1:4–5; 3:21; 2 John 1:4; 3 John 1:4; Rev 21:23
Catechism: God is light, 214; living in the truth, 2470

In the prologue John proclaimed Christ himself to be "the Word of life." Here he is proclaiming a message that he has **heard from** Christ. And what is this message? **God is light, and in him there is no darkness at all**. This is the only place in the Bible where it says that God *is* light. To say that God is light means that he is "the source and essence of holiness and righteousness, goodness and truth; in him there is nothing that is unholy or unrighteous, evil or false."[1] In God there is absolutely nothing that can be faulted.

The Gospel of John identifies Jesus as the "light" (John 1:4–5; 8:12; 9:5). Here in 1 John, it is Jesus who reveals that "God is light." There is no opposition between the two accounts. Both Father and Son are light and equally the source of light: "The city had no need of sun or moon to shine on it, for the glory of God gave it light, and its lamp was the Lamb" (Rev 21:23).

1:6   John now begins a string of †conditional sentences ("if . . . then . . .") that he uses to distinguish the way of light from the way of darkness. In particular he employs the conditional form "if we say" with great effectiveness to strip away our self-deception. **If we say, "We have fellowship with him," while we continue to walk in darkness, we lie and do not act in truth**. "To walk" is a common biblical expression for living a way of life—a lifestyle. "To walk in darkness" means to live a sinful way of life and to fail to keep the commandments. In 1 John, light and darkness refer primarily to moral character and action. They denote opposing ways of living.[2]

The logic runs like this: God is light and in him there is no darkness, so if we continue to walk in darkness, we cannot possibly have †fellowship or communion with God. If we claim to have this fellowship while continuing in sin, then we are speaking falsely. The point is that "walking in darkness" is incompatible with divine fellowship.

When John says "we lie," he is not necessarily saying that we are intentionally deceiving others or ourselves. For John, "to lie" is to speak falsely, to not be in accord with the truth, but it also indicates an underlying hostility to the truth.[3] The phrase translated as "act in truth" is literally "do the truth."[4] A parallel appears in John 3:21: "Whoever does the truth comes out into the light, so that what he is doing may plainly appear as done in God" (NJB). To our ears this is an odd expression; we normally do not speak this way. We think of truth as simply propositional, as a statement of fact. But John sees truth as something that we do, something that we practice. To live according to the truth is to live in a way that is faithful to God and his commandments.

1. F. F. Bruce, *The Epistles of John: Introduction, Exposition and Notes* (London: Pickering & Inglis, 1970), 41.
2. "The dualistic language in 1 John has primarily an ethical focus" (Rudolf Schnackenburg, *The Johannine Epistles*, trans. Reginald and Ilse Fuller [New York: Crossroad, 1992], 74).
3. Raymond Brown observes that John is not speaking about "a lie of self-deception but a lie involving active hostility to the truth" (*The Epistles of John: Translated, with Introduction, Notes, and Commentary*, AB 30 [Garden City, NY: Doubleday, 1982], 199).
4. The NRSV has "do what is true"; the ESV has "practice the truth." A similar phrase, "walking in the truth," appears in 2 John 1:4; 3 John 1:4.

Light and Darkness

The contrast between light and darkness appears in the very first verses of Genesis (1:3–4), but the use of the metaphor of light and darkness to describe two different ways of living, an ethical contrast, occurs only occasionally in the Old Testament (e.g., Eccles 2:13–14; Isa 5:20). In the New Testament, however, we find numerous instances of the light-darkness metaphor to distinguish two different ways of living (e.g., Matt 6:23; Acts 26:18; Rom 13:12; Eph 5:8). This ethical contrast reflects a similar use of the light-darkness metaphor widespread in Jewish literature from approximately 200 BC to AD 100, especially in the †Dead Sea Scrolls. The apostle Paul, like John, uses the light-darkness metaphor primarily to describe moral character and action: "For all of you are children of the light and children of the day. We are not of the night or of darkness. Therefore . . . let us stay alert and sober" (1 Thess 5:5–6).

John now offers the positive side of the conditional statement, showing the 1:7 consequences of walking in the light: **But if we walk in the light as he is in the light, then we have fellowship with one another, and the blood of his Son Jesus cleanses us from all sin**. God is light and always acts in a way in keeping with this light. If we imitate him by walking in the way of light empowered by our relationship with him through the eternal life that has come to dwell in us, two consequences follow: we have fellowship with each other, and the blood of Jesus cleanses us from all sin. Each requires some explanation.

We would expect John to have said, "then we have fellowship *with God*," as he did in verse 6.[5] Why does he change the terms and speak of fellowship "with one another"? John probably is assuming that walking in the light goes hand in hand with fellowship with God, and he wants to underline the communal impact of walking in the light. We should recall that, given the departure of some former members from the church (see the introduction), John is intensely concerned with the unity of the body and the mutual love of the brothers and sisters.[6] Walking in the light establishes communion not only with God but also with one another.

The logic of the second consequence—cleansing from sin by the blood of Jesus—requires some unpacking. The "blood of Jesus" is shorthand for his sacrificial death on the cross that brings about the forgiveness of our sins. Is John saying that first we must walk in the light, and only then will the blood

5. This reading is in fact found in one early manuscript and in the writings of several Church Fathers.
6. "The author's worst fear was a continuing drain of defections from within the Johannine network of churches" (John Painter, *1, 2, and 3 John*, SP 18 [Collegeville, MN: Liturgical Press, 2002], 148).

Didymus on Walking in the Light

Didymus "the Blind" (d. 398) was a renowned teacher and biblical commentator from the city of Alexandria. His commentary on the Epistles of John, existing now only in fragments, is the earliest recorded commentary on these letters.

> Since God is light, there is no darkness in him at all, and he has nothing to do with darkness. The person who is enlightened by his light walks in the light, according to the words of the Savior himself: "While you have the light, walk in the light, lest the darkness take hold of you." Anyone who walks in the darkness of sin but claims that his mind is not darkened and that he has a relationship with God is lying.[a]

a. Quoted in ACCS 11:171–72.

of Jesus cleanse us from our sins? How could we walk in the light if we have not first been cleansed from our sins? This would make no sense and would be contrary to John's teaching later in the letter (4:9–10). It is better to conclude that John is not making the cleansing of our sins dependent on our walking in the light. Rather, he is saying that walking in the light is evidence that we are in fact in communion with God, and that by continuing to walk in God's ways we avail ourselves in an ongoing way of the cleansing power of Christ's blood.

Acknowledge and Confess Sin (1:8–10)

⁸If we say, "We are without sin," we deceive ourselves, and the truth is not in us. ⁹If we acknowledge our sins, he is faithful and just and will forgive our sins and cleanse us from every wrongdoing. ¹⁰If we say, "We have not sinned," we make him a liar, and his word is not in us.

OT: Exod 34:6–7; Pss 32:1–5; 51:3–14
NT: Matt 4:17; 2 Tim 2:13; James 5:16
Catechism: sin, 827, 1425, 1846–69

1:8   John now takes up the topic of sin directly. If the blood of Jesus cleanses us from all sin (v. 7), how can we say, **"We are without sin"**? It is probable that the claim "We are without sin" was being made by those who had left the church. Possibly they were saying that they never had sin that needed cleansing by Jesus (see v. 10), but at least they were claiming that they now existed on a spiritual plane that was above all sin. John decisively rejects this position. If we say we are without sin, then **we deceive ourselves, and the truth is not in us**; that is, we are not speaking what is true. We will take up the apparently conflicting claims John makes about sin in the commentary on 3:6–9.

To the contrary, John says, **If we acknowledge our sins, he is faithful and just and will forgive our sins and cleanse us from every wrongdoing**. This pattern of confession and forgiveness, true not only for initial conversion but also for the whole of our lives (see James 5:16), is rooted in the Old Testament: "Then I declared my sin to you; / my guilt I did not hide. / I said, 'I confess my transgression to the †Lord,' / and you took away the guilt of my sin" (Ps 32:5). **1:9**

In what sense is God "faithful and just" when he forgives our sins? It is not because we have earned this and are getting our "just" deserts. On the contrary, we do not deserve his forgiveness. When God forgives those who acknowledge their sin, he is in fact being faithful to his own character and to his promise that if his people come to him in repentance, he will forgive them. This is the kind of God that he is: "a God gracious and merciful, slow to anger and abounding in love and fidelity, continuing his love for a thousand generations, and forgiving wickedness, rebellion, and sin" (Exod 34:6–7 [see 2 Tim 2:13]). John adds something crucial at this point: God not only forgives our sins but also cleanses us. We are not just pardoned; we are also purified within and so enabled to "walk in the light" in a new way of life.

Reflection and Application (1:8–9)

When we acknowledge our sin, God is merciful. He forgives us, cleanses us, and offers us a new beginning. In Ps 32, attributed to King David, we have a vivid picture of a sinner who finds deep relief and joy when he finally confesses his sin to God. At first, the psalmist refused to acknowledge his sin, and the result was bodily and emotional suffering. But then, as we noted above, he says, "Then I declared my sin to you; / my guilt I did not hide. / I said, 'I confess my transgression to the Lord,' / and you took away the guilt of my sin" (Ps 32:5).

There is great relief and blessedness when we come to our senses, recognize our sin, and speak directly to God. It is important to remember that God is not surprised by our sin; he knows us perfectly. By his †grace he helps us to recognize our sin, and he waits for us to come to him, so that he can show his mercy and restore us.

In Ps 51, also attributed to David, we see the fruits of confession. After admitting his sin (vv. 3–6), David prays for a full restoration:

Fill me with joy and gladness;
  let the bones which thou hast broken rejoice.
Hide thy face from my sins,
  and blot out all my iniquities.
Create in me a clean heart, O God,
  and put a new and right spirit within me.
Cast me not away from thy presence,
  and take not thy holy Spirit from me.
Restore to me the joy of thy salvation,
  and uphold me with a willing spirit. (vv. 8–12 RSV [vv. 10–14
  NABRE])

The psalms provide a language for us to confess our sins, and we can make these powerful lines our own. As a crisp summary, 1 John 1:9 is worth memorizing, both for ourselves and for giving pastoral encouragement to others: "If we acknowledge our sins, he is faithful and just and will forgive our sins and cleanse us from every wrongdoing." Blessed be God!

1:10   John restates his point (from v. 8) but with a new variation. Now the false claim to be without sin is put into the past tense: **If we say, "We have not sinned," we make him a liar**. Why does our denial of having sinned make God a liar? Because God has told us through his word in the Scriptures that we have sinned and that he has provided the remedy for sin through his Son.[7] Denial of our sin also shows that **his word is not in us**. If we deny that we have sinned, this shows that we have failed to receive the word of the †gospel that calls us to turn from our sin: "Repent, for the kingdom of heaven is at hand" (Matt 4:17).

John is concerned throughout this letter with what truly abides in us: Christ, the Spirit, the truth, and here "his word." If these do not abide *in us*, then we do not have life; we do not have †fellowship with the one who *is* life. Divine indwelling is a central theme of this letter.

Christ Our Advocate and Atonement (2:1–2)

---

[1]**My children, I am writing this to you so that you may not commit sin.
But if anyone does sin, we have an Advocate with the Father, Jesus Christ**

7. For the testimony to human sinfulness in the Scriptures, see, e.g., Gen 8:21; 1 Kings 8:46; Pss 14:3; 53:4; Rom 3:9–11.

Confession of Sin

Confession of sin always begins in the heart: we recognize that we have sinned and acknowledge our sin to God and ask his forgiveness. From the beginning, however, Christians were also expected to confess their sins in the context of the Church (see James 5:16). Exactly how confession of sin occurred in the apostolic Church is not spelled out in the New Testament, and "over the centuries the concrete form in which the Church has exercised this power received from the Lord [to forgive sins] has varied considerably" (Catechism 1447). The principal way that the faithful confess their sins is through the sacrament of reconciliation, when we individually confess our sins to a priest and receive forgiveness in the name of Christ. Confession through the sacrament is required for the forgiveness of grave (mortal) sins and is strongly recommended for everyday faults (venial sins) (Catechism 1458). We also have recourse to the penitential rite of the liturgy of the Mass when we confess our sins together and ask the Lord for his mercy. In addition, the Christian faithful can profitably make use of prudent acknowledgment of sin and weakness in small discipleship groups where we can receive encouragement to become more like Christ.

the righteous one. ²He is expiation for our sins, and not for our sins only but for those of the whole world.

OT: Lev 25:9; Num 5:8
NT: John 14:16, 26; 15:26; 16:7; Rom 8:34; Heb 9:26
Catechism: Jesus as our advocate, 519, 692; Jesus' sacrifice for the sins of the world, 605–6
Lectionary: 3rd Sunday of Easter, Year B (1 John 2:1–5a)

The title of address, **My children** (or "my little children"),[8] shows John's intimate   2:1
knowledge of his audience and his affection for them, but it also demonstrates his authority as a spiritual father. And for the first time in the letter John speaks in the first person singular, **I am writing this to you**, thus further emphasizing his personal authority.

John now explains why he is writing to them about the topic of sin. He recognizes that he needs to clarify just what he is saying—and, importantly, what he is *not* saying—about sin in the life of the Christian. By exhorting them

---

8. The Greek word *teknia* ("children" or "little children") occurs seven times in 1 John (2:1, 12, 28; 3:7, 18; 4:4; 5:21) and only one other time in the NT (John 13:33). Thus in the NT it is unique to the †Johannine literature. In 1 John two other terms are used for "children": *tekna* (3:1–2, 10; 5:2) and *paidia* (2:14, 18).

to confess their sins, he is not thereby encouraging them to sin, or saying that sin is what they ought to expect and settle for. Far from it! He makes this quite clear: **I am writing this to you so that you may not commit sin**. As John will say in greater detail later in the letter (3:4–9), God's new life in us is intended to yield a life of righteousness such that we do not sin.

Though his readers are to aim for a life of holiness and freedom from sin, John assures them that **if anyone does sin, we have an Advocate with the Father, Jesus Christ the righteous one**. This is good news! If we sin—and all of us know that we do fall into sin—we have an advocate (literally, "paraclete")[9] who intercedes for us before our Father in heaven. We are sinners, but Jesus is entirely "righteous," the Lamb of God who has no sin, but who died for our sins.[10] Paul makes the same point regarding Christ as our advocate: "It is Christ [Jesus] who died, rather, was raised, who also is at the right hand of God, who indeed intercedes for us" (Rom 8:34). What extraordinary encouragement in the face of our human frailty!

2:2   John goes on to say that Jesus Christ is **expiation for our sins**. "†Expiation" is a technical term that requires explanation. The Greek word, *hilasmos*, occurs in the New Testament only in 1 John (here and 4:10). In the †Septuagint it is used to render Hebrew terms that can be translated as "atonement" (Lev 25:9; Num 5:8; see also 2 Macc 3:33) or "sin offering" (Ezek 44:27). Some English versions translate *hilasmos* in 1 John 2:2 as "expiation" (NABRE, NJB, RSV), while others translate it as "†propitiation" (KJV, ESV).[11] What is the difference between "expiation" and "propitiation"?

"Expiation" refers primarily to the removal of our sins and the guilt that they bring. Jesus expiates our sins by removing them and cleansing us from them. "Propitiation" refers primarily to our relationship with God. By acting as our advocate before the Father, Jesus reconciles us to the Father, though we should always recall that it is equally true that the Father has reconciled us to himself through Christ (2 Cor 5:18). Perhaps the best way to render this verse is this: "He is the atoning sacrifice for our sins" (NRSV, NIV). This rendering captures both senses of Christ's work. As our "atoning sacrifice," Jesus both cleanses us from our sin and puts us in a right relationship with God as two aspects of one redemptive work.[12]

---

9. The Greek word *paraklētos* ("advocate, counselor") occurs just five times in the NT: here in 1 John 2:1 and four times in the Gospel of John (14:16, 26; 15:26; 16:7). In the Gospel, *paraklētos* always refers to the Holy Spirit, though in 14:16 Jesus implies that he himself is also a "paraclete" for us.

10. Jesus is identified as "righteous" or "the righteous one" also in Acts 3:14; 7:52; 22:14.

11. The Latin Vulgate for 1 John 2:2 uses the term *propitiatio*; the Douay-Rheims Catholic edition, based on the Vulgate, renders this as "propitiation."

12. Raymond Brown argues that "there are connotations both of expiation and of propitiation" in this term and recommends the translation "atonement" to best express both aspects (*Epistles of John*, 220–21).

St. Ambrose on Christ as Our Advocate

LIVING TRADITION

Saint Ambrose (339–97), †bishop of Milan, was an outstanding teacher and pastor. The testimony of his words and his example contributed significantly to the conversion of St. Augustine:

> I will not glory because I have been redeemed. I will not glory because I am free of sins but because sins have been forgiven me. I will not glory because I am profitable or because anyone is profitable to me but because Christ is an advocate on my behalf before the Father, because the blood of Christ has been poured out on my behalf.[a]

a. Quoted in ACCS 11:176.

John underlines the universal reach of Christ's work by adding that his sacrifice is **not for our sins only but for those of the whole world**. Jesus' atoning sacrifice is not limited to a select group of people or to a particular time period. His saving work is effective for the whole †world and for all times: "But now once for all he has appeared at the end of the ages to take away sin by his sacrifice" (Heb 9:26). Paul makes the same point with great force, showing how Christ's universal work motivates us as missionaries of God's mercy: "For the love of Christ impels us, once we have come to the conviction that one died for all; therefore, all have died. He indeed died for all, so that those who live might no longer live for themselves but for him who for their sake died and was raised" (2 Cor 5:14–15).

Reflection and Application (2:1–2)

To many readers, John's teaching on sin seems contradictory. On the one hand, he states categorically that those who say that they have no sin are liars, but on the other hand, he tells us that he is writing these things so that we may not sin. Which is it? What should we expect of ourselves and others regarding sin? In fact, John is not contradicting himself but is addressing two deficient views on sin, both of which are quite common today. The first view, which denies or redefines the reality of sin, runs rampant in our Western culture and has infected many who identify as Christians. Instead of acknowledging our sin (and sinfulness), we excuse our actions, we place the blame for our missteps on other people or causes, and we legitimize what God calls sin as new and valid lifestyles. There is a deep repugnance in our culture to confessing candidly, "I have greatly sinned."

The second view, found today in certain Christian circles, is quick to acknowledge sin but has lost sight of the goal for which Christ died, namely, that we might not sin! Sometimes this is expressed in the slogan that "Christians are not perfect, just forgiven." Christians certainly are not yet perfected, but we are more than just forgiven: we have been given the Spirit so that we might walk in a new way of life. Have we sinned? Absolutely. Are we still liable to lapse into sin through weakness and personal failure, at least on occasion? Yes. Do we still battle with certain habitual sins that stubbornly refuse to go away? Most of us do. But we should also expect that as we cooperate with the transforming power of God at work within us, we will become more and more free from sin. This is one of the main fruits of God's life at work within us.

Keeping the Commandments and Loving the Brothers and Sisters

1 John 2:3–17

The theme of light and darkness continues in this section, but John now introduces two new topics: keeping the commandments and loving the brothers and sisters. These are all closely related: for John, to walk in the light is to keep the commandments of God, and the preeminent commandment is to love one another.

Walk the Way That Christ Walked (2:3–6)

> ³The way we may be sure that we know him is to keep his commandments. ⁴Whoever says, "I know him," but does not keep his commandments is a liar, and the truth is not in him. ⁵But whoever keeps his word, the love of God is truly perfected in him. This is the way we may know that we are in union with him: ⁶whoever claims to abide in him ought to live [just] as he lived.

NT: Eph 5:1–2
Catechism: keeping the commandments, 2052–55; love of God in us, 1424, 1822, 1974, 2067; living the way Jesus lived, 2470
Lectionary: 3rd Sunday of Easter, Year B (1 John 2:1–5a)

The implied question that John is answering in these verses is this: How can **2:3–5a** we be sure that we know God and are in union with him? He begins with an answer to this implied question: **The way we may be sure that we know him is to keep his commandments**. John's concern here is not just whether we know God, but how to be sure that we know him. The issue here is one of assurance, of being convinced that we are in a right relationship with God. John wants to give his readers a criterion by which they can judge whether they and others truly know God. And this is the criterion: Are they keeping the commandments of God or not? These would certainly include the Ten Commandments, but as we will see, John is especially concerned with fulfilling the command to love one another.

John first offers a negative illustration of this criterion: **Whoever says, "I know him," but does not keep his commandments is a liar, and the truth is not in him.** If we claim to know God and be in right relationship with him but are not keeping his commandments, then we are deceiving both ourselves and others. As a counterpoint, John then gives a positive statement of the criterion, but with a variation that adds something important: **But whoever keeps his word, the love of God is truly perfected in him**. "Keeping his word" is equivalent to "keeping his commandments," but John now shows more clearly what he means by keeping the commandments: the true disciple is the one who hears God's word and puts that word into practice in daily life. We do not just follow

The Biblical Meaning of "To Know"   BIBLICAL BACKGROUND

In the Bible, "to know" often conveys more than just knowing information, more than just the possession of factual data. To know someone or something often includes an experiential and relational dimension as well. When Pharaoh says to Moses, "I do not know the †Lᴏʀᴅ" (Exod 5:2), he is not saying that he has never heard about the God of Israel, but that he does not acknowledge him as God and will not yield to his demands. When we hear that Samuel "did not yet know the Lᴏʀᴅ" (1 Sam 3:7 NRSV), this does not mean that Samuel did not know of the Lord's existence, but that he had not yet heard the Lord speak to him personally. In other words, Samuel did not yet have a personal knowledge of the Lord. In the same way, when Jesus says to those who refuse to obey his word, "I never knew you" (Matt 7:23), this means not that Jesus did not know who they were but that they are not in a good relationship with him. In 1 John, "to know God" includes a right understanding of who he is and what he has done. But it is much more than this. "To know God" is to be in a right relationship with him and to know him personally through the indwelling Spirit.

St. Augustine on the Perfection of Love

LIVING
TRADITION

Saint Augustine probes what it means to say that God's love is perfected in us. His answer is that we love our enemies so that they become our brothers and sisters: "What is perfection in love? To love one's enemies, and to love them to the degree that they may be brothers. For our love must not be fleshly. . . . Love your enemies in such a way that you wish them to be brothers; love your enemies in such a way that they are brought into your fellowship."[a]

a. *Homilies on 1 John* 1.9 (*Homilies on the First Epistle of John*, trans. Boniface Ramsey, ed. Daniel E. Doyle and Thomas Martin, WSA 3/14 [Hyde Park, NY: New City Press, 2008], 30).

a set of commands by rote; rather, we hear God's word, take it into our hearts, and then keep that word by living it out in practical ways.

In a compressed phrase, John says that "the love of God is truly perfected" in the one who keeps his word. Is John referring here to God's love for us or our love for God? The answer is both, in fact. God has shown his love for us by sending his Son. When we keep his word—by obeying his commandments and loving one another—we show that God's love for us has reached its intended goal in us. And now we are the ones acting in love. "Perfection" means not that our love is flawless but that we are genuinely loving God and neighbor. "The author of 1 John does not regard the fulfillment of the commandments as simply a first step toward a higher mystical life with God. On the contrary, when a person faithfully observes the word of God, the divine love is realized to the full."[1]

We should note that this is the first appearance of the word "love" in the letter. John will develop the theme of love much more extensively, especially in 4:7–21.

2:5b–6 John now expands and reframes the criterion in terms of how we know that we abide in God: **This is the way we may know that we are in union with him: whoever claims to abide in him ought to live [just] as he lived**. In Greek, this is literally "to walk [just] as he walked." The point is simple: whoever claims to "abide in him" ought to be "walking"—that is, living a consistent way of life—in the way that he walked. To say this in a contemporary idiom: how we talk must be backed up by how we walk, and we can walk as Christ did only if we have his very life abiding in us. This is the first appearance of the verb "abide" (*menō*) in 1 John (it occurs twenty-four times in 1 John, the highest concentration of

1. Rudolf Schnackenburg, *The Johannine Epistles*, trans. Reginald and Ilse Fuller (New York: Crossroad, 1992), 98.

157

this word in any New Testament book). The call to "abide" or "remain" in God is a major theme of the letter.

But here we face a question that recurs throughout the letter: Who is the one in whom we are to abide, and who is "he" that we are called to imitate? Is John referring to God the Father or to Jesus his Son? Throughout the letter John often seems to move back and forth between the Father and Son without clearly telling the reader who is the intended subject. God the Father is the one in whom we abide, but Jesus must be the one whom we imitate, since only he lived a life on earth that we can emulate. We might rephrase this verse as follows: "This is how we may know that we are in God: whoever claims to abide in God must walk the way that Jesus walked."[2]

The New Commandment: Love Your Brother and Sister (2:7–11)

[7]Beloved, I am writing no new commandment to you but an old commandment that you had from the beginning. The old commandment is the word that you have heard. [8]And yet I do write a new commandment to you, which holds true in him and among you, for the darkness is passing away, and the true light is already shining. [9]Whoever says he is in the light, yet hates his brother, is still in the darkness. [10]Whoever loves his brother remains in the light, and there is nothing in him to cause a fall. [11]Whoever hates his brother is in darkness; he walks in darkness and does not know where he is going because the darkness has blinded his eyes.

OT: Lev 19:18
NT: John 13:34; 2 John 1:5
Catechism: the new commandment of love, 782, 1823, 1970, 2842

2:7–8   In this section John specifies what he means by keeping the commandments of God. At the heart of the commandments (plural) is the primary commandment (singular), which is to love our brothers and sisters. John's address to his readers, **Beloved**, is entirely fitting for a section in which he calls us to love one another. He will use this term of affection five more times in the letter (3:2, 21; 4:1, 7, 11).

John now makes a somewhat puzzling distinction between a new commandment and an old commandment: **I am writing no new commandment to you but an old commandment that you had from the beginning**. A parallel passage, 2 John 1:5, makes clear that John is referring to the command to love one

2. The NIV (1984) inserts the name "Jesus" in v. 6 to make this distinction clear: "Whoever claims to live in him must walk as Jesus did."

another: "[It is] not as though I were writing a new commandment but the one we have had from the beginning: let us love one another."

But what does John mean by an "old" commandment that they had "from the beginning"? Is John referring to the Old Testament, where we discover the commandment to love one's neighbor as oneself (Lev 19:18)? Possibly. But more likely he is referring to the occasion when his readers first heard the †gospel of Jesus Christ and were called to love God and one another. **The old commandment is the word that you have heard**, the word that they received from the beginning of their faith in Christ. The point is that John is not speaking to them about something novel that they have never heard before.

Still, John says that there is something "new" in this commandment: **And yet I do write a new commandment to you, which holds true in him and among you, for the darkness is passing away, and the true light is already shining**. In what sense is this command new? Jesus himself calls it a new commandment: "I give you a new commandment: love one another. As I have loved you, so you also should love one another" (John 13:34). Just as it holds true for Jesus (he loved us and continues to love us), so it holds true among us (we are called to love one another). What is new is that we are to love one another *as Jesus loved us*, and this gives a new depth to our love. But this commandment is also new in the sense that Christ's presence in the †world—his light in us his people—continues to shine while the darkness recedes. As we walk "today" in the way of love, waiting for Christ's return, God's light is breaking in anew.[3] His love is made new among us every day as we fulfill the command to love one another.

In verses 9–10, John contrasts hatred and love. He begins with the nega-   **2:9–11**
tive case: **Whoever says he is in the light, yet hates his brother, is still in the darkness**. What does it mean to be in the light? It means that we are loving our fellow Christians ("brother" means "brothers and sisters"). For John, "to hate" does not signify so much a deep emotional dislike as a serious failure to love. If by our actions we fail to love our fellow Christians—by providing for them in need, for example—then we are still walking in darkness, no matter what we may claim.

Then we get the positive statement: **Whoever loves his brother remains in the light, and there is nothing in him to cause a fall**. If we truly love our brothers and sisters in Christ, this shows that we are abiding in the light, which, of course, is to abide in God. The result is that "there is nothing in him to cause

---

3. "The newness of the commandment is eschatological; it is part of the realization of God's promises in the last times" (Raymond E. Brown, *The Epistles of John: Translated, with Introduction, Notes, and Commentary*, AB 30 [Garden City, NY: Doubleday, 1982], 267).

a fall."[4] This could mean that there is nothing in the one who loves that would cause that person to fall or stumble, but it could also mean that there is no stumbling caused for others. If we claim one thing (to walk in the light) but do the opposite (hate our brother or sister), then †scandal arises. Those who observe our failure to live according to the message that we profess may be led to doubt the truth of it. But when our words are confirmed by our actions, then there is no "cause for stumbling" either for ourselves or others.

John concludes by restating the negative case: **Whoever hates his brother is in darkness; he walks in darkness and does not know where he is going because the darkness has blinded his eyes**. What does this add? John shows that hating our brother or sister actually envelops us in darkness so that we can no longer see what is true. The darkness that John is talking about "is not a neutral absence of light; it is a force that causes lack of sight."[5] Sin—especially the failure to love—blinds our eyes and ushers us into greater moral darkness. Only through repentance, through confessing our sins and finding life in Jesus, can we break out of this darkness and come back into the light.

Address to Children, Fathers, and Young Men (2:12–14)

---

[12]**I am writing to you, children, because your sins have been forgiven for his name's sake.**
[13]**I am writing to you, fathers, because you know him who is from the beginning.**

I am writing to you, young men, because you have conquered the evil one.
[14]**I write to you, children, because you know the Father.**

I write to you, fathers, because you know him who is from the beginning.

I write to you, young men, because you are strong and the word of God remains in you, and you have conquered the evil one.

OT: Joel 3:1
NT: Eph 5:22–6:9; Col 3:18–4:1; 1 Pet 2:18–3:7
Catechism: forgiveness of sin, 1846–48

2:12–14 This section has proved puzzling for readers across the centuries. Who exactly is John addressing here? Why does he identify these three specific groups within

---

4. The RSV, ESV, and NRSV translate this as "There is no cause for stumbling."
5. Brown, *Epistles of John*, 275.

the church? And how does this passage fit within the wider context of the letter? We will first examine the structure of the whole section and try to understand the context before looking at what John says to each particular grouping.

John addresses three groupings within the church—**children**,[6] **fathers**, and **young men**[7]—in two cycles. Here again we see John using repetition with variation to drive home and fill out his meaning. In the first cycle, he begins each address with **I am writing to you**; in the second cycle he changes this to **I write to you**.[8] The central question for interpretation concerns the identity of the three groups. Is John speaking to three groups, two groups, or just one group of people in the community? We can make a plausible argument for all three options.

According to the first view, John is addressing three distinct groupings within the community, probably distinguished by spiritual maturity rather than natural age.[9] We know from other New Testament letters that the apostolic writers sometimes addressed distinct groups within the community in order to give particular exhortations to those in each situation.[10] Many conclude that this is what John is doing here, speaking in turn to new converts (children), seasoned believers (fathers), and emerging younger leaders (young men).

According to the second view, John is addressing only two groups.[11] On this view, the title "children" best applies to the whole community, given that John employs the very same two words for "children" elsewhere in the letter to designate the entire community, not a distinct grouping.[12] John then distinguishes two groups within the church: those who are mature ("fathers") and those who are newer in the faith ("young men").[13]

According to the third view, John is speaking to the entire community, both men and women, as "children," "fathers," and "young men."[14] Why might John

---

6. John uses two synonymous words for "children": *teknia* in v. 12 and *paidia* in v. 14.

7. The Greek term for "young men" (*neaniskoi*) is sometimes used in the †Septuagint and other early Jewish literature to identify those who fight for the Lord or stand for his cause (Josh 2:1; 2 Sam 10:9; Dan 1:17; *4 Maccabees* 14:12).

8. In the Greek text, "I write to you" is in the past tense—"I wrote to you" or "I have written to you" (NJB)—but most modern translations (NABRE, RSV, NRSV, ESV) render it in the present tense. A majority of scholars conclude that the change in verb tense is stylistic and does not indicate two different times of writing. For a detailed discussion of the issues and options, see Brown, *Epistles of John*, 294–97.

9. Those who support this interpretation include (from the early Church) Clement of Alexandria and Origen of Alexandria and (in modern times) John Stott and F. F. Bruce.

10. E.g., Eph 5:22–6:9; Col 3:18–4:1; 1 Pet 2:18–3:7.

11. This view has strong support among modern interpreters, including Rudolf Schnackenburg, Raymond Brown, John Painter, and Francis Martin.

12. John addresses the whole community as *teknia* in 2:1, 28; 3:7, 18; 4:4; 5:21, and as *paidia* in 2:18.

13. Joel 3:1 offers a similar division, speaking first of "sons and daughters," and then distinguishing between "old men" and "young men."

14. This view was proposed by St. Augustine; among modern proponents are C. H. Dodd and Ignace de la Potterie.

choose to address the whole church under three distinct titles? Perhaps he would do so to point out the complementary qualities that they have attained—and are called to attain—in Christ.

Though it remains uncertain whether John is addressing one, two, or three groups, I favor the third view because the qualities that John ascribes to each of the three groups fittingly apply to all members of the church and are in fact applied to the whole church elsewhere in the letter (see below).

What are the distinct qualities that John ascribes to each group? John addresses them as "children" because their **sins have been forgiven for his name's sake** and because they **know the Father**. These two qualities point to basic Christian initiation and identity. When we become Christians, we come to know God as our Father and we receive the forgiveness of our sins through Jesus Christ. But these are also qualities that pertain to the ongoing identity of God's people. As already noted, John addresses the whole community as "children" on seven occasions in the letter; he also reminds them all that their sins are forgiven in Christ (1:9).

John speaks to them as "fathers" because they **know him who is from the beginning**. This is a reference to Jesus, the Word of life, who is "from the beginning" (1:1) and has been manifested to us. The term "fathers" may speak to spiritual maturity and depth of faith: they are fathers in the faith because they have come to know Christ as the one who is from the beginning and has appeared in the †flesh for our salvation. Elsewhere John addresses the whole community, men and women both, as those who have come to know and confess the Lord Jesus come in the flesh (2:22–23; 4:2–3, 15).

Finally, John addresses them as "young men" because they **are strong and the word of God remains** in them and because they **have conquered the evil one**. As "young men" they are assured by John of their strength in God and their victory over the evil one. God's word—God's "seed" (3:9)—abides in them. Therefore, they are fit for the spiritual battle and should have confidence that God is with them. John elsewhere tells the whole community, both men and women, that they have overcome the evil one by the power of God (4:4; 5:18–19).

How does this section fit into the wider context of the letter? John uses these titles of address to encourage the whole community and all its members, and so all of us who are readers of the letter, about what we have attained in Christ. He underlines what we have attained, so that we may have confidence to continue to walk in the light and to contend for the faith. It is a statement of fact but at the same time an encouragement to press on.

Do Not Love the World (2:15–17)

¹⁵Do not love the world or the things of the world. If anyone loves the world, the love of the Father is not in him. ¹⁶For all that is in the world, sensual lust, enticement for the eyes, and a pretentious life, is not from the Father but is from the world. ¹⁷Yet the world and its enticement are passing away. But whoever does the will of God remains forever.

OT: Gen 3:6; Ps 119:37; Wis 5:8
NT: Matt 4:1–11; Luke 4:1–13; Rom 13:14; 1 Cor 7:31; James 4:4, 16
Catechism: mastery over the world, 377; overcoming sinful desire or concupiscence, 2514, 2534

John now moves from encouragement to exhortation. This is the first direct **2:15** command in the letter: **Do not love the world or the things of the world**. As readers, we have just heard John speak about the love of God (2:5) and love for our brothers and sisters (2:10). Now John turns the tables and tells us what *not* to love: the †world and the things in the world.

The term "world" (*kosmos*) occurs frequently in the letter (twenty-three times). It can refer to that part of the created order—especially the human

Figure 7. The amphitheater in Ephesus, where plays, concerts, and civic functions took place

163

race—that is the recipient of God's salvation (2:2; 4:9, 14) or to the material necessities of human life (3:17). But most often in 1 John "world" refers to human society that is set against God (3:1), that is the home of sinful patterns of life (2:16) and is under the power of the evil one (4:4). When John calls us to "not love the world or the things of the world," he is referring not to the created order as such, which is good, but to a system of values and a sphere of temptation in human society that is hostile to God.

This is why love for the Father and love for the world are mutually exclusive: **if anyone loves the world, the love of the Father is not in him**. The Letter of James concurs: "Do you not know that to be a lover of the world means enmity with God?" (4:4). The two are set against each other and inescapably opposed. When God loves the world, in the sense of the human race, by sending his Son (John 3:16), the world is transformed into the kingdom of God; when we love the world in the pejorative sense that John warns against here, we are transformed and become worldly.

2:16–17   Verse 16 gives a diagnosis of **all that is in the world**, identifying three negative qualities that are **not from the Father** but are **from the world**. The first is **sensual lust,** literally, "desire of the flesh." The NJB translation, "disordered bodily desires," captures the sense well. The "world" is the place where all the disordered appetites of our body, not only sexual desire, are fanned into flame. Paul gives a similar exhortation: "Put on the Lord Jesus Christ, and make no provision for the desires of the flesh" (Rom 13:14).

The second quality found in the world is **enticement for the eyes**, literally, "the desire of the eyes."[15] From the world comes the allurement of our eyes, drawing them away from God to things that are sinful. The psalmist prays to be delivered from the enticement of the eyes: "Avert my eyes from what is worthless; / by your way give me life" (Ps 119:37).

The third negative quality is **a pretentious life,** literally, "the boastfulness of life." The Greek word for "life," *bios,* often refers to property, possessions, or livelihood.[16] John, then, is warning us against an arrogant or boastful manner of life, especially in regard to our material possessions. James cautions against the same: "Now you are boasting in your arrogance. All such boasting is evil" (James 4:16). The book of Wisdom neatly sums up the futility of this manner of life: "What did our pride avail us? / What have wealth and its boastfulness afforded us?" (Wis 5:8).

15. NJB: "disordered desires of the eyes."
16. Several translations reflect this emphasis on material possessions: "pride in possession(s)" (NJB, ESV); "pride in riches" (NRSV).

The Sin of Adam and Eve

In describing what is "in the world," John may be making a subtle reference to the sin of Adam and Eve in the garden. After being tempted and lied to by the serpent, Eve looks on the fruit of the tree and sees that it is "good for food," "pleasing to the eyes," and "desirable for gaining wisdom" (Gen 3:6). These three qualities are similar to what John warns against here, especially when we recognize that Eve's "desire for wisdom" was in fact a desire to "be like God" (Gen 3:5 NRSV) in a prideful way.

Moreover, there may be a link with the three temptations that Jesus faced in the wilderness (Matt 4:1–11; Luke 4:1–13). The first Adam succumbed to temptations in the garden, disobeyed God, and was exiled from the garden; the second Adam resisted these temptations in the wilderness and proved obedient to God, bringing us back to the garden of God. The Catechism (377) makes the link between 1 John 2:16 and Adam, observing that "the first man [Adam] was unimpaired and ordered in his whole being because he was free from the triple concupiscence that subjugates him to the pleasures of the senses, covetousness for earthly goods, and self-assertion." Saint Augustine explicitly links these three qualities found in the world with the temptations that Christ faced and overcame in the wilderness.[a] Our task, according to John, is to follow in the footsteps of Christ, rejecting the allurements of the world and doing the will of God.

a. *Homilies on 1 John* 2.14.

John concludes this section by contrasting two destinies. On the one hand, **the world and its enticement are passing away**. The fallen world with its enticements to sin will not endure, and when Jesus returns, the "world" in this sense will definitively pass away. Paul says the same: "The world in its present form is passing away" (1 Cor 7:31). On the other hand, **whoever does the will of God remains forever**. The one who keeps the commandments of God and walks in the light has eternal life. John's point is plain: if we choose to love the world and its ways, we are loving something deceitful that will pass away; if we choose to love the Father and do his will, we will enjoy everlasting life with him.

Reflection and Application (2:15–17)

John's directive, "Do not love the world or the things of the world," would seem a nearly impossible task today. "Sensual lust" has become a god in our culture, and we now have easy and constant access to a burgeoning pornography industry. Fighting off "enticement for the eyes" has never been more challenging: estimates are that more than a thousand images per day flash before the eyes of the average person. In our intensely materialistic society, the acquisition of things is constantly paraded before our eyes as the ideal for which we ought to strive. All this leads to an arrogant posture that we have control over our own lives through the things we possess and the power we wield—we have no need for God.

Though the enticements in the world may be more potent than ever, we are not without hope, because the †grace of Christ is superabundant. Many and various strategies are needed to resist this invasion of worldliness, but perhaps what we need most is to reacquire the practices of fasting, prayer, and almsgiving. Through prudent fasting we gain steady mastery over the disorderly desires of our physical appetites. Through daily prayer we draw near to God and set our eyes on "things that are above" (Col 3:2 NRSV), and so "disenchant" the enticements of the world. Through regular almsgiving we counter the temptation to boast in our riches and are reminded that our treasure is in heaven, where "moth and rust" do not consume (Matt 6:19 NRSV). Above all, we need to draw strength and courage from the truth that the One who is in us is greater than the one who is in the world (1 John 4:4).

Antichrist and Denial of the Truth

1 John 2:18–27

In this section John takes direct aim at those who have departed and their false teaching. Here we can see with particular clarity John's oscillating technique, as he moves back and forth between denunciation of falsehood and the positive statement of the truth, between those who have the spirit of †antichrist and those who carry the anointing of God. Through it all, John's core message shines through with piercing brightness: eternal life consists of true abiding in the Father, Son, and Spirit.

The Coming of Antichrist and the Departure from the Church (2:18–19)

[18]Children, it is the last hour; and just as you heard that the antichrist was coming, so now many antichrists have appeared. Thus we know this is the last hour. [19]They went out from us, but they were not really of our number; if they had been, they would have remained with us. Their desertion shows that none of them was of our number.

OT: Dan 9:27; 11:31; 12:11
NT: Acts 2:17; 2 Thess 2:3–10; 2 Tim 3:1; 2 John 1:7; 1 Pet 1:5; 2 Pet 3:3; Jude 1:18
Catechism: living in the last hour, 670–72; the deception of the antichrist, 675–76

Addressing his readers as **Children**, John now speaks plainly of the departure   2:18
of a group of people from the local church, and he links them with the coming

167

of the †antichrist and **the last hour** of this age of the †world. "The last hour" is
a reference to the final stage of world history before Christ returns and brings
in a new age. It is equivalent in meaning to "the last days" (Acts 2:17; 2 Tim
3:1; 2 Pet 3:3) and "the last time" (1 Pet 1:5 NRSV; Jude 1:18). To say that it is
the last hour does not necessarily mean that the end is temporally close, but
only that we are now in the final stage of history and waiting for Christ's return.

John, in fact, is presuming that his readers have already heard from previous
teaching that **the antichrist was coming**. Who is this figure? The word "antichrist"
appears only in the †Johannine Epistles (1 John 2:18, 22; 4:3; 2 John 1:7),[1] but Paul
is almost certainly referring to the same figure when he speaks of "the lawless
one" (2 Thess 2:3). Plainly, in the apostolic period there was a common teaching,
based on the teaching of Christ, about a human figure who would appear in the
last days, doing wonders through the power of †Satan and leading many astray.[2]
This figure would be decisively defeated by Jesus when he returned in glory.

2:19   But John now adds a startling claim: **so now many antichrists have appeared**.[3] He points to the same phenomenon in 2 John 1:7: "Many deceivers have
gone out into the world. . . . Any such person is the deceiver and the antichrist!"
(NRSV). Who are these multiple antichrists who have already emerged on the
scene? John probably is referring to former members of the church who broke
communion and departed: **they went out from us, but they were not really
of our number**. In John's understanding, these people already display the signs
of the antichrist; they are like a vanguard, a first installment, of what will come
when the antichrist appears (on those who departed, see "Those Who Left the
Church" in the introduction, pp. 129–30).

John's particular concern at this point is to mark off these false teachers who
are former members as never really having belonged to the †fellowship that John
and his readers share together: **their desertion shows that none of them was
of our number**. They failed to persevere, thus showing that they were not truly
among the faithful. "The fact that the dissenters had left the apostolic fellowship simply showed that at heart they had never belonged to it."[4] Why is John

1. The term "†antichrist" is not found in Jewish intertestamental literature. It appears that this word
was coined by the author of the Johannine Epistles.
2. Paul also reminds the Thessalonians that he already told them about the man of lawlessness:
"Do you not recall that while I was still with you I told you these things?" (2 Thess 2:5). The book of
Revelation points symbolically to the figure of the antichrist when describing the "beast" and the "false
prophet" that will arise in the last days (Rev 13).
3. Paul says something similar concerning the "man of lawlessness": "The mystery of lawlessness is
already at work" (2 Thess 2:7).
4. F. F. Bruce, *The Epistles of John: Introduction, Exposition and Notes* (London: Pickering & Inglis,
1970), 69.

Background to the Antichrist

Both John (1 John 2:18) and Paul (2 Thess 2:3) indicate that basic Christian teaching includes a prediction of the coming of the "antichrist" or the "lawless one." This was simply part of what the first Christians were taught to expect. From where does this teaching arise? We find it anchored authoritatively in the teaching of Jesus himself. Shortly before his death, Jesus warned the disciples about the difficult days to come, when deceivers would multiply: "False Christs and false prophets will arise and show signs and wonders, to lead astray, if possible, the elect" (Mark 13:22 RSV). On the same occasion, Jesus quotes the book of Daniel (Dan 9:27; 11:31; 12:11) and gives warning about a coming ruler who will desecrate the house of God: "When you see the desolating abomination standing where he should not (let the reader understand), then those in Judea must flee to the mountains" (Mark 13:14). The emergence of an evil ruler performing signs and wonders and persecuting the people of God was also a common theme in the †intertestamental Jewish literature (200 BC–AD 100). Paul clearly has this figure in mind when he identifies the "lawless one" as seating himself in the temple of God, claiming to be a god, working signs and wonders, and leading many astray (2 Thess 2:3–12). And in Rev 13 we witness the appearing of the "beast" and his false prophet who seek to deceive the people of God. Though all this amounts to only a sketch of a figure or figures who will appear, the Church is clearly forewarned about a human figure who will arise and powerfully oppose the work of Christ.

so intent on drawing a sharp line between those who departed and those who remained? Because he wants to prevent further desertion from the church, and for this he needs to show that the teaching of those who deserted the church is false and inimical to true fellowship with God.

Contrast: The Anointing Received versus the Lie of Antichrist (2:20–27)

[20]But you have the anointing that comes from the holy one, and you all have knowledge. [21]I write to you not because you do not know the truth but because you do, and because every lie is alien to the truth. [22]Who is the liar? Whoever denies that Jesus is the Christ. Whoever denies the Father and the Son, this is the antichrist. [23]No one who denies the Son has the Father, but whoever confesses the Son has the Father as well.

²⁴Let what you heard from the beginning remain in you. If what you heard from the beginning remains in you, then you will remain in the Son and in the Father. ²⁵And this is the promise that he made us: eternal life. ²⁶I write you these things about those who would deceive you. ²⁷As for you, the anointing that you received from him remains in you, so that you do not need anyone to teach you. But his anointing teaches you about everything and is true and not false; just as it taught you, remain in him.

OT: Exod 29:7; 30:25; 40:9
NT: John 5:23; 14:17; 15:26; 2 Pet 1:12; 2 John 1:9
Catechism: the anointing of the Spirit, 695; supernatural knowledge of the truth, 91–93

2:20   John now speaks to the faithful who have remained. In contrast to those who "went out," to those identified as "†antichrists," are those who **have the anointing that comes from the holy one**. There is a wordplay here that we could easily miss in English translation. The Greek term *christos* means "anointed one." In contrast to the antichrists (*antichristoi*) just mentioned, who falsely claim to have the anointing, are those who have received the true "anointing" (*chrisma*).

What is John referring to when he speaks of "the anointing" (as he does also in 2:27)?[5] It could refer to the gift of God's word that abides within us and teaches the truth (1:10; 2:14), but most probably "the anointing" refers to the gift of the Spirit himself, who comes to live and act in our hearts: "You know [the Spirit of truth], for he dwells with you, and will be in you" (John 14:17 RSV). When David was anointed king by Samuel, the Spirit of God came upon him: "Then Samuel, with the horn of oil in hand, anointed him in the midst of his brothers; and from that day on, the spirit of the †Lord rushed upon David" (1 Sam 16:13). Just as Jesus himself was anointed with the Holy Spirit at his baptism for his messianic mission, so he anoints Christians with the Holy Spirit at their baptism. John may, in fact, be referring to an anointing with oil that accompanied the early baptismal rite as signifying the gift of the Spirit in the hearts of the faithful.[6]

The "holy one" could refer to either God the Father or Jesus the Son, though it is more likely that John sees the "anointing" (*chrisma*) coming from Jesus the "anointed one" (*christos*). In the Gospel of John the Spirit is said to be "sent"

5. For a detailed discussion of the options for interpreting "the anointing," see Raymond E. Brown, *The Epistles of John: Translated, with Introduction, Notes, and Commentary*, AB 30 [Garden City, NY: Doubleday, 1982], 341–47. He favors the view that "anointing" refers to the Holy Spirit (p. 347). John Painter takes the view that "anointing" refers to the word that was preached (*1, 2, and 3 John*, SP 18 [Collegeville, MN: Liturgical Press, 2002], 197–98).
6. In the †Septuagint the Greek term *chrisma* is used to refer to an anointing with oil (e.g., Exod 29:7; 30:25; 40:9).

both by the Father (14:26) and by the Son (15:26). The result of this anointing is that **you all have knowledge** (literally, "you all know").[7] The anointing of the Spirit is for all the faithful, not for a special spiritual elite. With that anointing comes a knowledge of the truth, in contrast to the lies being circulated by false teachers. "The Spirit of truth," John tells us in the Fourth Gospel, "will guide you into all truth" (John 16:13 RSV).

John now gives two reasons why he is writing. The first might strike us as counterintuitive: **I write to you not because you do not know the truth but because you do**. He is not intending to impart new information but rather is reminding them of what they already know, so that they might stand fast in it. We encounter a similar expression in Peter's second letter: "I will always remind you of these things, even though you already know them and are established in the truth you have" (2 Pet 1:12).

The second reason for writing is **because every lie is alien to the truth**. John wishes to draw the contrast clearly between "the truth" and the lies being told by those who have left the community. There is no room for hedging our bets: truth and falsehood have nothing to do with one another. They cannot coexist in the life of the disciple.

Taking up the topic of lying from verse 21, John asks, **Who is the liar?** The answer: **whoever denies that Jesus is the Christ**. Then he adds: **Whoever denies the Father and the Son, this is the antichrist**. It is evident that John is concerned here for the basic confession of faith regarding the true identity of Jesus Christ.

But what exactly were these "antichrists" denying? This is not entirely clear, but as we piece together the evidence from the letter, it appears that they were denying that the Son of God (who was "in the beginning" with the Father) actually took †flesh and became a human being in the †incarnation. They were denying that Jesus was truly the "Christ"—that is, the †Messiah or anointed one—who had come from the Father for our salvation. "The Lie *par excellence* is that which refuses to see the Godhead shine in the human life and death of Jesus."[8] For John, this is the core activity of the antichrist: to deny the true incarnation of the Son of God sent from the Father.

John then makes the link between confession of the Father and confession of the Son explicit: **No one who denies the Son has the Father, but whoever confesses the Son has the Father as well**. This is mirrored in 2 John: "Everyone who does not abide in the teaching of Christ, but goes beyond it, does not have God; whoever

2:21

2:22

2:23

---

7. Early manuscripts are equally divided between "you *all* know" and "you know *all things*," but most scholars conclude that "you all know" is more likely the original text.

8. Bruce, *Epistles of John*, 73.

St. Polycarp on the Lie of Antichrist

Polycarp (c. 70–156), †bishop and martyr, is reputed to have been a disciple of the apostle John. In his *Letter to the Philippians* (dated between 108 and 120) he offers the following commentary on the antichrist:

> For everyone who does not confess that Jesus Christ has come in the flesh is antichrist; and whoever does not acknowledge the testimony of the cross is of the devil; and whoever twists the sayings of the Lord to suit his own sinful desires and claims that there is neither resurrection nor judgment—well, that one is the firstborn of Satan. Therefore let us leave behind the worthless speculations of the crowd and their false teachings and let us return to the word delivered to us from the beginning.[a]

a. *Letter to the Philippians* 7.1–2 (Michael W. Holmes, trans. and ed., *The Apostolic Fathers in English* [Grand Rapids: Baker Academic, 2006], 138).

abides in the teaching has both the Father and the Son" (2 John 1:9 NRSV). If we deny the truth about the Son, then we lose the Father as well; if we confess and believe in the Son as the faith teaches, then we gain the Father as well. "Whoever does not honor the Son does not honor the Father who sent him" (John 5:23).

2:24–25   How, then, can we be sure to abide in the Father and the Son? **Let what you heard from the beginning remain in you**, John tells his readers. **If what you heard from the beginning remains in you, then you will remain in the Son and in the Father.** John is referring to the word of the †gospel that they heard at the start of their life in Christ (see 2:7). What, then, are the weapons we have to defend against the lies of the antichrist? We have both the anointing of the Spirit within us (v. 20) and God's word abiding in us (v. 24). By clinging to God's word and Spirit, we hold fast to the faith and remain in communion with the Father and the Son. John underlines the importance of true teaching ("what you heard"). It is not just information; it is a word that dwells in the believer and gives life, resulting in communion with the Father and the Son.

The result is that we partake of **the promise that he made us: eternal life**. John circles back here to the theme that he announced at the beginning. By yielding to the anointing of the Spirit and by holding fast to the word of God, we receive a living communion with God himself—Father, Son, and Spirit—that lasts forever (see 5:11–12).

2:26–27   John now sums up what he has been saying in verses 18–25. He informs his readers that he is writing explicitly **about those who would deceive you.**

These are former members of the local church (the "liars" and "antichrists") who are denying fundamental truths of the faith, and they pose a present and ongoing threat to John's hearers. In direct contrast to this deceptive teaching, John points once again to the "anointing" that the faithful have received: **As for you, the anointing that you received from him remains in you**. This anointing is not a temporary or occasional reality; it is an ongoing, abiding presence of God through the Spirit.

But strikingly John then adds, **so that you do not need anyone to teach you**. To expand on this, he explains, **But his anointing teaches you about everything and is true and not false**. We might have expected John to position himself as the true teacher, in contrast to the false ones. Instead, he identifies "the anointing" from God that they have received as their primary teacher.

Is John then rejecting the role of human teachers in the church, as if they have no place or function? Clearly not, since he himself is teaching them in this letter. John also positively refers to the original proclamation of the gospel and basic catechesis that they received from human teachers: "Let what you heard from the beginning remain in you" (v. 24). But it is crucial to recognize that John envisions the role of ongoing teaching primarily as reminding the faithful of what they already know. He believes that the Spirit is the true and fundamental teacher of the faithful.[9] Human teachers have the task of instructing, reminding, clarifying, and exhorting—exactly what John himself is doing in this letter. But the primary teacher of the faith is God himself, through his word and Spirit. It is the Spirit who takes what is taught and reveals it as true to the believer in an existential way.

John closes by saying, **Just as it** (the anointing) **has taught you, remain in him**. He seems to have Jesus in mind here, as the one in whom we are to abide (on the basis of what follows in v. 29). In other words, by the anointing of God's Spirit we are fitted to repel the false teaching that assaults us and to retain our communion with the One who is eternal life.

Reflection and Application (2:20–27)

To postmodern ears, John could seem to be vindicating the attitudes of our culture by saying that we really have no need of external teachers because we have within ourselves everything necessary to discern what is true and good. But John is neither validating the self as the source of truth nor rejecting a teaching authority. On the contrary, the anointing that we have within us is

9. For the role of the Spirit as the teacher of the faithful, see especially John 14:26; 16:13.

St. Augustine on the Teacher Within

Saint Augustine comments on teachings from without versus the teacher from within:

> Teachings and admonitions that come from without are of some help. He who teaches hearts has his chair in heaven. Hence even he himself says in the gospel, "Do not call anyone on earth your teacher; one is your teacher, the Christ" (Matt 23:8–9). Let him, then, speak to you within. . . . He who teaches, then, is the inner teacher: Christ teaches; his inbreathing teaches. Where his inbreathing and his anointing don't exist, words sound to no avail. These words which we are speaking from without, brothers, are like a farmer in respect to a tree. He works from without; he employs water and careful cultivation. Whatever he may employ from without, does he form the fruit? . . . This is what I tell you, then: whether by our speaking we plant or water (1 Cor 3:6–7), we aren't anything, but he who gives the growth, God—that is, his anointing, which teaches you about everything.[a]

a. *Homilies on 1 John* 3.13 (*Homilies on the First Epistle of John*, trans. Boniface Ramsey, ed. Daniel E. Doyle and Thomas Martin, WSA 3/14 [Hyde Park, NY: New City Press, 2008], 63).

not from ourselves but is the Holy Spirit—God himself—teaching us through his word. And by writing this letter, John is acting as an authoritative teacher for the church. John is, in fact, pointing us to the great gift of God that has been given to each of us, a living relationship with God through the Spirit that enables us to be taught by God and know the truth. Thomas Aquinas calls this "the instinct of the Holy Spirit" at work in the believer.[10]

Echoing 1 John 2:20–27, the Second Vatican Council gives eloquent voice to this supernatural sense of faith (*sensus fidei*) that comes through the gift of the Spirit:

> The entire body of the faithful, anointed as they are by the Holy One, cannot err in matters of belief. They manifest this special property by means of the whole people's supernatural discernment in matters of faith [*sensus fidei*] when "from the Bishops down to the last of the lay faithful" they show universal agreement in matters of faith and morals. That discernment in matters of faith is aroused and sustained by the Spirit of truth. It is exercised under the guidance of the sacred teaching authority, in faithful and respectful obedience to which the people of God accepts that which is not just the word of men but truly the word of God. (*Lumen Gentium* 12)

10. See, e.g., *Summa theologiae* III, q. 25, a. 3 ad 4; III, q. 36, a. 5.

Second Movement:
Walk in Righteousness

1 John 2:28–4:6

The Children of God

1 John 2:28–3:10

We now begin the second overall movement of the letter (2:28–4:6), with the focus on righteousness, a term that appears three times in this opening section (2:29; 3:7, 10). Many of the same themes continue to be sounded, but the emphasis shifts to the purity and righteousness that ought to characterize the children of God. In this section (2:28–3:10), John uses †antithesis to highlight the contrast between the children of God and the children of the devil. The children of the devil follow the way of sin marked out by the devil, who "sinned from the beginning," whereas the children of God, born of God's "seed," practice righteousness and so abide in him.

God's Righteous Children (2:28–3:2)

---

²⁸And now, children, remain in him, so that when he appears we may have confidence and not be put to shame by him at his coming. ²⁹If you consider that he is righteous, you also know that everyone who acts in righteousness is begotten by him.
³:¹See what love the Father has bestowed on us that we may be called the children of God. Yet so we are. The reason the world does not know us is that it did not know him. ²Beloved, we are God's children now; what we shall be has not yet been revealed. We do know that when it is revealed we shall be like him, for we shall see him as he is.

OT: Exod 34:29–30

NT: John 1:12–13; 3:5; 1 Cor 13:12; 2 Cor 3:18; 4:6; 1 Pet 1:23

Catechism: confidence before God, 2633, 2777–78; revelation that we are children of God, 1692; seeing God in the beatific vision, 163, 1023, 1028, 2519

Lectionary: 4th Sunday of Easter, Year B (1 John 3:1–2); Holy Family, Year C (1 John 3:1–2, 21–24); All Saints (1 John 3:1–3)

2:28–29   These verses act as a kind of hinge, connecting what comes before with a new section that follows. For this reason, some commentators place verses 28–29 with the previous section, others with the section that follows—there are good reasons for both. We will treat them as beginning a new section primarily because they introduce new words and themes that will be developed at greater length in the following chapter.

John again addresses his readers as **children** and repeats the call to **remain in him** (Jesus). What does it mean to "remain" or "abide" in Jesus? It means that we, like branches to the vine, cling to him through faith, hope, and love (John 15:1–10). We "remain" in him by keeping his commandments from the heart and by drawing near to him in prayer, asking for all that we need (John 15:10; 16:24). In short, to remain in Jesus means that we have a living relationship with the Father, Son, and Spirit, who have come to dwell within us, and that we are bearing fruit in our lives, pleasing to God (John 15:8). Why should we remain, or abide, in Christ Jesus? **So that when he appears we may have confidence and not be put to shame by him at his coming.** John is saying that if we truly abide in the Son now and allow his atoning sacrifice to cleanse us from all sin, we have no need to fear the final judgment that will take place when he comes.

John uses the same verb, "appear," to describe the two comings of Christ: the first in his †incarnation to take away sins (1:2), the second at his final coming when he will come to judge (2:28).

John expects us to stand in confidence at the coming of Christ.[1] The term "confidence" (*parrhēsia*), which appears four times in the letter,[2] displays the attitude that we should have as children before God our Father. This is not arrogant presumption, but a humble assurance that we can ask God for what we need now and stand before him without terror on the day of judgment (see sidebar, "*Parrhēsia* in the New Testament").

In verse 29 we encounter two new words, "righteousness" and "begotten," both of which play an important role in the next section of the letter: **If you consider that he is righteous, you also know that everyone who acts in righteousness is begotten by him.** To be righteous is to be just, and in particular to conform

---

1. Readers of the Greek would catch the similarity in sound between "confidence" (*parrhēsia*) and "coming" (*parousia*). John is assuring them that they will have *parrhēsia* at Christ's *parousia*.

2. 1 John 2:28; 3:21; 4:17; 5:14.

Parrhēsia in the New Testament

The Greek word *parrhēsia* plays an important role in the New Testament writings. To act with *parrhēsia* can mean simply to act "openly," "plainly," or "publicly" (e.g., John 7:4; 16:29), but more commonly *parrhēsia* means "boldness" or "confidence." The apostles spoke the word of God with "boldness" in the face of great opposition (Acts 4:13, 29–31; Eph 6:19). Paul testifies to the "boldness" that he expressed in his pastoral care of the churches (2 Cor 7:4; Philem 1:8). Most profoundly, *parrhēsia* expresses the "boldness" and "confidence" that we have as sons and daughters of God to stand before God in worship and ask for what we need (Eph 3:12; Heb 4:16; 10:19). In 1 John, *parrhēsia* conveys the confidence and boldness that we possess as children of God to ask for what we need and to stand before God on the day of judgment. *Parrhēsia* is not confidence in ourselves (arrogant pride) but the confidence that we gain because God has loved us and has given us his Spirit. It is a "humble boldness" that characterizes how we live as Christians before God and among others in the †world.

to a standard. Often in Scripture, righteousness indicates conformity to God's ways expressed in his law and in his own conduct (Deut 6:25). Jesus conforms perfectly to God's standards in his conduct, and when our conduct conforms to God's standards, we act in righteousness. John has already told us that Jesus is "the righteous one" (1 John 2:1) who has cleansed us from sin. Now he draws out the implication of this: if we know and recognize that Christ himself is righteous, then we can be sure that everyone who "acts in righteousness" has been begotten of God.

John's readers would have recognized the phrase "begotten by him [God]" as a reference to baptized believers who are living a life of righteousness through the indwelling Spirit. In the Gospel of John, Jesus assures Nicodemus that "no one can enter the kingdom of God without being born of water and the Spirit" (John 3:5). The Greek verb for "born" in John 3:5 is the same as the one for "begotten" here. By receiving the word of the †gospel, believers are born of or begotten by God through the water of baptism and the gift of the Spirit. But there is also a word of caution here. Merely receiving the sacrament of baptism does not qualify people as truly "begotten of God" in John's eyes. Those who fail to show the fruits of this new life (e.g., those who departed from the community or those who fail to love their fellow Christians) are not counted among those who have been truly begotten by God (see 1 John 3:9–10).

This is another instance in 1 John where the masculine pronoun ("him") could refer grammatically either to the Son or to the Father. But given that the phrase "begotten by" unambiguously refers to the Father elsewhere in 1 John, it is highly probable that this is what John has in mind here.[3] In other words, if we have been begotten from "God's seed" (3:9), then this will be manifested in a godly, righteous way of life. As we read in 1 Peter: "You have been born anew, not from perishable but from imperishable seed, through the living and abiding word of God" (1 Pet 1:23).

3:1–2   In one of the most exhilarating passages in the New Testament, John speaks about what we are now, God's children, in order to point to something even greater that awaits us: becoming fully like Jesus. He begins by bringing the theme of being God's children to center stage: **See what love the Father has bestowed on us that we may be called the children of God**. God the Father has loved us to such an extent that we have the immense privilege of being called his children. But John immediately adds, **Yet so we are**. We are children of God not in name only or merely as a title of honor. Christians truly have become God's children in a new way through the saving work of Christ: "To all who received him, who believed in his name, he gave power to become children of God, who were born, not of blood or of the will of the flesh or of the will of man, but of God" (John 1:12–13 NRSV).

John continues: **The reason the world does not know us is that it did not know him**. The fact that we are the children of God explains why the "world" does not recognize us for what we are. Just as those who belong to the world failed to recognize Christ himself and his Father, so they clearly will not know or recognize those who are begotten of God. As children, we are like the Father and the true Son, Jesus Christ, and so we should expect to experience the same rejection that Christ received.

In a remarkable and unexpected development, John speaks in verse 2 of what we will become when Jesus appears in his second coming. He begins by restating what we already are: **Beloved, we are God's children now**. This is the starting point and a strong affirmation that we are already "like" him as children are like their father. Then he adds: **What we shall be has not yet been revealed**. Is John saying that Christians have received no revelation whatsoever about what we can expect in eternal life, in the kingdom to come? No, but he is pointing to the fact that we do not fully know the form of what our life will look like after Jesus returns, when we will live as children of God in our resurrected bodies. This

---

3. For the phrase "begotten by" referring to God the Father, see 1 John 3:9; 4:7; 5:1, 4, 18; see also John 1:13.

Children of God

BIBLICAL BACKGROUND

The title "children of God" is not found as such in the Old Testament, though there are occurrences of the title "sons of God" (Hosea 2:1; NABRE: "children of the living God"), and certainly the revelation of the people of Israel as God's children is deeply rooted in the Old Testament (Exod 4:22–23). In the New Testament, Paul freely uses the title "children of God" of Christians: "The Spirit itself bears witness with our spirit that we are children of God, and if children, then heirs" (Rom 8:16–17 [see also Rom 8:21; Eph 5:1; Phil 2:15]). He also employs the parallel title "sons of God" to designate all believers (Rom 8:14). John, however, never uses the word "sons" to designate Christians, reserving "son" for the only-begotten Son, Jesus. "Children of God," therefore, is John's special title to denote our adoption by God and close resemblance to him (John 1:12; 11:52; 1 John 3:1–2, 10; 5:2).

is because "what we shall be" is far more wonderful than we can now imagine: "Now to him who is able to accomplish far more than all we ask or imagine, by the power at work within us, to him be glory in the church and in Christ Jesus to all generations, forever and ever. Amen" (Eph 3:20–21).

Though we may not fully know what our life will be like then, John assures us, **We do know that when it is revealed we shall be like him, for we shall see him as he is**. Most translations have "when *he* is revealed," referring to Christ.[4] When Jesus comes again and brings in the fullness of the kingdom of God, we will be like him, for we will see him in his full glory. We are already God's children right now; this is a present reality. Though we do not know precisely the form that this will take in the next life, we do know that we will be "like him": we will be sons and daughters who are like the Son of God (see sidebar, "The Deification of the Christian"). "For now we see in a mirror dimly, but then face to face. Now I know in part; then I shall understand fully, even as I have been fully understood" (1 Cor 13:12 RSV).

John seems to make a connection between "seeing" Jesus and "being like" him. Paul speaks in strikingly similar terms: "And we all, with unveiled face, beholding the glory of the Lord, are being changed into his likeness from one degree of glory to another" (2 Cor 3:18 RSV). "Seeing" or "beholding" the Lord in his glory is transformative. Just as Moses' face shone because it reflected the

4. For example, the RSV, NRSV, NJB, ESV, NIV. The Greek text permits either translation, as the NABRE footnote acknowledges.

The †Deification of the Christian

When John says that "we are God's children now," and that when Christ returns "we shall be like him, for we shall see him as he is" (3:2), he is speaking about what the later Christian tradition would call our deification or divinization. Deification does not mean that we "turn into God" or that we simply "become God," but that we share so fully in God's divine life and power that we become "like God." Paul describes this as becoming conformed to the image of Jesus (Rom 8:29). Our deification begins in this life—we are God's children now—but it reaches completion only in eternal life, when we will be fully transformed into the likeness of God. All this is possible only because God has come to dwell in us and has granted us †fellowship with himself. Maximus the Confessor (c. 580–662), an outstanding teacher who suffered torture and exile in defense of the faith, describes the goal of our deification in these words:

> The fullness of God permeates [the faithful] wholly as the soul permeates the body. . . . He directs them as he thinks best, filling them with his own glory and blessedness, and bestows on them unending life beyond imagining and wholly free from the signs of corruption that mark the present age. He gives them life, not the life that comes from breathing air, nor that of veins coursing with blood, but the life that comes from being wholly infused with the fullness of God.[a]

a. *On the Cosmic Mystery of Jesus Christ: Selected Writings from St. Maximus the Confessor*, trans. Paul M. Blowers and Robert L. Wilken (Crestwood, NY: St. Vladimir's Seminary Press, 2003), 63.

glory of God as he stood in God's presence (Exod 34:29–30), so when we behold *fully* the glory of God in the face of Christ (2 Cor 4:6), his life will be fully manifested in us, both spiritually and physically through our resurrected bodies.

Purity and Sin Contrasted (3:3–6)

³Everyone who has this hope based on him makes himself pure, as he is pure.

⁴Everyone who commits sin commits lawlessness, for sin is lawlessness. ⁵You know that he was revealed to take away sins, and in him there is no sin. ⁶No one who remains in him sins; no one who sins has seen him or known him.

NT: John 8:46; Rom 6:2; 2 Cor 5:21; Heb 4:15; 1 Pet 2:22
Catechism: imitating the purity of Christ, 2345; the reality of human sin, 386–89; Christ taking away our sins, 601–5
Lectionary: All Saints (1 John 3:1–3)

In this section John insists on the incompatibility between purity and sin. The   3:3
opening verse states the positive goal: **Everyone who has this hope based on
him makes himself pure, as he is pure**. What is the logic at work here? John
is saying that all who possess the hope of becoming like the Lord in the age to
come purify themselves now in order to grow in our likeness to him. Just as he is
pure, so we seek to become pure. Even now we have God's Holy Spirit dwelling
within us, and the Spirit inspires us to seek the purity that Christ himself has.
Our hope that we will be fully like him when he comes again gives us motivation in the present to press on toward the goal of purity.

What does it mean to make oneself pure, literally, "to purify oneself"?[5] In
the New Testament, the verb "purify" (*hagnizō*) always refers to what one does
for oneself, often through a rite of cleansing (John 11:55; Acts 21:24, 26; 24:18).
The purpose of purifying something is to cleanse it so that it will be in the right
condition to enter God's presence. John does not specify what he means by purifying ourselves, but the wider teaching of the letter provides a basic answer:
to be pure and righteous is to avoid sin (2:1), to obey the commandments of
the Lord (2:3–4), and to live in the way that Jesus lived (2:6).

The opposite of a life of purity is a life marked by sin: **Everyone who com-**   3:4–6
mits sin commits lawlessness, for sin is lawlessness. Sin by its very nature is
a form of lawlessness.[6] "Lawlessness" is one of the most negative terms that the
Bible uses to describe human conduct. It is the opposite of righteousness. To
be lawless is to manifest active rebellion against God and his ways. For John,
Christians who persist in unrepentant sin manifest a serious disregard for God
and his standards. The accent here is on *the ongoing practice* of sinning. The
fact that John uses the present tense when speaking about sinning in verses 4–6
indicates ongoing or habitual sinful actions.[7] The ESV translation, "Everyone
who makes a practice of sinning," is preferable to the NABRE, "Everyone who
commits sin," because it brings out the ongoing practice of sin. John, then, is
contrasting two ways of life, one marked by the practice of sinning, the other
by the practice of righteousness: "Everyone who practices righteousness has
been born of him" (2:29 ESV).

John then turns our attention back to Christ Jesus himself: **You know that
he was revealed to take away sins**. The eternal Son did not become incarnate

---

5. For the call to purify one's heart, see especially James 4:8; 1 Pet 1:22.

6. This is the only occurrence of "lawlessness" (*anomia*) in the †Johannine writings, but the term
appears in other NT writings (e.g., Matt 7:23; Rom 6:19). Notably, Paul identifies the †antichrist as "the
man of lawlessness" (2 Thess 2:3 RSV).

7. Those who support this interpretation include John Painter (*1, 2, and 3 John*, SP 18 [Collegeville,
MN: Liturgical Press, 2002], 227) and Peter Rhea Jones (*1, 2 & 3 John*, SHBC [Macon, GA: Smith &
Helwys, 2009], 122).

to leave us burdened by sin, but so that we would be free from sin and live a life of purity. To make clear that Christ had nothing to do with sin, John adds: **and in him there is no sin**. The New Testament speaks with one voice about the sinlessness of Christ. Paul says that Jesus "did not know sin" (2 Cor 5:21), Hebrews tells us that he was "without sin" (Heb 4:15), and Peter says that he "committed no sin" (1 Pet 2:22). Just as Christ is "pure" and "in him there is no sin," so we are to pursue a life of righteousness because we desire to be like him.

John concludes with a sharp contrast: **No one who remains in him sins; no one who sins has seen him or known him**. The idea of an ongoing practice of sin is captured by the ESV: "No one who abides in him keeps on sinning." In other words, those who truly abide in Christ will not live in sin or lawlessness. If we are living a life that continues to be characterized by serious sin, this is evidence that we have not truly come into †fellowship with the Father and the Son. The more deeply we are in communion (*koinōnia*) with God, the more we love his will and aim to live a life of purity and righteousness.

Is John contradicting what he said earlier in the letter? There he stated, "If we say, 'We are without sin,' we deceive ourselves, and the truth is not in us" (1:8). He also explained the remedy for sin available to Christians: "If anyone does sin, we have an Advocate with the Father, Jesus Christ the righteous one" (2:1). Now he seems to be saying that if we sin, then we neither truly see nor know Christ. How can these statements be reconciled?

When John says here that "no one who remains in him sins," he is not primarily concerned with an occasional lapse or even with habitual sins of personal weakness that we are making every effort to overcome through regular repentance. He is speaking, rather, about a pattern of sinful living for which we are not repenting. He is speaking about the person who claims to be a Christian yet continues to live a life characterized by sin.[8] For John, the new life that we have received in Christ through the Spirit leads us *out of* sin: "I am writing this to you so that you may not commit sin" (2:1). John expects that Christians will cooperate with the †grace of God to lead a life of substantial purity and righteousness.

Children of God versus Children of the Devil (3:7–10)

[7]**Children, let no one deceive you. The person who acts in righteousness is righteous, just as he is righteous. [8]Whoever sins belongs to the devil,**

8. Many scholars believe that John is directing this word against his opponents, those who left the church, because they were claiming to be true disciples of Christ yet were still living in sin and lawlessness.

because the devil has sinned from the beginning. Indeed, the Son of
God was revealed to destroy the works of the devil. ⁹No one who is
begotten by God commits sin, because God's seed remains in him; he
cannot sin because he is begotten by God. ¹⁰In this way, the children of
God and the children of the devil are made plain; no one who fails to
act in righteousness belongs to God, nor anyone who does not love his
brother.

OT: Gen 3:1–6
NT: John 8:40–41, 44; 13:2; Heb 2:14–15; 1 Pet 1:23
Catechism: the primordial sin of the devil, 391–93; Christ destroying the devil's work, 394; Christians born from the seed of God's word, 1228

John wants to ensure that no one is deceived about the utter incompatibility   **3:7–8**
between sin and righteousness: **Children, let no one deceive you**. Who is
deceiving them? John seems to be referring here to the false teachers who
were boasting of their standing before God but who in fact were living lawless
and sinful lives. Who, then, is truly righteous? **The person who acts in righteousness**. Just as we are to live in purity following the example of Christ, so
we are to act in righteousness, **just as he is righteous**. John is circling around
his theme, calling us to pursue similar qualities—purity and righteousness—to
emphasize the contrast between two fundamental types of living.

In contrast to righteousness, **Whoever sins belongs to the devil, because
the devil has sinned from the beginning**. Once again, the ESV translation,
"Whoever makes a practice of sinning is of the devil," more accurately expresses
the present continuous tense of the verb and points to the ongoing pattern of
sin that John seems to have in mind. Why would John introduce the devil at
this point? Because he wants to show the personal *source* of the two contrasting
ways of life. Christ Jesus is the source of our purity and righteousness, but the
devil is at the origin of sin, because it was through the devil that sin entered the
†world. "From the beginning" may refer to the devil's own primordial rebellion
against God, but more likely refers to the occasion when the devil lured Adam
and Eve to disobey the command of God (Gen 3:1–6).⁹ In either case, the devil
is the personal origin of sin in the world, and those who live a life characterized
by sin show that they belong to him.

Then, in a striking statement, John says that **the Son of God was revealed
to destroy the works of the devil**. When we think about why Christ became
incarnate, we usually think of other (true) reasons: to reveal the Father, to redeem

9. When Jesus says that the devil was "a murderer from the beginning" (John 8:44), he is clearly
referring to Gen 3:1–6, when the devil lured Adam and Eve into the disobedience that led to death.

St. Augustine on "Belonging to the Devil"

LIVING TRADITION

John's phrase "belongs to the devil" (3:8) is more literally "is of the devil." On this, St. Augustine wrote, "You know that 'of the devil' means 'imitating the devil.' For the devil has made no one, has begotten no one, has created no one. But whoever imitates the devil, as though having been born of him, becomes the devil's child by imitation, not, strictly speaking, by birth."[a]

a. *Homilies on 1 John* 4.10 (*Homilies on the First Epistle of John*, trans. Boniface Ramsey, ed. Daniel E. Doyle and Thomas Martin, WSA 3/14 [Hyde Park, NY: New City Press, 2008], 73).

us from sin, to give us new life, and so forth. But here John declares that the Son took on our nature in the †incarnation to do away with the works of our adversary. Christ's *work* destroys the devil's *works*. Sin is one of the primary works of the devil that Christ came to destroy. John is revealing here the cosmic battle between two figures, Christ and the devil. Just as the devil sought to destroy Christ and have him put to death (John 13:2), so by dying Jesus in fact destroyed the works of the devil (see John 12:31; Heb 2:14–15). The Christian cannot avoid taking sides in this battle. If we make a practice of sin, we show that we belong the devil and are doing his work; if we avoid sin and practice righteousness, we show that we are abiding in Christ.

3:9–10   John deepens this contrast through the metaphor of two incompatible parentages: in the end, we are either children of God or children of the devil. And our parentage is made evident by what we are like and how we live.

John already introduced the idea that we are "begotten" by God (2:29). Now he develops this theme: **No one who is begotten by God commits sin** (ESV: "No one born of God makes a practice of sinning"). Why? **Because God's seed remains in him**. This is a striking truth: the Christian has God's own "seed" (*sperma*) abiding within. In the Christian tradition, some commentators interpret "seed" to mean God's word (see 1 Pet 1:23; James 1:18), while others see it as a reference to the Holy Spirit (John 3:5). Whether we understand God's "seed" to be a reference to his word or to the Spirit or simply to his new life within us, John is using the analogy of biological fatherhood to show that we truly have God's very life in us and that the result is the desire and ability to live free of the dominating power of sin. Saint Paul makes a similar point in Romans about the very real and profound change that occurs in us through faith and baptism. We have died with Christ so that "we might no longer be in

Figure 8. Baptistery at the Basilica of St. John in Ephesus

slavery to sin" (Rom 6:6). Where Paul speaks of dying and rising with Christ, John speaks of being born of God's seed.

At this point we encounter a perplexing and troubling statement: **he cannot sin because he is begotten by God**. Is John saying that for those who have been truly born of God, sinning is now an impossibility? This conclusion would contradict what John said in chapter 1, and further it goes against our universal experience as Christians, that in fact we still can and do sin. It is crucial to see that John is speaking here about the principle in us (the life of God) and what it produces. God's seed cannot give birth to sin, for there is no sin in him. In other words, insofar as we live and abide in God, we will not sin. When we do sin, even occasionally or through habitual weakness, this is evidence that the life and power of God are not yet reigning fully in our lives.

Notably, John does not push the parallel with the devil; he never speaks about being begotten of the devil's *seed*. We consent to the devil's sin and lawlessness, and so we become enslaved to him spiritually, but we are never born from him in the same sense that we are born anew in God through the Spirit. The devil "does not give life but takes it away."[10]

10. Raymond E. Brown, *The Epistles of John: Translated, with Introduction, Notes, and Commentary*, AB 30 (Garden City, NY: Doubleday, 1982), 405.

The Catechism on the Devil's Sin

LIVING
TRADITION

The Catechism (392, 394) comments on the sin of the devil and the angels who followed him.

> Scripture speaks of a sin of these angels [see 2 Pet 2:4]. This "fall" consists in the free choice of these created spirits, who radically and irrevocably rejected God and his reign. We find a reflection of that rebellion in the tempter's words to our first parents: "You will be like God" [Gen 3:5]. The devil "has sinned from the beginning"; he is "a liar and the father of lies" [1 John 3:8; John 8:44].
>
> Scripture witnesses to the disastrous influence of the one Jesus calls "a murderer from the beginning," who would even try to divert Jesus from the mission received from his Father [John 8:44; see Matt 4:1–11]. "The reason the Son of God appeared was to destroy the works of the devil" [1 John 3:8]. In its consequences the gravest of these works was the mendacious seduction that led man to disobey God.

The section concludes with a compact summary: **In this way, the children of God and the children of the devil are made plain**. Those who are children of God show this through a life of righteousness and purity; those who are children of the devil manifest this by living a life of sin and lawlessness. As if to emphasize this truth, John reminds his readers that **no one who fails to act in righteousness belongs to God, nor anyone who does not love his brother**. To put this positively: those who belong to God will demonstrate this by keeping the commandments, especially the command to love one another.

Reflection and Application (3:1–10)

John's teaching on being children of God is, at one and the same time, a profound revelation and a tremendous challenge. The revelation comes first. The Father's love is so great that he has called us his children and genuinely made us his children. We do not have to wait for this; we are already the children of God. Do we know this personally? This is one of the deepest works of the Holy Spirit in us: "The Spirit himself bears witness with our spirit that we are children of God" (Rom 8:16 ESV). What will we become in eternal life? We do not fully know, but we have the assurance that "we will be like him" and "we will see him as he is." These are momentous promises of transformation and life in God's presence, both now and in the age to come.

But John does not stop with the revelation; he goes on to describe the task of living as God's children and the danger of turning away from the Lord. We are called to make ourselves pure and to pursue a life of righteous conduct free from sin. Yes, as God's children, we have his seed living in us, but we are obliged to live according to that seed by acting in righteousness and loving our brothers and sisters. John challenges us to look to the fruits of our lives. Are we showing the signs of being the children of God, or are we acting in ways that show us to be "children of the devil"?

God our Father, through his love, has bestowed on us a great privilege: to be his children. With this privilege comes a responsibility: to live as the children of God by living in union with and imitating Jesus Christ.

Loving One Another in Truth

1 John 3:11–24

In this section the theme of living righteously continues, but John turns our attention anew to the love of our brothers and sisters and then addresses our need to be reassured of our forgiveness before the Lord. He concludes with a pithy statement that sums up the entire letter and what God requires of us.

Genuine Love Contrasted with Murder (3:11–18)

[11]For this is the message you have heard from the beginning: we should love one another, [12]unlike Cain who belonged to the evil one and slaughtered his brother. Why did he slaughter him? Because his own works were evil, and those of his brother righteous. [13]Do not be amazed, [then,] brothers, if the world hates you. [14]We know that we have passed from death to life because we love our brothers. Whoever does not love remains in death. [15]Everyone who hates his brother is a murderer, and you know that no murderer has eternal life remaining in him. [16]The way we came to know love was that he laid down his life for us; so we ought to lay down our lives for our brothers. [17]If someone who has worldly means sees a brother in need and refuses him compassion, how can the love of God remain in him? [18]Children, let us love not in word or speech but in deed and truth.

OT: Gen 4:1–16
NT: John 5:24; 8:44; 15:12–13, 19; James 2:15–16
Catechism: call to love one another, 459, 1823–25; eternal separation from God, 1033; charitable works of mercy, 2447–48

For the second and final time in the letter, John speaks about a **message** that 3:11–12
was delivered in the original preaching of the †gospel. In 1:5–7 that message
was that "God is light" and that we must walk in the light. Here, the message
heard **from the beginning** is that **we should love one another**. John briefly
introduced this theme in 2:9–10, but now he expands on it by condemning
its opposite: Christians must avoid being like **Cain who belonged to the evil
one and slaughtered his brother**. This is the only direct reference to the Old
Testament in 1 John.

Why does Cain's murder of his brother, Abel, show him to be "of the evil
one"? Because the devil "was a murderer from the beginning" (John 8:44), who
"murdered" our first parents by leading them to spiritual death. By hating and
murdering his brother, Cain shows himself to be a child of the devil (see 3:10).

John then says, **Why did he slaughter him? Because his own works were
evil, and those of his brother righteous**. Genesis reports that Cain and Abel
both offered sacrifices but that, for reasons not perfectly clear in the text, Abel's
sacrifice was acceptable to the Lord, while Cain's was not. Rather than accept
God's invitation to change his ways and offer an acceptable sacrifice himself
(Gen 4:7), Cain killed his brother out of envy. Jewish and Christian tradition

Cain in Scripture and Jewish Tradition

BIBLICAL BACKGROUND

Surprisingly, Cain appears only once in the Old Testament (Gen
4:1–25). There we hear how the firstborn son of Adam and Eve,
despite direct warning from the Lord God, killed his brother, Abel,
out of envy—the first act of murder in the Bible—and for his punishment was placed under a curse and exiled as a fugitive. Cain is
then briefly identified in two New Testament passages (Heb 11:4;
Jude 1:11), where he serves as a "†type" of one who does evil. The
figure of Cain, however, became prominent in Jewish literature in
the first century AD. Philo of Alexandria describes Cain as "full of
impiety" (*On the Cherubim* 65). Josephus calls Cain "very wicked" in contrast
to Abel, who was "the lover of righteousness" (*Jewish Antiquities* 1.53). The
Apocalypse of Abraham (24:5) says that Cain was "led by the adversary to break
the law," and the *Testament of Benjamin* (7:5) speaks of "those who are like Cain
in the envy and hatred of brothers." When John describes Cain as "belonging
to the devil" and a worker of evil, he is not only drawing on the story in Gen
4:1–25 but also reflecting the wider Jewish tradition of his day that identified
Cain and Abel as "types" of two contrasting ways of life: Cain as the epitome
of evil and Abel as the righteous one, pleasing to God.

came to regard Abel as a †type of the persecuted righteous person and Cain as a type of the wicked. It is important that we recognize the link that John is making between living righteously and loving our brothers and sisters, on the one hand, and doing evil and hating them, on the other. Cain is the prime biblical example of someone whose deeds were not pleasing to the Lord, and who then killed his brother out of envy and hatred.

3:13–15   When John says in verse 13, **Do not be amazed, [then,] brothers, if the world hates you**, he is making a subterranean connection between Cain's hatred of his brother and the †world's hatred of Christians. As Jesus said, "If you belonged to the world, the world would love its own; but because you do not belong to the world, and I have chosen you out of the world, the world hates you" (John 15:19).

In verse 14, John gives a criterion by which we can know that we really belong to Christ: **We know that we have passed from death to life because we love our brothers**. To pass "from death to life," to move from a state of separation from God to having communion with the One who is "eternal life," is to become a Christian. Jesus said, "Whoever hears my word and believes in the one who sent me has eternal life and will not come to condemnation, but has passed from death to life" (John 5:24). We know that this has happened for us when we love our brothers and sisters.

John then offers several statements contrasting love and murder. **Whoever does not love remains in death**. Someone may claim to be a Christian, but if love is not present, then that person remains in a state of separation from God. Furthermore, **Everyone who hates his brother is a murderer**. If we hate our brother or sister, then we are already breaking the commandment "You shall not kill." John is making the same startling connection between hatred and murder that we find in Jesus' teaching in the Sermon on the Mount: "You have heard that it was said to those of ancient times, 'You shall not murder.' . . . But I say to you that if you are angry with a brother or sister, you will be liable to judgment" (Matt 5:21–22 NRSV). Hatred of a brother or sister is no light matter. By linking hatred to murder, John shows the seriousness of the command to love one another.

John is assuming that we **know that no murderer has eternal life remaining in him,** because murder is a grave sin that cuts us off from a living relationship with God. By contrast, if we are loving our brothers and sisters, then we know that we have eternal life abiding in us.

3:16–18   John now recalls us to the source of our love (he will develop this at length in 4:8–19): **The way we came to know love was that he laid down his life for**

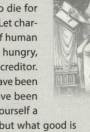

St. Augustine on Charity in Action   **LIVING TRADITION**

In one of his homilies on 1 John, St. Augustine comments,

> Look, this is where charity begins. If you aren't yet ready to die for
> your brother, be ready to give of your goods to your brother. Let char-
> ity strike your heart now, so that you don't act for the sake of human
> display but out of mercy's inmost marrow. . . . Your brother is hungry,
> he is needy. Perhaps he is anxious and is being pressed by a creditor.
> He has nothing, you have something. He is your brother. You have been
> purchased together; your price is the same; both of you have been
> redeemed by the blood of Christ. . . . For if you don't show yourself a
> Christian by your deeds, everyone may call you a Christian, but what good is
> the name where there is no reality?[a]

a. *Homilies on 1 John* 5.12 (*Homilies on the First Epistle of John*, trans. Boniface Ramsey, ed. Daniel E.
Doyle and Thomas Martin, WSA 3/14 [Hyde Park, NY: New City Press, 2008], 85–86).

us; so we ought to lay down our lives for our brothers. The RSV states this
in a more striking way: "*By this we know love,* that he laid down his life for us"
(italics added). We are not the originators or authors of love. We come to know
what love is only by seeing with faith how Jesus himself laid his life down for
us. There is an echo here of Jesus' own words: "This is my commandment, that
you love one another as I have loved you. Greater love has no man than this,
that a man lay down his life for his friends" (John 15:12–13 RSV). There is
also an implied contrast here between Christ and Cain. Cain envied and then
murdered his brother, but Christ offered his own life for the sake of those who
would become his brothers and sisters.[1]

By means of a rhetorical question, John challenges us to make our love active
and real: **If someone who has worldly means sees a brother in need and refuses
him compassion, how can the love of God remain in him?** This is practical
Christian life. Our love for one another is not merely a sentiment, a feeling,
but rather concrete action stemming from real concern and compassion.[2] If
we see a brother or sister in real physical, material, or spiritual need but fail to
meet that need when we could have done so, how can this be a manifestation of
real love, the love that God has poured out on us? Obviously, it cannot. And so

1. Peter Rhea Jones, *1, 2 & 3 John*, SHBC (Macon, GA: Smith & Helwys, 2009), 141.
2. The Greek word translated as "compassion" is literally "inner parts" (heart, lungs, liver, intestines).
This anatomical region of the body (often translated as "heart") was commonly seen as the center of
mercy and compassion and is applied to God (Luke 1:78) and the Christian faithful (Phil 2:1; Col 3:12;
Philem 1:7).

John concludes with a direct exhortation: **Children, let us love not in word or speech but in deed and truth**. Those who are truly the children of God display love in concrete ways; they do not simply claim to love or talk about loving, but show their love in action (see James 2:15–16).

Reflection and Application (3:16–18)

As much as any passage in the Bible, 1 John 3:16–18 explains what love is and what imitating Christ's love means for Christians. Many Christians think of love as a feeling. But here it is described as a concrete action. Most of us assume that the opportunity to lay down our lives for others will happen only rarely. But John tells us here that laying down our lives includes making our livelihood—our material possessions—available to help our brothers and sisters in need. For John, almsgiving is not just the exercise of personal virtue; it is the test of whether the love of God dwells in us.

No one has been more insistent and eloquent than Pope Francis in calling for the Church to remember the poor and needy. Citing this passage from 1 John, he beckons us to hear the cry of the poor and contribute to their need:

> Each individual Christian and every community is called to be an instrument of God for the liberation and promotion of the poor, and for enabling them to be fully a part of society. This demands that we be docile and attentive to the cry of the poor and to come to their aid. A mere glance at the Scriptures is enough to make us see how our gracious Father wants to hear the cry of the poor. . . . If we, who are God's means of hearing the poor, turn deaf ears to this plea, we oppose the Father's will and his plan; that poor person "might cry to the Lord against you, and you would incur guilt" (Deut 15:9). A lack of solidarity towards his or her needs will directly affect our relationship with God: "For if in bitterness of soul he calls down a curse upon you, his Creator will hear his prayer" (Sir 4:6). The old question always returns: "How does God's love abide in anyone who has the world's goods, and sees a brother or sister in need and yet refuses help?" (1 John 3:17). (*Evangelii Gaudium* 187)

Confidence before God (3:19–22)

---

[19][Now] this is how we shall know that we belong to the truth and reassure our hearts before him [20]in whatever our hearts condemn, for God is greater than our hearts and knows everything. [21]Beloved, if [our] hearts

do not condemn us, we have confidence in God ²²and receive from him
whatever we ask, because we keep his commandments and do what pleases
him.

NT: John 14:13–14; 15:7; 16:23–24

Catechism: God's mercy greater than our hearts, 208, 1781, 2845; praying with confidence for
   our needs, 2631

Lectionary: 5th Sunday of Easter, Year B (1 John 3:18–24)

John turns our attention back to how we know that we belong to God: **[Now]**   **3:19–20**
this is how we shall know that we belong to the truth and reassure our hearts
before him in whatever our hearts condemn. To what does "this" refer? It
points back to loving our brothers and sisters "in deed and truth" (v. 18). The
point is that if we are indeed loving others, then this enables us to "reassure
our hearts" about our standing before God. "Reassure" could also be translated
as "convince" (NJB).³

Why is John speaking about reassuring our hearts? And what does he
mean by this? Because the grammatical structure of verses 19–20 is unclear,
we cannot determine John's meaning with certainty. There are two main interpretations. John may be saying that despite the just condemnation that arises
from the heart or conscience because of sin, God's mercy in Christ is greater
than our sin, and if we are truly striving to obey him, we can stand before
him in confidence: **God is greater than our hearts and knows everything.**
But John may instead be saying that whenever our hearts falsely condemn
us,⁴ our love of our brothers and sisters—manifest by sharing our time, tal-
ent, and treasure with those in need—is evidence to us that we are in a good
relationship with God.⁵

The difference between the two interpretations hinges on whether the "condemnation" of our hearts is true or false, accurate or inaccurate. Both interpretations are in fact true. Our hearts do often condemn our conduct or intentions,
sometimes truly and sometimes falsely. But God knows us better than we do
ourselves, and he is greater than our hearts. His true knowledge is greater than
our false perceptions of ourselves, and his mercy is greater than our genuine

---

   3. For this Greek verb meaning "convince" or "persuade," see Acts 21:14; 23:21; for the meaning
"reassure," see 2 Macc 4:34; Matt 28:14.
   4. The NJB translation seems to adopt this interpretation: "even if our own feelings condemn us."
   5. For a summary of what Raymond Brown calls a "severe" interpretation of 3:19–20 in the Christian
tradition that presents God as a stricter judge of our lives than our own consciences, see *The Epistles
of John: Translated, with Introduction, Notes, and Commentary*, AB 30 (Garden City, NY: Doubleday,
1982), 459–60. Most commentators, however, believe that John's purpose here is not to warn the faithful
of God's stringent judgment but rather to reassure troubled consciences.

failures and sins. If we hold fast to God and his truth, then we can stand confidently and not give way to condemnation.

3:21–22   John now sets forth a benefit of standing before the Lord in confidence: **Beloved, if [our] hearts do not condemn us, we have confidence in God**.[6] If in fact our hearts, now reassured, do not truly condemn us, then we can entrust ourselves fully to God. God himself—and not our own hearts—is the source of our confidence. The result of this confidence is that we **receive from him whatever we ask, because we keep his commandments and do what pleases him**. Later in the letter, John qualifies "whatever we ask" by adding "according to his will" (5:14). The point is that we can ask boldly and expect to receive from God what we ask because we are in a good relationship with him. In other words, keeping his commandments and living in a way pleasing to God is evidence to us that we are in the kind of relationship with God in which we can ask freely for what we need.[7]

Summary: Believe and Love (3:23–24)

---

[23]**And his commandment is this: we should believe in the name of his Son, Jesus Christ, and love one another just as he commanded us.** [24]**Those who keep his commandments remain in him, and he in them, and the way we know that he remains in us is from the Spirit that he gave us.**

OT: Gen 6:3

NT: John 1:33; 3:18; 14:17; 15:10; 20:31

Catechism: believing in Jesus Christ, 151; keeping the commandments, 2052–55, 2072; the gift of the Spirit, 733–36

Lectionary: 5th Sunday of Easter, Year B (1 John 3:18–24)

3:23   Here, in midletter, John gives a compact summary of the whole letter. He has just named keeping the commandments (v. 22) as one of the main criteria for what pleases God, and now he gives a concise summary of what pleasing God entails: **And his commandment is this: we should believe in the name of his Son, Jesus Christ, and love one another just as he commanded us**. It is noteworthy that John speaks of a "commandment" in the singular but then names

---

6. For John's first invitation to have confidence before the Lord, see 2:28.

7. We find close parallels in the Gospel of John (14:13–14; 15:7; 16:23–24), where Jesus assures his disciples that they can now ask freely of the Father in his name.

two parts to this commandment: "believe" and "love." Faith and love together are the heart of Christian life; they are inseparable.[8]

We have just considered the second part on loving one another (in vv. 11–15), and John will treat this topic again in greater detail in 4:7–21. It is the first part of this commandment that calls for attention here.

John says that God's commandment is that we "believe in the name of his Son, Jesus Christ." This sounds strange in our ears. How can we be commanded to believe? For John, faith is not only assent to propositions; it also includes an act of internal trust and surrender to God and an outward confession of faith.[9] The Father has sent the Son as savior of the †world, and he sets before us the basic choice to believe or not to believe. "Whoever believes in him will not be condemned, but whoever does not believe has already been condemned, because he has not believed in the name of the only Son of God" (John 3:18). Belief is not just a matter of having adequate information; rather, it reflects the attitude of our heart toward God. By referring to God's commandment that we believe in Jesus Christ, John is underlining the necessity of true faith for being in good standing with God. This is what God requires: that we believe in Jesus and love one another.

In the remainder of the letter John offers four more variations of this call to believe, and it is instructive to gather and view them together:

- "Everyone who believes that Jesus is the Christ is begotten by God" (5:1).
- "Who . . . is the victor over the world but the one who believes that Jesus is the Son of God?" (5:5).
- "Whoever believes in the Son of God has this testimony within himself" (5:10).
- "I write these things to you so that you may know that you have eternal life, you who believe in the name of the Son of God" (5:13).

Clearly, to believe in the "name" of God's Son is to believe that he is the Christ, the Son of God, who has cleansed us from all sin. For John, believing in Jesus Christ for our salvation is central to true Christian life (John 20:31). To believe in Jesus is a fundamental part of being obedient to God and his word.

John returns to speaking of the commandments in the plural, and now he   3:24
links keeping the commandments with mutual abiding: **Those who keep his**

---

8. Peter Jones calls vv. 23–24 a "synthesis scene" that "sums up the thrust of the Epistle" (*1, 2, & 3 John*, 154). Here we find joined together the two commandments that "are the very essence of Johannine Christianity."

9. For the importance of "confessing" or "acknowledging" our faith in Jesus, see 2:23; 4:2–3, 15.

St. Bede on Faith and Love

LIVING
TRADITION

Bede the Venerable comments, "At first [John] wrote 'commandment' in the singular and then subsequently added two commandments, namely, faith and love, because undoubtedly these cannot
be separated from one another. For without faith in Christ we are
not able to love one another properly nor can we truly believe in
the name of Jesus Christ without brotherly love."[a]

a. *The Commentary on the Seven Catholic Epistles*, trans. David Hurst, CSS 82 (Kalamazoo,
MI: Cistercian Publications, 1985), 198.

commandments remain in him, and he in them. We can hear an echo of Jesus'
own words: "If you keep my commandments, you will remain in my love, just
as I have kept my Father's commandments and remain in his love" (John 15:10).
The idea of *mutual* abiding—God abiding in us, we abiding in God—is a recur-
ring theme in 1 John (2:24, 27; 4:13, 15–16). We abide in God through faith and
love; God abides in us through the Holy Spirit, who graciously imparts divine
power and life to us. When we keep the commandments from the heart by the
power of God, we strengthen our relationship with God; we "remain" in his
†grace and in a life-giving relationship with him. Faithful obedience cultivates
our †fellowship with the Trinity.

John makes the presence of the Spirit a further criterion by which we can
know that we abide in God: **the way we know that he remains in us is from
the Spirit that he gave us**.[10] This is the first direct mention of the Spirit in
the letter, though John's reference to the "anointing" (2:20, 27) most likely
refers to the Spirit as well. From this point onward the role of the Spirit will
be more pronounced (4:1–6, 13; 5:6–8). The gift of the indwelling Spirit,
through which the Father and Son come to dwell in us, is one of the primary
marks of the new †covenant: "You know [the Spirit], because he abides with
you, and he will be in you" (John 14:17 NRSV). In the New Testament, the
presence of the Spirit is not simply believed in as an article of faith but is
something experienced by Christians. The Spirit not only often acts powerfully in the midst of the believers (see Acts 4:31; 10:44–47) but also witnesses
internally to the hearts of the faithful that they are truly children of God
(Rom 8:15–17; Gal 4:6).

10. John offers a nearly identical restatement of this verse in 4:13: "This is how we know that we
remain in him and he in us, that he has given us of his Spirit."

The Spirit Abiding in the Human Race

BIBLICAL BACKGROUND

In Gen 6:3 the Lord God announces, "My spirit shall not abide in man for ever, for he is flesh" (RSV). Certain Fathers of the Church saw in these words evidence for a progressive removal of the Spirit from the human race because of the multiplication of sin (Gen 6:5). In John's Gospel, John the Baptist gives testimony to seeing the Spirit descend upon Jesus at his baptism: "I saw the Spirit descend as a dove from heaven, and it remained on him" (John 1:32 RSV). The word "remain" or "abide" (*menō*) is decisive here. The Spirit of God could not "abide in" or "remain with" the descendants of the old Adam, who were captive to sin, but now finds a new place of abiding in Christ, the second Adam. According to John, Jesus is the one who "gives the Spirit without measure" (John 3:34 NRSV); he promises the disciples that the Spirit will abide with them and be in them (John 14:17); and he breathes the Spirit upon them (John 20:22) in a way that recalls the original breathing by God upon Adam (Gen 2:7). For John, the gift of the Spirit signals that God's purpose from the beginning has been fulfilled. The Spirit, who was withdrawn from the descendants of the first Adam, has found a permanent dwelling place in Jesus and in those who belong to him.

Reflection and Application (3:23–24)

In the course of chapter 3, John teaches us what it means to be the children of God who abide in him. He concludes this section with the first direct reference in the letter to the Spirit of God and says that we "know" that God abides in us because he has given us his Spirit. But what does this mean? How do we "know" that the Spirit is abiding in us? What is the evidence? What are the signs? One sign is the witness of the Holy Spirit in our hearts assuring us that we are truly children of God (Rom 8:15–17). Other signs include the fruit of the Spirit manifested in our daily lives (Gal 5:22–23), the charismatic gifts of the Spirit that build up the body (1 Cor 12:3–13; Gal 3:5; Heb 2:4), and a new ability to follow the commandments through the power of the Spirit (Rom 8:1–14; Gal 5:16–17). But John himself in this letter points to two other signs of the Spirit's work. The first he names explicitly: "This is how you can know the Spirit of God: every spirit that acknowledges Jesus Christ come in the flesh belongs to God" (4:2). One clear and sure sign that we have the Spirit is our confession of Jesus Christ. As Paul says, "No one can say 'Jesus is Lord' except by the Holy Spirit" (1 Cor 12:3 RSV). A second undoubted sign of the Spirit's work is that we love one another. As Paul says, "God's love has been poured into our hearts through the Holy Spirit that has been given to us" (Rom 5:5 NRSV). As John makes abundantly clear, we can love only because God has loved us first. Thus for John, believing in and confessing Jesus Christ and loving one another as God has loved us are the sure signs that we have the Spirit of Christ effectively at work in us.

Test the Spirits

1 John 4:1–6

This section circles back to themes raised in 2:15–23 and draws a sharp contrast between those who belong to God and those who belong to the †world and the †antichrist. The new aspect of John's teaching here is the distinction between opposing "spirits" and the need to discern which spirit is from God.

The Spirit of God versus the Spirit of Antichrist (4:1–3)

---

¹**Beloved, do not trust every spirit but test the spirits to see whether they belong to God, because many false prophets have gone out into the world. ²This is how you can know the Spirit of God: every spirit that acknowledges Jesus Christ come in the flesh belongs to God, ³and every spirit that does not acknowledge Jesus does not belong to God. This is the spirit of the antichrist that, as you heard, is to come, but in fact is already in the world.**

NT: Matt 7:15; 24:24; John 1:14; 1 Cor 12:3; 1 Thess 5:20–21; 2 John 1:7
Catechism: Jesus coming in the flesh, 423, 463–65; the deception of the antichrist, 675–76

Addressing his audience as **Beloved**,[1] John opens with a command: **do not**   4:1–3
trust every spirit but test the spirits to see whether they belong to God. What does John mean by "spirit" or "spirits" here? The use of the plural shows that John means something like the root spiritual influence or the animating force

---

1. For this title of address, see also 2:7; 3:2, 21; 4:7, 11.

behind teaching and prophecy (e.g., 1 Cor 12:8–11). John will clarify shortly that the spirit that is from God is in fact the Holy Spirit, and that the spirits that are not from God draw their power from the spirit at work in the †antichrist. John cautions his readers not to "trust" or "believe" everything that purports to be from God. They must "test"—that is, discern—whether a given prophecy or teaching is truly from God or not. Paul offers similar counsel: "Do not despise prophetic utterances. Test everything; retain what is good" (1 Thess 5:20–21).

It is essential to recognize that both the spirit that is from God—the Holy Spirit—and the spirit of the antichrist work through human agents. This is why John straightaway raises the specter of false prophets: **many false prophets have gone out into the world**. John is echoing a warning against the rise of false prophets that Jesus himself gives: "Beware of false prophets, who come to you in sheep's clothing, but underneath are ravenous wolves" (Matt 7:15 [see 24:24]).

These false prophets have "gone out into the world" by going about and promoting their teaching in public. They are almost certainly the teachers and others whom John identifies in 2:19 as having left the church. The false prophets have departed spiritually and gone out into "the world" in a second sense, showing their true colors. By their teaching and practice they indicate that they are not from God. Does not the Church today experience the reality of false teachers who have "gone out into the world," disseminating teaching that purports to be Christian truth but that in fact denies that Jesus Christ has come in the †flesh as the unique Savior for the salvation of the world?

In verse 2, John turns his attention to how we can discern the spirits—that is, determine what spiritual teaching is from God and what is not. **This is how you can know the Spirit of God: every spirit that acknowledges Jesus Christ come in the flesh belongs to God**. The test is whether the human being through whom the "spirit" speaks confesses that Jesus Christ has come in the flesh. In this case, the discernment of spirits is based on the confession of faith. If Jesus Christ is confessed as incarnate, as having come "in the flesh," then this must be the Holy Spirit speaking. "No one can say 'Jesus is Lord' except by the Holy Spirit" (1 Cor 12:3 NRSV). We should also recognize here John's emphasis on the genuine †incarnation of the Son: "And the Word became flesh and dwelt among us" (John 1:14 RSV).

To the contrary, **every spirit that does not acknowledge Jesus does not belong to God**. John offers a variation on this in his second letter: "Many deceivers have gone out into the world, those who do not acknowledge Jesus Christ as coming in the flesh; such is the deceitful one and the antichrist" (2 John 1:7). Every prophet or teacher who denies that Jesus is the Son of God who has become incarnate is simply not from God; rather, this is **the spirit of the antichrist**. John is simply restating and rephrasing what he said in 2:18–23: the faithful have been taught that the antichrist **is to come**, but John reminds them that the antichrist **in fact is already in the world** (see sidebar, "Background to the Antichrist," p. 169). In other words, the battle against the antichrist is not just for some time in the distant future; it is the task of the Christian faithful already in the present.

From God, Not from the World (4:4–6)

> ⁴You belong to God, children, and you have conquered them, for the one who is in you is greater than the one who is in the world. ⁵They belong to the world; accordingly, their teaching belongs to the world, and the world listens to them. ⁶We belong to God, and anyone who knows God listens to us, while anyone who does not belong to God refuses to hear us. This is how we know the spirit of truth and the spirit of deceit.

NT: John 14:17; 15:26; 16:13, 33
Catechism: victory over the world, 377; the Spirit of truth, 692, 1848

John now develops the contrast between those who belong to God and those   4:4–6
who belong to the †world. He assures his readers, **You belong to God, children**, and he adds, **and you have conquered them**, referring to the false prophets who have departed from the church and gone out into the world. How have they "conquered" these false teachers? By refusing to accept their false teaching and by holding to the confession that Jesus Christ has come in the flesh for our salvation. John then identifies the source of their strength to conquer: **for the one who is in you is greater than the one who is in the world**. Jesus himself assured his disciples, "In the world you will have trouble, but take courage, I have conquered the world" (John 16:33). Through the indwelling Spirit, Christ himself—the one who conquered the world—now lives in them, and so they have power to be victorious over "the evil one." Earlier in the letter John twice told his hearers, "You have conquered the evil one" (2:13–14). Now he tells them how they conquer the evil one, the one who is in the world: through the Spirit of Christ who dwells within them.

In verse 5, John offers this further description of the false prophets: **They belong to the world; accordingly, their teaching belongs to the world, and the world listens to them**. Here John uses the "world" to refer to human society as dominated by sin and under the power of the devil. These false teachers have the spirit of the world. They speak from this spirit, and predictably the world listens to them because they are saying things that are pleasing to those who are in the world. John does not describe here the content of this "worldly" teaching, but given his description of the "world" in 2:15–17, we can assume that it includes elements that stir up sensual desire and entice the mind away from God and toward boasting in worldly possessions and power.

In verse 6, John restates his main point—**We belong to God**—but at the same time situates himself as part of the apostolic teaching authority that speaks the truth of God's word: **anyone who knows God listens to us, while anyone who does not belong to God refuses to hear us**. Who is the group represented by "us" here? It could refer to all the faithful—to the entirety of the Church—but probably it has special reference to John and others as authoritative teachers who heard, saw, and touched the "Word of life" (see 1:1–3). In other words, John is presenting himself as part of the apostolic teaching authority, in contrast to the false teachers and prophets who have departed from the Church and denied the faith.

John presents this authority as a criterion for discerning a true from a false spirit; it **is how we know the spirit of truth and the spirit of deceit**. If we heed the true apostolic teachers, this is a sign that we know God and are of him. If we follow those who contradict the apostolic testimony, this shows that we "belong to the world," because we are following the spirit of "deceit," which is the spirit of †antichrist.

Reflection and Application (4:1–6)

The need to "test the spirits" is every bit as crucial in our time as it was in John's. We face an array of philosophies, ideologies, and worldviews that barrage us from every direction, and many of these have made deep inroads among the Christian people. We could easily miss the fact that in these verses John is calling us to develop a discerning mind, to distinguish what is of God and what is not, to discern what is true from what is deceitful. What tools does John point to that can help us in this very difficult and demanding task? First, we have the Holy Spirit dwelling within us, teaching us the truth and leading us into all truth (see 2:20, 27). Second, we have the faith itself and especially the fundamental truth that the Son of God—the Word of life—has become incarnate for our salvation (see 4:2). Any teaching that denies or ignores this truth cannot be from God. Finally, we have the apostolic witness (now enshrined in the Scriptures) and the ongoing teaching authority in the Church (see 4:6). It

The Two Spirits

BIBLICAL BACKGROUND

John's distinction between the "spirit of truth" (the Holy Spirit) and the "spirit of deceit" (the spirit of antichrist) finds an echo in several Jewish writings of his day, and in particular in the writings of the Jewish community that lived in Qumran on the shore of the Dead Sea from approximately the second century BC until AD 70. The Qumran community collected a library of various Jewish writings, and they also wrote texts of their own. The remains of this library are known as the †Dead Sea Scrolls.

In their writings we find a sharp distinction between two spirits, one from God and another from the devil: "God has appointed for human beings two spirits in which to walk until the time of his visitation: the spirits of truth and iniquity. . . . All the sons of righteousness are under the rule of the prince of light and walk in the ways of light, but all the sons of iniquity are under the rule of the angel of darkness and walk in the ways of darkness."[a] In Qumran theology, it is God who appoints which spirit we are to walk in; it is fixed by him. For John, however, we have the choice whether to follow the "spirit of truth" or "the spirit of deceit." John calls the faithful to critically "test the spirits" and to abide in the Holy Spirit, whom they have received.

a. *The Community Rule* 3.17–21 (cited in Raymond E. Brown, *The Epistles of John: Translated, with Introduction, Notes, and Commentary*, AB 30 [Garden City, NY: Doubleday, 1982], 487).

is no easy task to test the spirits of our age and to discern what is of God and what is not, but as children of God we have been equipped with what we need to do this. Our task is to take up the challenge and, in courage and humility, to make use of these gifts for discernment.

Third Movement:
Walk in Love

1 John 4:7–5:12

Walking in Love

1 John 4:7–21

This section, one of the most powerful in the New Testament, brings John's treatment of love to its climax. John has already addressed the call to love one another on two occasions (2:5–11; 3:10–18), but now he offers an extended meditation on what love is, where it originates, and how it must be expressed. What John makes abundantly clear is that love originates in God, because God is love, and is manifested preeminently in the gift of his Son to die for us. Our love for one another is essential but is entirely dependent on God's prior love for us.

The Order of Love (4:7–10)

⁷Beloved, let us love one another, because love is of God; everyone who loves is begotten by God and knows God. ⁸Whoever is without love does not know God, for God is love. ⁹In this way the love of God was revealed to us: God sent his only Son into the world so that we might have life through him. ¹⁰In this is love: not that we have loved God, but that he loved us and sent his Son as expiation for our sins.

OT: Lev 25:9; Num 5:8; Ezek 44:27; 2 Macc 3:33
NT: John 3:16
Catechism: call to love one another, 459, 1823–25; God is love, 221, 733; God loving us by sending his Son, 457–58, 604, 620
Lectionary: 6th Sunday of Easter, Year B (1 John 4:7–10); Solemnity of the Most Sacred Heart of Jesus (1 John 4:7–16); Memorial of St. Augustine

4:7–8   John begins by renewing the call to mutual love (see 3:11, 23): **Beloved, let us love one another**. The call to love our brothers and sisters in fact functions as bookends to this entire section (see v. 21). It is John's primary message and charge to the Christian community. But John is not just renewing his exhortation to love one another; he is intent on explaining why we should love one another and where love originates. And so he continues: **because love is of God**. Love has its origin in God; the source of love is in God himself. Furthermore, **everyone who loves is begotten of God and knows God**. In other words, if we truly display love, this proves that we have been begotten of God, because if we were not born of God's seed, we could not truly love (see 2:29; 3:9). Our practice of love also demonstrates that we know God, because if we were not in a living relationship with God, we could not truly love. Conversely, **Whoever is without love does not know God**. If we fail

---

St. Augustine on the Centrality of Love

These verses (4:7–8) were among St. Augustine's favorite texts of Scripture. The revelation that "God is love" and that "God's love has been poured into our hearts through the Holy Spirit" (Rom 5:5 ESV) provided the heart of Augustine's theology and spirituality. He writes in his work on the Trinity, "Therefore God the Holy Spirit, who proceeds from the Father, when he has been given to man, inflames him to the love of God and of his neighbor, and is himself love. For man has not whence to love God, unless from God; and therefore he says a little after, 'Let us love him, because he first loved us.'"[a] For Augustine, love is also the key that opens the door to a true understanding of the Bible: "Scripture enjoins nothing but love"; thus, "Anyone who thinks that he had understood the divine scriptures or any part of them, but cannot by his understanding build up this double love of God and neighbor, has not yet succeeded in understanding them."[b] Finally, love is the true mark of the Church, the "city of God": "Two cities have been formed by two loves: the earthly by the love of self, even to the contempt of God; the heavenly by the love of God, even to the contempt of self."[c] In the judgment of Pope John Paul II, "It is no small merit of Augustine's to have narrowed all of Christian doctrine and life down to the question of charity."[d]

a. *De Trinitate* 15.17.31 (*NPNF*[1] 3:217 [modified]).
b. *On Christian Teaching* 2.10.15; 1.36.40 (*On Christian Teaching*, trans. R. P. H. Green, OWC [Oxford: Oxford University Press, 1997], 76, 27).
c. *The City of God* 14.28 (*NPNF*[1] 2:282–83).
d. *Augustinum Hipponensem* 2.5 (Apostolic Letter, August 28, 1986).

to love, this shows that we do not have a living knowledge of God himself. And for John, to be "without love" is especially failing to love our brothers and sisters in concrete, practical ways (see the commentary on 3:17–18).

At this point John adds a short explanatory phrase that is momentous: **for God is love** (he will repeat this verbatim in 4:16). God not only *shows* love but *is* love. John identifies the very being of God with love (and love with God). According to the Catechism (221), "God's very being is love. By sending his only Son and the Spirit of love in the fullness of time, God has revealed his innermost secret."[1] Saint Augustine expresses how astounding this revelation is: "If nothing at all were said in the other pages of the scriptures, and this were the one and only thing that we heard from the voice of the Spirit of God, that *God is love*, we wouldn't have to look for anything else."[2]

Now that we know that love is *from* God and that in fact God *is* love, John **4:9–10** goes on to state how love was preeminently made known in human history: **In this way the love of God was revealed to us: God sent his only Son into the world so that we might have life through him**. There is a clear echo here of the famous text from John 3:16: "God so loved the world that he gave his only Son, so that everyone who believes in him might not perish but might have eternal life." God's love, of course, is manifested in many ways in the †world. But John points here to the primary and full revelation of this love: the Father sent the Son—his only-begotten Son[3]—into the world so that we might have life in him.

In order to underline that love originates with God and not with us, John adds: **In this is love: not that we have loved God, but that he loved us and sent his Son as expiation for our sins**. In other words, our human efforts to love do not define what love is. It is God—who *is* love—who defines what love is. How has he done this? By sending his Son to take away our sins. Jesus came to give us life (v. 9) but also to be the "†expiation for our sins" (on the meaning of "expiation," see commentary on 2:2). He came to take away our sins, reconcile us to the Father, and bring us eternal life. *This* is what love is. As Paul says, Jesus showed his greatest love for us while we were helpless and sinful: "God proves his love for us in that while we were still sinners Christ died for us" (Rom 5:8). Jesus offered himself entirely to the Father out

---

1. See 1 Cor 2:7–16; Eph 3:9–12.
2. *Homilies on 1 John* 7.4 (*Homilies on the First Epistle of John*, trans. Boniface Ramsey, ed. Daniel E. Doyle and Thomas Martin, WSA 3/14 [Hyde Park, NY: New City Press, 2008], 107).
3. To describe the uniqueness of Jesus, John here uses the same word, *monogenēs* ("only" or "only-begotten"), used of Jesus in the Gospel of John (1:14, 18; 3:16, 18).

St. Bede on God's Love for Us

Bede the Venerable comments, "Grace, in truth, precedes man, that he might love God with that love by which he might do what is good.... And this is the greatest evidence of the divine charity towards us, because when we ourselves did not know how to entreat him for our sins, he sent his Son who might gratuitously give pardon to us who believed in him and call us to the fellowship of the Father's glory."[a]

a. *The Commentary on the Seven Catholic Epistles*, trans. David Hurst, CSS 82 (Kalamazoo, MI: Cistercian Publications, 1985), 204.

of love for us, so that we, his "enemies" (see Rom 5:10), might become his friends.

Reflection and Application (4:7–10)

On one level, John's call to "love one another" does not sound at all revolutionary to our contemporary culture. Christians know that they are supposed to love each other, and even our wider secular society values love and praises those who show love in culturally approved ways. All this is a good thing, and it shows that a Christian ethic of love has penetrated our culture to some degree.

The problem that we face is that our cultural understanding of love is often superficial, sentimental, and unanchored. It often boils down to being nice. Our notion of love has become unmoored from the very source of love, which is God himself, and from the prime example of love: Christ coming to redeem us from our sins. John's insistence on the true origin of love is a reminder that all of us need to hear. We should be careful not to reverse the terms of John's famous saying, "God is love." Yes, God is love, but not all that passes for love is therefore "God." We cannot begin with our own safe and secure notions of love and then apply them to what God is like. No, "in *this* is love," John insists, that God sent his Son to atone for our sins. This is costly love that has led us out of darkness and into God's light. This love is ready to die for one's friends. Shockingly, this love is even ready to die for one's enemies. When we hear John's words about loving one another, our main task is to be more deeply converted to what love truly is, and then by God's †grace to manifest that love in action to both friends and enemies alike.

The Perfection of Love (4:11–18)   #14

¹¹**Beloved, if God so loved us, we also must love one another.** ¹²**No one has ever seen God. Yet, if we love one another, God remains in us, and his love is brought to perfection in us.**

¹³**This is how we know that we remain in him and he in us, that he has given us of his Spirit.** ¹⁴**Moreover, we have seen and testify that the Father sent his Son as savior of the world.** ¹⁵**Whoever acknowledges that Jesus is the Son of God, God remains in him and he in God.** ¹⁶**We have come to know and to believe in the love God has for us.**

God is love, and whoever remains in love remains in God and God in him. ¹⁷**In this is love brought to perfection among us, that we have confidence on the day of judgment because as he is, so are we in this world.** ¹⁸**There is no fear in love, but perfect love drives out fear because fear has to do with punishment, and so one who fears is not yet perfect in love.**

OT: Pss 19:9; 34:9, 11; Prov 1:7

NT: John 1:18; 13:35; 14:9; 17:14; Acts 9:31; Rom 8:15; 2 Cor 5:11; Eph 5:21; 1 Pet 1:17

Catechism: God's love given through the gift of the Spirit, 735; the call to love another, 459, 1823–25; love overcoming servile fear, 1828, 1964, 1972

Lectionary: 7th Sunday of Easter, Year B (1 John 4:11–16); Solemnity of the Most Sacred Heart of Jesus (1 John 4:7–16)

With the true origin of love now in place, John renews the call to love one **4:11–12** another: **Beloved, if God so loved us, we also must love one another.** *Since* God has loved us (the "beloved"), we also ought to love one another in the same way. Obviously we cannot love one another in exactly the same way that God has loved us. We cannot send our only-begotten Son to die for the sins of the whole †world! But we can participate in Christ's own love for us by laying down our lives for one another—that is, by caring for one another, both spiritually and materially, and by being ready even to die for one another.

Why would John add at this point, **No one has ever seen God**? This is a clear echo of John 1:18: "No one has ever seen God. The only Son, God, who is at the Father's side, has revealed him." The point is that we cannot see the invisible God with human eyes. It is Jesus, the Word made †flesh, who reveals the Father to us: "Whoever has seen me has seen the Father" (John 14:9). But now with Jesus ascended to the Father's right hand, how is God to be "seen" among the faithful? Through the practice of loving one another: **Yet, if we love one another, God remains in us.** "Now that the Son has returned to the Father, God is made known on earth by those who through faith in his Son have become his

What Does It Mean to Love One Another?

BIBLICAL BACKGROUND

When John calls us to "love one another," he is speaking first of all about love for our brothers and sisters in Christ, those who are part of the Christian community. He is by no means excluding love for those outside the body of Christ but is directly addressing here how Christians are meant to love one another in concrete ways. This is consistent with teaching on love for one another elsewhere in the Bible. Jesus taught that the second great commandment is, "You shall love your neighbor as yourself" (Matt 22:34–40; Mark 12:28–34; see Luke 10:25–28). He is quoting here from Lev 19:18, and when we examine this verse in context, it is clear that "neighbor" is equivalent to "brother": "You shall not hate your brother in your heart, but you shall reason with your neighbor, lest you bear sin because of him. You shall not take vengeance or bear any grudge against the sons of your own people, but you shall love your neighbor as yourself: I am the †Lord" (Lev 19:17–18 RSV) (for the equivalence of "brother" and "neighbor," see also Deut 15:2). In the Old Testament, "neighbor" normally refers to someone who is part of the people of Israel, or by extension to "sojourners" from other nations who have come to dwell in Israel and who either share Israel's way of life or are favorable to the people of Israel (see Deut 10:18–19). One's neighbor, then, is part of the wider family. In the New Testament, "neighbor" normally carries the same connotation. When Paul and James quote the commandment "You shall love your neighbor as yourself," the context is caring for one another within the

continued on next page

children—if they love one another."[4] The word "remains" (NABRE) is perhaps better translated as "abides" (RSV). If we truly love one another, this is a sign and manifestation that God really is abiding in us, and it enables God to be seen among us. This has profound implications for Christian community: where there is genuine mutual love, God is truly present, dwelling in the community, manifested in the members' mutual love.

Further, as we love our brothers and sisters, God's **love is brought to perfection in us**. "God abides in us and the love that comes from him reaches perfection in our love for others."[5] In other words, the love that God has shown to us in Christ reaches its "perfection"—its "completion" or "culmination"—when we show this same love to one another. This is one of the main reasons God

4. F. F. Bruce, *The Epistles of John: Introduction, Exposition and Notes* (London: Pickering & Inglis, 1970), 109.

5. Raymond E. Brown, *The Epistles of John: Translated, with Introduction, Notes, and Commentary*, AB 30 (Garden City, NY: Doubleday, 1982), 521.

Christian community (Gal 5:13–15; James 2:8–9), though Paul also applies "love of neighbor" more broadly (see Rom 13:8). The Christian community, like the family, is a "school of love" where we learn to love in concrete ways. A special responsibility remains to care for one another within the body of Christ (Gal 6:10; 1 Pet 2:17).

Nevertheless, this mutual love within the Christian community is meant to overflow into all our relationships, which is why the portrayal of one's "neighbor" in the parable of the good Samaritan is so powerful. The man who was beaten and left by the side of the road for dead had a special claim on the priest and the Levite: they were part of the same nation (the Jews) and were objectively "neighbors" to one another. But his compatriots walked past and refused to act as a neighbor should. It was left to a Samaritan to fulfill the role of neighbor, though Samaritans and Jews normally had no dealings with each other (John 4:9). At the close of the parable, Jesus asks, "Which of these three, do you think, proved himself a neighbor to the man who fell into the bandits' hands?" (Luke 10:36 NJB). The point of the parable is to reveal what the "love of neighbor" looks like in action and at the same time to teach us that the love that we show to our brothers and sisters in the faith should also be extended to those outside the community of faith. This is the radical newness of Jesus' teaching on love: we are called to love not just our neighbor but even our enemy (Matt 5:43–45; Luke 6:27–35). And we do this because God has first done this for us (Rom 5:8, 12) and has poured his own love into our hearts so that we can love the way he does (Rom 5:5).

has shown his love: that we should be changed by this love and show the same love to one another. John is recalling and reapplying a phrase that he first used in 2:5: "Whoever keeps his word, the love of God is truly perfected in him." In this earlier passage, God's love is perfected as we obey his word; here, his love is perfected as we love one another. There is no opposition between these two: the primary "word" of God that we are called to keep is his command to love one another. The two statements on the perfection of God's love in us are closely connected and mutually illuminating.

In verses 13–15, John steps aside from his treatment of love to take up   4:13–15
the theme of abiding in God (picking up the theme just stated at the end of v. 12). Francis Martin calls this a "remarkable Trinitarian passage" on the theme of the indwelling of God.[6] John is answering an implied question: How do we know that we truly abide in God? His answer: **This is how we**

6. Francis Martin, "1 John," in *The International Bible Commentary*, ed. William R. Farmer (Collegeville, MN: Liturgical Press, 1998), 1831.

know that we remain in him and he in us, that he has given us of his Spirit. This is a slight variation on 3:24: "The way we know that he remains in us is from the Spirit that he gave us." In 3:24 John speaks of "the Spirit that he gave us"; here in 4:13 he says, "he has given us *of* his Spirit" (NJB: "a share in his Spirit"). Is there a difference between being given his Spirit and being given *of* his Spirit? Probably not. For John, one of the hallmarks of the Christian life is the presence and activity of the Holy Spirit within us. God has given us his Spirit through Christ, and therefore we have a share in his life and power.

We should also recognize here a return to the theme of *mutual* abiding: "we abide in him and he in us" (NRSV). Mutual abiding is one of the characteristic truths of both 1 John (2:24, 27; 4:15–16) and the Gospel of John (6:56; 15:4, 7). God abides in us through his word and Spirit; we abide in God through faith and love. Mutual abiding is another way of speaking of the "†fellowship" or "communion" that we have with the Father and the Son (1:3, 6, 7).

Then in verse 14 John restates and sums up what he said in 1:1–3: **Moreover, we have seen and testify that the Father sent his Son as savior of the world**. This is the unique and special testimony that John and other eyewitnesses were privileged to give because they saw, heard, and touched "the Word of life" (1:1–3).[7] The title "savior of the world" appears only twice in the New Testament, here and in John 4:42 when the Samaritans profess their faith in Christ: "We no longer believe because of your word; for we have heard for ourselves, and we know that this is truly the savior of the world."

John then applies this to the whole Church: **Whoever acknowledges that Jesus is the Son of God, God remains in him and he in God**. Mutual abiding is not reserved for the original eyewitness followers of Jesus; everyone who acknowledges Jesus as the true Son of God abides in God. Thus, the confession of Jesus as the Son of God serves as another criterion of mutual abiding in God. In sum, John recalls and restates in verses 13–15 two criteria by which we can know that there is mutual abiding between the believer and the trinitarian God: we have the Spirit dwelling in us, and we confess that Jesus is the Son of God, the true savior of the world.

4:16–18   John now returns to the theme of love and connects it with mutual abiding: **We have come to know and to believe in the love God has for us**. In other words, believers in Christ have come to know experientially God's love for

---

7. The combination of the verbs "see" and "testify" links this passage to the opening proclamation in 1:1–2 as the eyewitness testimony to the Son.

St. Thomas Aquinas on the Greatness of Love

LIVING TRADITION

Thomas Aquinas observed, "In this way charity is greater than the other [theological virtues]. Because the others, in their very nature, imply a certain distance from the object, since faith is of what is not seen, and hope is of what is not possessed. But the love of charity is of that which is already possessed, since the beloved is, in a manner, in the lover, and, again, the lover is drawn by desire to union with the beloved; hence it is written (1 John 4:16): 'He who abides in love, abides in God, and God in him.'"[a]

a. *Summa theologiae* I-II, q. 66, a. 6 (*Summa Theologica*, trans. Fathers of the English Dominican Province [New York: Benzinger, 1947], 1:870–71, modified).

them and to believe in this love because they believe that the Father sent the Son out of love for the world. John repeats the remarkable revelation that **God is love** and adds that whoever **remains** or "abides" in the love of God **remains in God** himself—and **God in him** or her. There is a certain logic at work here: since God is love, if we abide in love, then we also abide in God. The two are inseparable.

Then in verse 17 John picks up the theme (from v. 12) of how love is brought to completion in us: **In this is love brought to perfection among us, that we have confidence on the day of judgment**. What John means by this is not perfectly clear, both because the grammar of verses 16–17 is difficult and because the connection between perfect love and confidence on the day of judgment is not obvious. One clue to John's meaning appears in what immediately follows: **because as he is, so are we in this world**. This is "†Johannine shorthand" intended to show how we are like Christ and therefore can stand in confidence before him.

A glance over to John 17:14 helps explain what John means: "I gave them your word, and the world hated them, because they do not belong to the world any more than I belong to the world." Just as Jesus is the one who knows the Father's love and came into the world but is not of the world, so the faithful are those who know this love as God's children and are in the world but are not of the world. John is saying, then, that God's love comes to maturity ("perfection") in us when we are living as faithful disciples of Christ in the world; and this gives us confidence rather than terror before God on the day of judgment. In the words of Peter Jones, the result is that "in such a moment of intense reckoning when one's whole being comes under scrutiny, the Christian will actually experience boldness rather than frantic fear."[8]

The perfection of love at the judgment is further illustrated in verse 18: **There is no fear in love, but perfect love drives out fear**. If we have perfect love—that is, love that is brought to maturity—then fear has no place. Why? **Because fear has to do with punishment, and so one who fears is not yet perfect in love**. John has in mind a fear or terror of God that exists when we see him as an exacting judge hovering over us and waiting to punish us, both in the present and in the future at the day of judgment. If we know the love of God and are confident that he watches over us to show us his mercy (see Isa 30:18), then this kind of fear is expelled. The casting out of this fear shows that we have "perfect love"—that is, love that is fully active and mature.

It is helpful to make a distinction between two kinds of fear. The fear that John is referring to here is sometimes called "servile fear," the fear of a slave who does not know the love of God but is motivated only by the threat of punishment. Paul makes this distinction between the fear of a slave and the confidence of a son or daughter of God: "You did not receive a spirit of slavery to fall back into fear, but you received a spirit of adoption, through which we cry, 'Abba, Father!'" (Rom 8:15). The Scriptures of both the Old and the New Testament also speak of "fear" or "reverence" in a positive sense, as something that ought to mark our mature relationship with God.[9] It is in fact one of the gifts of the Spirit (Isa 11:2).[10] This is often called "filial fear"—that is, the reverence that a son or daughter has for the Father. This reverence for God is not inconsistent with "perfect love" but is an irreplaceable element of our love for God.

Summary on the Love of God (4:19–21)

[19]We love because he first loved us. [20]If anyone says, "I love God," but hates his brother, he is a liar; for whoever does not love a brother whom he has seen cannot love God whom he has not seen. [21]This is the commandment we have from him: whoever loves God must also love his brother.

NT: Rom 5:5
Catechism: call to love one another, 459, 1823–25

8. Peter Rhea Jones, *1, 2 & 3 John*, SHBC (Macon, GA: Smith & Helwys, 2009), 192.
9. See, e.g., Pss 19:10; 34:10, 12; Prov 1:7; Acts 9:31; 2 Cor 5:11; Eph 5:21; 1 Pet 1:17.
10. For "the fear of the Lord" as one of the seven gifts of the Spirit, see Catechism 712, 1831, 2217.

If we were in any doubt that our love is always a response to God's love, John
underlines this truth concisely and clearly one final time: **We love because he
first loved us.**[11] All of our love, whether for God or one another, is based on the
fact that God loved us first. This means that our love is never self-originating;
it does not arise from within ourselves. Instead, we can love because he first
loved us and has given us a share in his own love: "God's love has been poured
into our hearts through the Holy Spirit who has been given to us" (Rom 5:5
ESV). This also means that we must love in return. We cannot truly receive
God's love and have †fellowship with a loving God if we are unwilling to love
in return. To sum this up: we *can* love because he first loved us, and we *must*
love because he first loved us.

Here John returns to the incompatibility between claiming to love God and
refusing to show love to God's children, our brothers and sisters in Christ: **If
anyone says, "I love God," but hates his brother, he is a liar**. John Painter
remarks, "For our author, not to love is to hate."[12]

This incompatibility between our words and our actions is heightened by
a comparison: **whoever does not love a brother whom he has seen cannot
love God whom he has not seen**. The logic is this: if we are not showing love
to those who are visible and right before our eyes, then we are lying if we say
that we are loving the One who is invisible.

There is a deeper logic at work here. For John, the Christian is by definition
one who is begotten of God: "Everyone who loves is begotten by God" (4:7).
If we are failing to demonstrate love for our brothers and sisters in Christ, this
shows that we are not abiding in God and so do not have his love freely at work
in and through our lives. If we are failing to show fraternal charity, this proves
not only that we are not loving God but also that we cannot love God because
we do not have his love acting through us. "If someone who has worldly means
sees a brother in need and refuses him compassion, how can the love of God
remain in him?" (3:17). It is easy to say and think that we love God, but in
reality our love for God is manifested in how we treat others.

John concludes by summing up his entire point: **This is the commandment
we have from him: whoever loves God must also love his brother**. The fundamental commandment that we have from God is to love God and neighbor:
if we claim to be, and genuinely are, those who love God, then we must also
love our neighbor.

11. This verse could also be translated as a command, "Let us love because he first loved us," but
most scholars conclude that John is stating a truth, not giving a command.
12. John Painter, *1, 2, and 3 John*, SP 18 (Collegeville, MN: Liturgical Press, 2002), 285.

Reflection and Application (4:11–21)

Mutual Abiding

Six times in this letter John speaks about mutual abiding, using the verb "abide" or "remain" to designate how God is in us and we are in God: "God is love, and whoever abides in love abides in God, and God abides in him" (4:16 ESV). But what does this look like in real life? God is always the one who takes the initiative: he comes to us. Scripture speaks about God coming to dwell in us through the Holy Spirit, communicating to us deeply that we are beloved sons and daughters of God (Rom 8:14–17). We respond to God's initiative by placing our faith in him, by welcoming him into our lives, and by loving him in return. We show this love by zealously keeping his word and obeying his voice. We seek to align our lives with his will. This mutual abiding grows as we draw near to God in daily prayer, as we partake of the sacraments with faith and expectation, and as we turn away from everything that is incompatible with God. Mutual abiding leads to a deeper friendship with God in which we can talk with him and hear his voice. It also leads to a deeper identification with the cross and with Christ's suffering, as Paul exemplifies when he says, "For his sake I have suffered the loss of all things, and count them as refuse, in order that I may gain Christ and be found in him, . . . that I may know him and the power of his resurrection, and may share his sufferings, becoming like him in his death, that if possible I may attain the resurrection from the dead" (Phil 3:8–11 RSV). Mutual abiding expresses our share in the divine life of the Trinity—Father, Son, and Spirit.

Love without Fear

Pope Francis made a deep impression on the whole world in the first few days of his pontificate. His striking example and provocative words moved many to show love to the poor and to step out of comfortable quarters to go to those in need. In his first Easter address, Francis called the faithful to receive God's mercy and make it known in the world: "Let us accept the grace of Christ's resurrection! Let us be renewed by God's mercy, let us be loved by Jesus, let us enable the power of his love to transform our lives too; and let us become agents of this mercy, channels through which God can water the earth, protect all creation, and make justice and peace flourish."[13] What is it that enables the Church—enables us—to go out freely and show love to others? It is a mature

13. Easter Address (March 31, 2013).

love (a "perfect" love) that is no longer hampered by fear. How is fear driven out? When we are so deeply aware of the love that God has for us that we become convinced that nothing can separate us from the love of God in Christ Jesus our Lord (Rom 8:39). In his remarks to the cardinals on the eve of the conclave, Francis warned against the danger of a Church that lives to protect itself and remain within itself. Instead, the Church must go out of itself and evangelize by the power of Christ. We are called to love our brothers and sisters—and even our enemies! But we can do this only when fear has been driven out and we are free to love with the same love that God showed to us by sending his Son.

Faith as the Foundation of Love

1 John 5:1–12

This section of the letter speaks about faith as the foundation of love. It is here that we see most clearly how John weaves together faith or believing and love. Love was the central theme of the last section; now faith comes to the fore as the foundation for our life in Christ. At the same time, John interweaves previous themes in new ways: keeping the commandments of God, overcoming the †world by our faith, and seeing eternal life as the central goal. By believing and loving, we participate in the very life of God, which is eternal life.

Children of God Living in Faith and Love (5:1–5)

¹Everyone who believes that Jesus is the Christ is begotten by God, and everyone who loves the father loves [also] the one begotten by him. ²In this way we know that we love the children of God when we love God and obey his commandments. ³For the love of God is this, that we keep his commandments. And his commandments are not burdensome, ⁴for whoever is begotten by God conquers the world. And the victory that conquers the world is our faith. ⁵Who [indeed] is the victor over the world but the one who believes that Jesus is the Son of God?

OT: Deut 30:11, 15–16
NT: Matt 11:29–30; John 14:15; 16:33; Acts 15:10; 2 John 1:6; Rev 2:7
Catechism: Jesus as the Christ, 436
Lectionary: 2nd Sunday of Easter, Year B (1 John 5:1–6)

John opens with two parallel statements that sum up the main theme: **Everyone** 5:1
who believes that Jesus is the Christ is begotten by God, and everyone who
loves the father loves [also] the one begotten by him. How are the two statements ("everyone who believes," "everyone who loves") related? John is uniting two of his major themes in the letter: faith in Jesus Christ and love for one
another. The one who truly believes that Jesus is the Christ, the Son of God,
shows that he or she has been begotten by God. This faith is evidence that the
seed of God is active and producing its fruit in the believer. Then John adds,
literally, "Everyone who loves the one begetting loves the one begotten from
him." Is John making a general reference to the begetting of offspring? Yes,
in the sense that he is using a human example to illustrate the essential link
between love of God and love for our brothers and sisters. John is assuming
that his readers understand and accept this principle: if we love the father (the
parents), we will love the offspring as well. "Love" here is not an emotion but
practical love in action. John then applies this to God the Father, as the one
who has begotten us to a new life in Christ. The "one begotten by him" could
refer to Jesus the unique Son, but the context shows that John has the Christian
believer in mind. The one who believes is begotten of God, and so if we love
the Father, who begets, then we should also love those begotten of God. John
is giving here a further rationale for what he said in 4:21: "Whoever loves God
must also love his brother."

Now John reverses the logic of his claim. Previously, he said we know that 5:2–3
we love God because we love the brothers and sisters; now he says, **In this way**
we know that we love the children of God when we love God and obey his
commandments. Is John confused here, giving a circular argument, proving
A from B and then turning around and proving B from A? In fact, he is not
being illogical, because he is grounding both claims on the reality that we are
begotten of God and abide in him. If we truly abide in God, then we will love
God and love the brothers and sisters—these always occur together.[1] Each one
becomes a kind of demonstration for the reality of the other.

For John, loving God consists primarily in keeping his commandments:
For the love of God is this, that we keep his commandments. This mirrors
2 John 1:6: "This is love, that we walk according to his commandments."[2] We

---

1. Raymond Brown describes the love of God and of one another as simultaneous: "The idea is not
that only after (or if) we love God and obey his commandments, do we then love God's children, but
that the two actions go together and are simultaneous" (*The Epistles of John: Translated, with Introduction, Notes, and Commentary*, AB 30 [Garden City, NY: Doubleday, 1982], 539).
2. A close parallel is 1 John 2:3: "The way we may be sure that we know him is to keep his commandments."

The Burdensomeness of the Law

The commandments to love God and one another are already
found in the Old Testament (Deut 6:5; Lev 19:18), and Moses tells
the people of Israel that the commandment of God "is not too hard
for you" (Deut 30:11 NRSV). In fact, living by the law of God was
intended to be a source of life and blessing for God's people (see
Deut 30:15–16). Why and in what way did the commandments of
God then become "burdensome"? There are several reasons why
the law proved to be burdensome, but two stand out. First, the
commandments of God became burdensome in part because of
the way that they were interpreted and applied. Jesus critiques the Pharisees
in his day for applying the law of God in such a strict way that they lay burdens
on the people: "They tie up heavy burdens, hard to bear, and lay them on the
shoulders of others; but they themselves are unwilling to lift a finger to move
them" (Matt 23:4 NRSV). But the deeper reason for the burdensomeness of
the law is uncovered by Paul: because the power of sin is living within us, we
cannot keep the law even when we desire to. The law itself is "holy and just
and good" (Rom 7:12 NRSV); the problem lies within ourselves. Christ has set
us free from the power of sin, and through the indwelling Spirit we are now
capable of keeping the commandments of God (see Rom 8:3–4).

also hear an echo of Jesus' words: "If you love me, you will keep my commandments" (John 14:15). What are his commandments? Certainly the †Decalogue
is included here, but for John the primary commandments are summed up
in 3:23: "We should believe in the name of his Son, Jesus Christ, and love one
another just as he commanded us." Faith and love sum up the primary obliga-
tions of the Christian life.

John then adds, **And his commandments are not burdensome**. The mention
of burden brings to mind Jesus' words in Matt 11:29–30: "Take my yoke upon
you, and learn from me; for I am gentle and humble of heart, and you will find
rest for your souls. For my yoke is easy, and my burden light" (NRSV). Peter
speaks of the burden of the Old Testament law in Acts 15:10: "Why, then, are
you now putting God to the test by placing on the shoulders of the disciples a
yoke that neither our ancestors nor we have been able to bear?" Are the commandments of God intrinsically burdensome? No, but because of the power of
sin living within us, we are not able to keep the commandments from the heart.
For Christians, however, because they have been begotten of God and have his
Spirit living within them, the commandments of God "are not burdensome" (see

Figure 9. St. John the Apostle's tomb in Ephesus

sidebar, "The Burdensomeness of the Law"). As Peter Jones says, "With great confidence in the power of the new birth, the apostolic writer sees the keeping of the divine commandments as doable."[3] This does not mean the elimination of all difficulty in living the Christian life and following the call of God (see Matt 16:24; Mark 14:36; Heb 5:7), but it does mean that as we live in Christ through the power of the Spirit, following God's ways is not a burden for us.

5:4–5 John now returns to the theme of Christians overcoming the †world: **whoever is begotten by God conquers the world**. Because we have the power of Christ at work within us, we can "conquer" the world and its desires (see 2:16; see also commentary on 4:4–6). But now John makes a new connection between conquering and our faith: **the victory that conquers the world is our faith**.[4] How is this so? Is it not Jesus himself who has conquered the power of the world and its desires through his death on the cross (John 16:33; 1 John 2:1–2)? Yes, but we share in this victory and become conquerors of the world

3. Peter Rhea Jones, *1, 2 & 3 John*, SHBC (Macon, GA: Smith & Helwys, 2009), 209.
4. This is the only occurrence of the noun "faith" (*pistis*) in both the Gospel of John and the †Johannine Epistles. Normally, John uses the verb "believe" (*pisteuō*) to describe the action of believing (ninety-eight times in John's Gospel, nine times in 1 John).

and its desires through our faith in him: **Who [indeed] is the victor over the world but the one who believes that Jesus is the Son of God?**[5] This is another case of †Johannine shorthand: by "faith" and "believes" John sums up all that comes *through* this faith—confession of Jesus as the true Son of God, abiding in Christ, the life and witness of the Spirit within, and the power of God through our fellowship with him. It is by our faith that we are enabled to overcome the disordered desires of the world, to proclaim the †gospel, to endure persecution, to love our enemies, even to change the world. As Rev 12:11 says, "They conquered him by the blood of the Lamb / and by the word of their testimony; / love for life did not deter them from death."

Reflection and Application (5:1–5)

The call to love *all* those begotten of God (1 John 5:1) has important ecumenical implications for today. †Ecumenism is the effort put forth by all Christians to make "the partial communion existing between Christians grow towards full communion."[6] Recognizing the action of the Holy Spirit, the Catholic Church embarked on a new path toward Christian unity at the Second Vatican Council and embraced Christians from other churches and ecclesial communities as brothers and sisters in Christ: "For men who believe in Christ and have been truly baptized are in communion with the Catholic Church even though this communion is imperfect."[7] The Church continues to call all the faithful to participate in this embrace and to work to increase the unity that we share with other Christians: "For that reason, all the faithful are called upon to make a personal commitment toward promoting increasing communion with other Christians."[8]

The first and crucial step in this process is to see other Christians as genuinely begotten by God, as really and truly our brothers and sisters in Christ. For example, in our relationships with non-Catholic Christians, our first goal should be to find what we have in common, to discover the *koinōnia*, or †fellowship, in Christ and the Spirit that we already share. Perhaps this will be a common concern for the protection of human life, or a common love of the word of God, or even our personal love for Jesus and prayer. When trust has

5. In the book of Revelation, the author ("John") speaks repeatedly about conquering in Christ (Rev 2:7, 11, 17, 26; 3:5, 12, 21; 21:7).
6. Pope John Paul II, *Ut Unum Sint* (That They May Be One) 14.
7. Second Vatican Council, *Unitatis Redintegratio* (Decree on Ecumenism) 3.
8. *Directory for the Application of Principles and Norms for Ecumenism*, Pontifical Council for Christian Unity (1993), 55.

been established and we have gained a mutual recognition of one another as brothers and sisters in the Lord, then we can have fruitful discussions about the matters in which we differ. The second step is to gain the wisdom we need so that our efforts at promoting greater unity are guided by the Spirit and faithful to the Church's teaching.[9]

In all this, we place our hope in God: "Human powers and capacities cannot achieve this holy objective—the reconciling of all Christians in the unity of the one and only Church of Christ. It is because of this that the Council rests all its hope on the prayer of Christ for the Church, on our Father's love for us, and on the power of the Holy Spirit."[10]

Threefold Testimony: Water, Blood, and Spirit (5:6–8)

> [6]This is the one who came through water and blood, Jesus Christ, not by water alone, but by water and blood. The Spirit is the one that testifies, and the Spirit is truth. [7]So there are three that testify, [8]the Spirit, the water, and the blood, and the three are of one accord.

OT: Deut 19:15
NT: John 1:32–34; 3:5; 15:26; 16:13; 19:34–35
Catechism: water as type of the gift of the Spirit, 694; blood and water as types of baptism and Eucharist, 1225
Lectionary: 2nd Sunday of Easter, Year B (1 John 5:1–6); Baptism of the Lord, Year B (1 John 5:1–9)

John's reference to the "three witnesses" (water, blood, and Spirit) intrudes into **5:6** this section like a bolt from the blue. Why does John apparently step aside from his main themes to take up this testimony of the three witnesses? The wider context of verses 1–12 helps us in our task of interpretation: John is concerned in this section with belief in Jesus Christ as the true Son of God. The three witnesses, then, are intended to strengthen and confirm our belief in Jesus.

John opens with a claim about Jesus: **This is the one who came through water and blood, Jesus Christ**. Then immediately he adds, **not by water alone, but by water and blood**.[11] What does John mean by "water and blood," and why does he emphasize that it is not by water alone but also by blood

9. For the Church's guidance on how to engage in ecumenical relationships, see the *Directory* (1993), 102–42; also, Pope John Paul II, *Ut Unum Sint* 77–87, 97–99.
10. Second Vatican Council, *Unitatis Redintegratio* 24.
11. There is a change of preposition from "*through* water and blood" in the first clause to "*by* water and blood" in the second. Most commentators see no significant difference in this variation.

that Jesus came? John himself provides no explanation in the text. He is assuming that his original readers will understand what "through water and blood" means. For our part, we have to look back to the Gospel of John to seek John's meaning.

Water and blood are joined together just once in the Gospel, when the soldier's lance pierces the side of Christ: "One soldier thrust his lance into his side, and immediately blood and water flowed out. An eyewitness has testified, and his testimony is true; he knows that he is speaking the truth, so that you also may [come to] believe" (John 19:34–35). Here "blood and water" refers in some sense to Christ's death and the fruits of that death, but we are still left with the question, "What exactly do the water and blood signify?"

First of all, the flow of blood and water confirms the real bodily death of the Lord. His body was pierced with a spear, and out flowed blood and water. But clearly the †evangelist sees more in this than just a physical manifestation of Jesus' real death. The blood and water signify something important about the death of Jesus and what it means for us.

It is interesting that the order of the terms is reversed in 1 John. In the Gospel, the evangelist says that he saw "blood and water" flow from Christ's side, and this is probably the order in which he saw them appear. But here in the letter John speaks about "water and blood." Why this change of order? Possibly because John is drawing attention to the order of Christ's own baptism and death.[12] Jesus came by water through his baptism, submitting to the Father's plan as the incarnate Son of God (see John 1:32–34); he came by blood through his crucifixion, offering himself to the Father as the sacrifice for our sins (see 1 John 1:7). These two events mark, respectively, the inauguration and the conclusion of his earthly ministry. Jesus was not simply anointed by God for ministry through the water of baptism; he also shed his blood and died for our sins so that we might share in his divine life.[13]

But "water and blood" also points to the effects of Christ's work in the Church. The water that poured forth from his side signifies the water of baptism and the gift of the Spirit,[14] and the blood that poured forth signifies the gift of his

12. Francis Martin applies "water and blood" first of all to Christ's own baptism and crucifixion ("1 John," in *The International Bible Commentary*, ed. William R. Farmer [Collegeville, MN: Liturgical Press, 1998], 1831).

13. The second-century heretical teacher †Cerinthus was reputed to teach that the Spirit descended upon Christ at his baptism but then fled from him before his passion and death; he denied that God's anointed Son actually shed his blood for our sins (see Irenaeus, *Against Heresies* 1.26.1–2). By insisting that Jesus came "through water and blood," John is refuting anyone who teaches that Jesus did not really shed his blood for the forgiveness of sins.

14. "Water" is linked to baptism and the gift of the Spirit in John 1:26, 31, 33; 3:5, 23; 4:7–15; 7:38.

St. Leo the Great on the Three Witnesses

In his renowned *Tome* (449), St. Leo the Great quotes these verses from 1 John to uphold the full humanity of Christ and sees in them a reference to baptism and the Eucharist. Writing against anyone who would deny Christ's full human nature, he says,

> Let him understand from what source the "blood and water" flowed, when the soldier's lance pierced the side of the crucified one so that the church might be moistened both by washing and by the cup.... "And it is the Spirit who bears witness, because the Spirit is truth, for there are three which bear witness—the Spirit, the water, and the blood—and the three are one" (1 John 5:6–8). This means the Spirit of †sanctification and the blood of redemption and the water of baptism.... The Catholic church lives and grows by the faith that in Christ Jesus there is neither humanity apart from real divinity nor divinity apart from real humanity.[a]

a. *Tome* (*Letter to Flavian*) 5 (quoted in Richard A. Norris Jr., trans. and ed., *The Christological Controversy* [Philadelphia: Fortress, 1980], 153–54, modified).

body and blood in the Eucharist.[15] In other words, "water and blood" points, at one and the same time, to Christ's work of salvation and our reception of that work through the sacraments of baptism and the Eucharist.

John then adds, **The Spirit is the one that testifies, and the Spirit is truth**. In the Gospel of John, the Spirit testifies to Jesus as the Son of God at his baptism by descending upon him and remaining with him (John 1:32–33). The Spirit is also the one who gives testimony to Jesus among the disciples: "When the Advocate comes whom I will send you from the Father, the Spirit of truth that proceeds from the Father, he will testify to me" (John 15:26). He is "the Spirit of truth" who will guide the disciples into all truth (John 16:13). In this context, the testimony of the Spirit "consists in that action by which the truth of Jesus' baptism and death is brought to life within the Church through the sacraments of baptism and the Eucharist."[16] The Holy Spirit "testifies" to us about Christ by making the redemptive power of his work manifest in our lives.

John sums up this section by pointing to the unified testimony of the three 5:7–8 witnesses: **So there are three that testify, the Spirit, the water, and the blood,**

15. "Blood" is linked to Christ's body and blood in the Eucharist in John 6:53–56.
16. Martin, "1 John," 1832.

The "Johannine Comma"

LIVING
TRADITION

The "Johannine Comma" is a short passage that scholars today believe was later inserted in the manuscripts of 1 John in the Western Church, probably in the late fourth or early fifth century. This brief text, embedded in 1 John 5:7–8, runs as follows (the Johannine Comma is the text in italics): "And there are three who give testimony *in heaven, the Father, the Word, and the Holy Spirit. And these three are one. And there are three that give testimony on earth:* the spirit and the water and the blood. And these three are one."[a] What does this insertion add? It provides the witness of the three persons of the Trinity "from heaven" and places them in parallel to the three witnesses to Christ "on earth."

We can only make a conjecture about how this short passage came to be added to the text of 1 John. It probably was a note originally written into the margin of the manuscript to show the parallel between the three witnesses and the three persons of the Trinity. Over time this handwritten note may have been copied and inserted into the text itself. Then in several stages the Johannine Comma became part of the standard Western version of the Bible (both Protestant and Catholic) until the early part of the twentieth century. This addition is entirely sound in its teaching but is considered now to be a later addition. Today no major English translation includes the Johannine Comma in the text of 1 John, including officially approved versions for use in the Catholic Church.

a. This translation of the Johannine Comma follows the Douay-Rheims Catholic edition with one change: "Holy Ghost" in the Douay version is rendered "Holy Spirit" to follow the Latin original (*spiritus*) and to maintain the parallel to "spirit" in the second part of the passage.

and the three are of one accord. Under the law of Moses, two or three witness were required to establish the truth of a matter (Deut 19:15; see John 8:17). For John, our faith in Jesus is based on three witnesses that agree in their testimony: the Spirit, the water, and the blood. Jesus' baptism by water signifies that he has come in the †flesh for our sake; he offered his blood on the cross that we might have forgiveness of sins and new life in him; and he sent the Spirit to testify about him and to give witness within us to his true identity as the Son of God.[17] Sharing in the gift of the Spirit, regenerated by the waters of baptism, and participating in Christ's flesh and blood in the Eucharist, we are given God's

17. Some commentators link the gift of the Spirit to the sacrament of confirmation (chrismation in the Eastern Church) and see in the three witnesses a reference to the three sacraments of initiation: baptism, confirmation, and the Eucharist.

own threefold witness to Jesus that he is God's Son, anointed with the Spirit, who came in the flesh and died for our salvation.

Reflection and Application (5:6–8)

How can we apply what John says about the three witnesses to our daily lives? In his book *Jesus of Nazareth*, Pope Benedict XVI identifies full sacramental participation as one important application of this text. He observes that "in this double outpouring of blood and water, the Fathers saw an image of the two fundamental sacraments—Eucharist and Baptism—which sprang forth from the Lord's pierced side." Why, Benedict asks, does John insist that Jesus came not by water only but also by blood? "We may assume that he is alluding to the tendency to place all the emphasis on Jesus' baptism while setting the Cross aside." By this Benedict means "an attempt to create a Christianity of thoughts and ideas, divorced from the reality of the flesh" and from the sacraments.[18] Just as Jesus offered his body and blood on the cross, so we are called to a faith-filled participation in the body and blood of Christ in the Eucharist.

John also draws our attention to the witness of the Spirit: "The Spirit is the one that testifies, and the Spirit is truth" (v. 6). Through the Spirit we know and can proclaim that Jesus Christ is Lord (1 Cor 12:3). Through the witness of the Spirit we know that we are beloved sons and daughters of God (Rom 8:14–17). Our bodies have become temples of the Holy Spirit (1 Cor 6:19), and he works within us to make us progressively like Jesus himself (2 Cor 3:18). There is, of course, no opposition between the witness of the Spirit and the witness of the "water and blood" through sacramental life. They are "one" and are "of one accord." Our life in the Spirit should include a full sacramental life, and our sacramental life should be fully alive in the Spirit.

The Testimony of God to His Son (5:9–12)

[9]**If we accept human testimony, the testimony of God is surely greater. Now the testimony of God is this, that he has testified on behalf of his Son. [10]Whoever believes in the Son of God has this testimony within himself. Whoever does not believe God has made him a liar by not believing the testimony God has given about his Son. [11]And this is the testimony: God**

18. Joseph Ratzinger (Pope Benedict XVI), *Jesus of Nazareth*, part 2, *Holy Week: From the Entrance into Jerusalem to the Resurrection* (San Francisco: Ignatius Press, 2011), 225–26.

gave us eternal life, and this life is in his Son. [12]Whoever possesses the Son has life; whoever does not possess the Son of God does not have life.

NT: Mark 1:11; 9:7; John 5:26, 36–37; 6:40; 17:3
Catechism: faith in Jesus Christ as the Son of God, 150–51; faith as the beginning of eternal life, 163
Lectionary: Baptism of the Lord, Year B (1 John 5:1–9)

5:9–10   John continues the theme of giving testimony to Jesus Christ, but now he turns to God himself as the one who has given testimony to his Son.[19] He begins with a comparison: **If we accept human testimony, the testimony of God is surely greater.** The point is this: if we are willing to accept the testimony of people—and we do so in all sorts of matters—then surely the testimony that God himself gives is greater and worthy of our full acceptance. And what is **the testimony of God**? It is this: **he has testified on behalf of his Son.** The question naturally arises: How has God the Father given testimony to his Son? In the Gospels, the Father gives explicit testimony at both Jesus' baptism and transfiguration: the Father's voice is heard, declaring that Jesus is his "beloved Son" (Mark 1:11; 9:7). But the Father also gives testimony throughout Jesus' ministry through the works of power that he performed (see John 5:36–37). John probably also has in mind here the three witnesses (the Spirit, the water, and the blood) as means by which the Father has given testimony to his Son.

John then moves immediately to the issue of believing in Jesus, the Son of God, thus circling back to the theme that opened the chapter (faith in Jesus Christ): **Whoever believes in the Son of God has this testimony within himself.** By believing God's word concerning his Son, we receive this "testimony" within ourselves. The act of receiving the word of the †gospel actually causes that word to take root in us and grow, so that we have a living testimony within us; we become interiorly convinced of the reality of the lordship of Jesus such that we experience it in our daily lives. And the Spirit of God also continues to witness within us to Jesus as the true Son of God (see 2:20, 27). Characteristically, John states his point in a negative form: **Whoever does not believe God has made him a liar by not believing the testimony God has given about his Son.** If we reject God's own testimony to his Son, then we make God to be a liar (see 1:10), and we do not have his living testimony within us, for the simple reason that we have cast it away.

19. The Greek words for "testimony" (noun and verb) are highly concentrated in this section of the letter. Four of six occurrences of the verb "give testimony" (*martyreō*) appear in 5:6–10, and all six occurrences of the noun "testimony" (*martyria*) appear in 5:9–11.

Pope Benedict XVI on Eternal Life

LIVING TRADITION

In his encyclical letter *Spe Salvi* (Saved in Hope), Pope Benedict XVI reflects on the meaning of life:

> Jesus, who said that he had come so that we might have life and have it in its fullness, in abundance (see John 10:10), has also explained to us what "life" means: "this is eternal life, that they know you the only true God, and Jesus Christ whom you have sent" (John 17:3). Life in its true sense is not something we have exclusively in or from ourselves: it is a relationship. And life in its totality is a relationship with him who is the source of life. If we are in relation with him who does not die, who is Life itself and Love itself, then we are in life. Then we "live."[a]

a. *Spe Salvi* 27.

John now declares directly just what this testimony is: **And this is the tes-**   5:11–12
timony: God gave us eternal life, and this life is in his Son. This succinct
statement marvelously sums up the message of the entire letter. For John, God
is eternal life, and the Son too possesses this eternal life in himself: "Just as the
Father has life in himself, so also he gave to his Son the possession of life in
himself" (John 5:26). The testimony of the gospel is this, that God has given
this eternal life to us through his Son, Jesus Christ, and we have this life within
us even now: "This is the will of my Father, that everyone who sees the Son and
believes in him may have eternal life" (John 6:40).

This is why believing in the Son is so essential, because **Whoever possesses
the Son has life**. If the purpose of God is to give us a share in his very life, and
the Son himself is this life, then we must literally "have the Son"—that is, have
communion with the Son. As Jesus says to the Father, "Now this is eternal life,
that they should know you, the only true God, and the one whom you sent,
Jesus Christ" (John 17:3). Conversely, **whoever does not possess the Son of
God does not have life**, because the Son *is* "the eternal life / that was with the
Father" (1 John 1:2). Once again John has steered us back to his primary theme:
"life" consists in true †fellowship and communion with God himself—Father,
Son, and Spirit.

Summary and Conclusion

1 John 5:13–21

In these final verses John sums up his message and concludes the letter. Though he draws together many of his main themes, he seems especially concerned that his readers know the truth and be assured in this knowledge (the verb "know" occurs seven times in these closing verses).

John arranges his closing words in the following way. He begins by stating the purpose of the letter: that his hearers might know that they have eternal life dwelling within them (v. 13). Next he speaks about our confidence in approaching the Father in prayer, first for our own needs (vv. 14–15) and then for our brothers and sisters who have become entangled in sin (vv. 16–17). Finally, he reminds us about the truth that we know: we are born of God, we belong to God, and we abide in Jesus Christ (vv. 18–21).

Purpose of the Letter and Confidence in Prayer (5:13–15)

> [13]I write these things to you so that you may know that you have eternal life, you who believe in the name of the Son of God. [14]And we have this confidence in him, that if we ask anything according to his will, he hears us. [15]And if we know that he hears us in regard to whatever we ask, we know that what we have asked him for is ours.

NT: Matt 6:11; 7:7; John 14:13; Rom 8:26
Catechism: prayer of petition, 2634–36

To close the letter John returns to the theme of eternal life with which he began: **5:13**
I write these things to you so that you may know that you have eternal life.
He sums up the whole letter in terms of the eternal life that believers in Jesus
have come to possess. Here we should recall that all six occurrences of the word
"eternal" are linked directly with the word "life" in 1 John. Eternal life is what
we most need. It is the deepest desire of the human heart and the fundamental
gift that we receive. The Son of God, Jesus Christ, *is* eternal life (1:2; 5:11, 20),
and we receive this eternal life by abiding and living in the Son (2:24). But John
wants to ensure that we know we have eternal life. This is not a presumption
that we will automatically receive final salvation, but the confident assurance
that we **who believe in the name of the Son of God** really do have God's own
life abiding within us. We can be confident that we have genuine †fellowship
with the Father and the Son through the Spirit.

We now move to an important manifestation of having God abiding in us,   **5:14–15**
namely, confidence to approach God through intercessory prayer: **And we
have this confidence in him, that if we ask anything according to his will,
he hears us**. How can we claim to be in a relationship with God our Father if
we are not confident to approach him with our needs? Earlier in the letter John
already assured us that we can approach God confidently in prayer: "We have
confidence in God and receive from him whatever we ask" (3:21–22 [see John
14:13–14]). Now he adds the qualification that we must ask "according to his
will." By this he means that we should ask for things that are consistent with
what God has already revealed as his purpose and will. This includes praying for
the material goods that we need to live (Matt 6:11), but also asking for growth
in faith, love, holiness, and unity (see Jesus' own prayer for the disciples in John
17:9–21) and for the salvation of those we love. This also means that we should
seek the things that are his will for us right now. Because of our communion
with God, we can become more conformed to his will and ask confidently for
what he desires to give us.

John encourages us to ask with confidence and boldness because we live
in the Son and already have his life dwelling within us. And so we can be sure
that "he hears us" and that our prayers will be answered: **And if we know
that he hears us in regard to whatever we ask, we know that what we have
asked him for is ours**. This assurance echoes many promises of Jesus in the
Gospels that our Father is eager to grant us what we need (Matt 7:7–11; Luke
11:9–13) and that requests asked "in my name" (i.e., united to Jesus) will be
granted (John 14:13–14; 16:23–24). Thus we should pray with expectant faith
(Mark 11:22–24).

What John does not say is that our prayers will be answered exactly as we have prayed. We can be assured that God will hear our prayers and provide for us, but we are not guaranteed that every prayer will be fulfilled just as we desire it to be. This is why we need to strive to pray according to God's will. The more we are in union with him, the more our desires will be conformed to his, and the more we will pray in accord with his will. In the end, our confidence is not in our perfect knowledge of how to pray (see Rom 8:26) but in our Father's providential care for us.

We should recognize again John's emphasis on what we should know: if we know that God hears us, then we can also know that what we request is already ours—no matter when and how God in his providence will choose to fulfill these requests.

Reflection and Application (5:13–15)

Do we pray confidently for ourselves and others, knowing that God hears our prayer? The burden of John's exhortation is that we should approach our Father confidently and boldly, asking for what we need and praying for the restoration of those who have stumbled. Why do we so often lack this boldness? One reason is that "we do not know how to pray as we ought" (Rom 8:26). We are not sure how to pray or what to pray for, and so we do not pray at all. But this is why the Spirit has been given to us: to help us in our ignorance and lead us to pray according to the will of God. As we step out in prayer, the Spirit will lead us and help us. It is often while I am praying that I discover what I should pray for and receive direction and encouragement for how to continue to pray. Prayer begets prayer. As we venture out in prayer, we will be led further on.

There is, however, another reason why we often fail to pray with boldness and confidence: we do not really know God as our Father and have not yet experienced Christ abiding in us. For John, we can pray with confidence because we know our Father and already have his life abiding in us. What we need in this case is a fresh outpouring of the Holy Spirit, who witnesses to us that we are God's sons and daughters and who leads us to pray with boldness as the children of God that we truly are (Rom 8:14–16). This is what the Father seeks: children who can approach him confidently in Christ through the Spirit and who can cooperate with him in the advance of his mission.

Praying for Fellow Christians (5:16–17)

> [16]If anyone sees his brother sinning, if the sin is not deadly, he should pray to God and he will give him life. This is only for those whose sin is not deadly. There is such a thing as deadly sin, about which I do not say that you should pray. [17]All wrongdoing is sin, but there is sin that is not deadly.

OT: Num 15:22–36; 35:31–34
NT: Acts 5:1–11; 1 Cor 5:1–5
Catechism: intercessory prayer, 2574–84; mortal and venial sin, 1854–64

We now come to a difficult passage concerning intercessory prayer for our broth-   5:16–17
ers and sisters entrapped in sin. The first difficulty is what John means by sin that "is not deadly": **If anyone sees his brother sinning, if the sin is not deadly, he should pray to God and he will give him life. This is only for those whose sin is not deadly.**[1] The second and even greater difficulty is why John would say that we are not obliged to pray for one whose sin is "deadly": **There is such a thing as deadly sin, about which I do not say that you should pray.** To finish, John adds one further qualification: **All wrongdoing is sin, but there is sin that is not deadly.** By this, John is saying that every form of disobedience to God is sin, but there is nonetheless a distinction between sin that is deadly and sin that is not (see sidebar, "Distinctions between Kinds of Sins in the Old Testament," p. 238).

What are we to make of the distinction between "deadly sin" and "sin that is not deadly"? One line of interpretation links "sin unto death" with the phys- ical death of the sinner. On this view, John would be saying that we should not pray for someone who has already died in sin (like Ananias and Sapphira in Acts 5:1–11); that is, we should not pray for the dead who have died in sin. A few commentators have recommended this interpretation,[2] but John seems in context to be speaking about how we should pray for those who are still living, and if in fact he was speaking about prayer for those who have already died, he probably would have made this clear.

The main school of interpretation identifies "sin unto death" with a sin of great seriousness that leads to spiritual death. On this view, John is speaking

---

1. The phrase is literally "sin not unto death." There are three main ways to translate this phrase: (1) "sin not leading to death / that does not lead to death" (ESV, NIV); (2) "sin [that] is not deadly / that is not deadly sin" (NAB, NJB); (3) "what is not a mortal sin / whose sin is not mortal" (RSV, NRSV).

2. In ancient times, Bede the Venerable points to this interpretation (*Commentary on the Seven Catholic Epistles*, trans. David Hurst, CSS 82 [Kalamazoo, MI: Cistercian Publications, 1985], 224); among modern interpreters, F. F. Bruce considers it a possible interpretation of the text (*The Epistles of John: Introduction, Exposition and Notes* [London: Pickering & Inglis, 1970], 124–25).

Distinctions between Kinds of Sins in the Old Testament

The distinction between different kinds of sins has its origin in the Old Testament. The most basic distinction is that between unintentional and intentional sin. The sacrifices offered by the priests in the tabernacle (and later the temple) were for the most part directed toward making atonement for unintentional sins (see Lev 4:1–3; Num 15:22–29). When someone sinned intentionally and defiantly in a serious matter, that person was "cut off" from the people and sometimes put to death (Num 15:30–36). There is also a distinction made on the basis of the gravity of the sin, between, on the one hand, lesser sins that could be compensated for by sacrifice or payment and, on the other hand, graver sins, capital sins, that could not normally be atoned for by sacrifice (see Num 35:31–34; Deut 22:25–26; see also Catechism 1854). When someone committed blasphemy, idolatry, murder, kidnapping, or adultery, the penalty was either death or being "cut off" from the people, which could mean banishment. Most scholars believe that John's distinction between "sin unto death" and "sin not unto death" is linked to these Old Testament distinctions, though by no means is identical to them. John's "sin unto death" appears to indicate not just serious sin but an unrepentant and defiant rejection of faith in Jesus or the way of life that he teaches.

about transgressions like the sin of apostasy, the direct denial of Jesus Christ (see Matt 10:33; Mark 8:38; Heb 6:4–6), or what Scripture elsewhere calls the "sin against the Holy Spirit" (see Mark 3:28–29).[3] It is also possible that when John speaks of "sin unto death," he is including those from his own time who denied faith in Jesus and broke the bonds of communion in the Church.[4]

It is difficult to determine with certainty just what John means by "sin unto death" or "deadly sin."[5] I believe that the best interpretation is that John is

3. Augustine identifies the "sin unto death" primarily with apostasy (*Sermon on the Mount* 1.22.73); Pope John Paul II links "sin unto death" both with apostasy and the "sin against the Holy Spirit" (*Reconciliatio et Paenitentia* [Reconciliation and Penance] 17). It is important not to equate the sin against the Holy Spirit with apostasy; otherwise there would be no hope of repentance and forgiveness for those who commit apostasy.

4. The link between those who left the church and the "sin unto death" is made by Raymond E. Brown, *The Epistles of John: Translated, with Introduction, Notes, and Commentary*, AB 30 (Garden City, NY: Doubleday, 1982), 617–18; John Painter, *1, 2, and 3 John*, SP 18 (Collegeville, MN: Liturgical Press, 2002), 317; Peter Rhea Jones, *1, 2 & 3 John*, SHBC (Macon, GA: Smith & Helwys, 2009), 230.

5. The Church later made a distinction between mortal and venial sin (see Catechism 1854–64), which is similar to the distinction John is making here but probably not identical. According to most commentators, ancient and modern, John's "sin unto death" is more serious than what the Church

St. Ignatius of Antioch on Praying for False Teachers

LIVING
TRADITION

Writing in the early second century, Ignatius warns the church in Smyrna (modern Izmir, Turkey) to avoid contact with false teachers who are leading many astray. Nevertheless, he calls the church to pray for them in the hope that they might repent, confident that Jesus has the power to bring this about: "I am guarding you in advance against wild beasts in human form—people whom you must not only not welcome but, if possible, not even meet. Nevertheless, do pray for them, that somehow they might repent, difficult though it may be. But Jesus Christ, our true life, has power over this."[a]

a. *Letter to the Smyrnaeans* 4 (Michael W. Holmes, trans. and ed., *The Apostolic Fathers in English* [Grand Rapids: Baker Academic, 2006], 122).

referring to those living in serious, unrepented sin who cannot be reconciled to the Church by prayer for restoration because they are rejecting faith in Jesus Christ or refusing to follow his commandments. John may be operating with the same framework that Paul shows in 1 Cor 5:1–5 when he directs that the man who refuses to repent of living incestuously be removed from the community of faith. For John as for Paul, this act of exclusion does not presume or wish for the final condemnation of the sinner but is a means of handing the person over to the consequences of his own sin, "so that his spirit may be saved on the day of the Lord" (1 Cor 5:5). It is noteworthy that John does not forbid praying for those whose sin is "unto death"; he simply does not urge his hearers to pray for their restoration, given their present state. It is even possible that John is speaking here not about praying to God *for* someone who is caught in sin unto death but about praying *with* that person for restoration to full †fellowship with God and the Church. If so, John would be saying that we should not pray with those living in "sin unto death," because they cannot be restored as long as they are living in this sin. This would be in accord with Paul's counsel (1 Cor 5:1–5) for how to deal with the man engaged in incest. However we understand John's advice here, the Church in fact calls us not to despair of anyone's salvation, and to pray for everyone, even hardened sinners and apostates, that they might repent and come back to the faith and way of life they have rejected.

---

understands as "mortal sin." Those in mortal sin can repent and be restored by the prayer of the Church through the sacrament of penance; John seems to be speaking of those who are hardened in their rejection of Christ and who *while hardened* cannot be reconciled by the prayer of the Church.

Conclusion: What We Know in Jesus Christ (5:18–21)

---

¹⁸We know that no one begotten by God sins; but the one begotten by God he protects, and the evil one cannot touch him. ¹⁹We know that we belong to God, and the whole world is under the power of the evil one. ²⁰We also know that the Son of God has come and has given us discernment to know the one who is true. And we are in the one who is true, in his Son Jesus Christ. He is the true God and eternal life. ²¹Children, be on your guard against idols.

NT: John 12:31; 14:30; 16:11; 17:15; 20:28; 1 Pet 5:8–9; Rev 14:4
Catechism: Christ as true God, 242, 464–69; warning against idolatry, 2112–14

5:18–20   In these final words, John offers a summary of the letter's message in three parallel statements concerning what "we know." By "we" he means all the faithful who have come to know Jesus Christ and abide in him.

John's first statement about what we should know (v. 18) concerns sin and the power of the devil: **We know that no one begotten by God sins; but the one begotten by God he protects, and the evil one cannot touch him**. The first part ("We know that no one begotten by God sins") is a capsule summary of what John said earlier in 3:9: "No one who is begotten by God commits sin, because God's seed remains in him; he cannot sin because he is begotten by God." It is not that we as Christian believers are incapable of sin, but that God's life within us leads us into a way of righteousness free of sin, and when we follow that way, we will not sin (see the commentary on 3:9).

The meaning of the second part of the verse is unclear because the grammar is ambiguous and because there are several different versions of the text in surviving manuscripts.[6] The NABRE has "the one begotten by God" (the believer) being protected by God (the Father). This is possible but difficult grammatically. The plain sense of the grammar has "the one begotten by God" (Jesus) as the one protecting "him" (the believer). Jesus, the one begotten by God, protects those who belong to him.

The believer, then, is protected from the evil one, who is not allowed to "touch him." This means not that the believer is completely free from any influence or assault by the devil (see 1 Pet 5:8–9) but that he or she is not under the devil's power. As believers in Christ, we are no longer subject to the devil but now belong to Christ and the Father. We no longer have to fear the devil, and no matter what temptations or harassments may come, we do not have to be conquered by them.

---

6. For a concise summary of the variations in the manuscripts, see Painter, *1, 2, and 3 John*, 320–21.

The second statement about what we should know (v. 19) contrasts two kingdoms: **We know that we belong to God, and the whole world is under the power of the evil one**. The contrast is between those born of God, who belong to him (see 3:9, 10; 4:4, 6–7), and the †world, which "lies under the power of the evil one" (NRSV). John is reminding his readers that those who belong to God have overcome the evil one (2:13–14), while the world and those who belong to the world are subject to the power of the devil (3:12).

This does not mean that everything in the physical world is under the devil's power. God is the sovereign ruler of the world that he has made, and all things are under his power. But the "world" in John's sense here is human society that resists God and is therefore under the power of the devil and is subject to his influence (see commentary on 2:15–17). The devil has a certain authority over the world governed by sin and death that those who belong to Christ are no longer under.[7] "They have been ransomed as the firstfruits of the human race for God and the Lamb" (Rev 14:4).

The third statement about what we know (v. 20) considers our ability to recognize the truth: **We also know that the Son of God has come and has given us discernment to know the one who is true**. Jesus has come in the †flesh to give us true understanding and insight about who God truly is and what he has done for us. "The one who is true" could be a reference to the Father, but given the explanatory phrase that follows—**And we are in the one who is true, in his Son Jesus Christ**—it seems that John means to point to Christ Jesus as "the one who is true." In either case, John is reframing what he said earlier about the anointing of the Holy Spirit within us: "His anointing teaches you about everything and is true and not false; just as it taught you, remain in him" (2:27). In other words, we now have the divine life within us that teaches us the truth.

The meaning of the second part of verse 20, **He is the true God and eternal life**, is hotly contested. Some commentators apply the phrase to God the Father. To achieve this result, the first part of the verse must be translated so that "the one who is true" refers to the Father, as we see in the NJB: "so that we may know the One who is true. We are in the One who is true as we are in his Son, Jesus Christ. He is the true God and this is eternal life." This translation is grammatically possible but more difficult. We would adopt it especially if we were persuaded that John would be unlikely to call Jesus "the true God."

7. In the Gospel of John, Jesus three times identifies the devil as "the ruler of this world" (12:31; 14:30; 16:11), and he prays to the Father for his followers: "I do not ask that you take them out of the world but that you keep them from the evil one" (17:15).

However, a majority of commentators, both ancient and modern, apply the phrase "he is the true God" to Jesus himself. This is the most natural reading of the Greek text and is quite plausible in light of John's testimony to Christ's divinity elsewhere (John 1:1). Read in this way, John's extraordinary statement, "He is the true God and eternal life," serves as the climactic announcement of the letter, similar to Thomas's confession of Jesus toward the end of the Gospel of John: "My Lord and my God!" (John 20:28). It is one of the strongest witnesses to the full divinity of Jesus in the Bible and provides the biblical basis for the phrase "true God from true God" in the Nicene Creed.

5:21   John ends the letter abruptly with no closing greeting. Addressing his readers for the final time as **Children** (or "little children"), he cautions them, **be on your guard against idols**. The vocabulary is new,[8] but the point is consistent with the overall message of the letter. John is writing because the churches are under threat, and true faith in Jesus Christ is being undermined.

While the recipients of John's letter probably experienced societal pressure to participate in actual idolatrous rites (see 1 Cor 8:10; Rev 2:14, 20), "idols" here may represent forms of belief and practice that in one way or another deny Jesus Christ and impede true life in him. "Any conception of [God] that is at variance with his self-revelation in Christ is an idol."[9] John concludes, then, by exhorting us to guard ourselves against anything that would become an idol, anything that would cause us to walk away from the true and eternal life that we possess through our †fellowship in Jesus Christ. In fact, the bold confession of Jesus Christ as "the true God" (v. 20) provides the context for the contrast with idols. If Jesus is genuinely "the true God," then anything presenting itself as a false god should be shunned.

In a sense, John leaves us off balance at the close of the letter. He does not provide closing greetings, the wish of peace, and a blessing in the name of God. Rather, the letter closes brusquely. John ends with a caution that gets to the heart of his message. We are to cling to Jesus Christ and avoid anything that would keep us from true and living fellowship with the One who is eternal life.

8. This is the only appearance of the term "idol" in John's Gospel and the †Johannine Epistles, and the only occurrence of the verb "guard" in the Johannine Epistles.

9. Bruce, *Epistles of John*, 128.

Introduction to 2 John

Second John is a brief letter of just thirteen verses, a length that neatly fills one sheet of ancient papyrus.[1] The author identifies himself as "the †presbyter," or "elder," writing to a church that he calls "the chosen Lady" (for the authorship of 2 John, see the general introduction to 1–3 John). This short letter has numerous thematic parallels with 1 John, while at the same time showing similarities to 3 John in format and expression. It serves as a kind of bridge between 1 John and 3 John, being closer to both of them than they are to each other.

The first reference to 2 John in the early Church appears in Irenaeus of Lyons (late second century), who treats the letter as part of the apostolic canon.[2] But doubts over the authenticity and apostolic authorship of the letter (and of 3 John as well) appear in the third century and run into the mid-fourth century.[3] By the end of the fourth century, these doubts were largely settled: all three letters of John appear in †canonical lists of the New Testament in both the Eastern and Western churches.[4]

The letter is far too short to have any developed themes, but John clearly has certain concerns and topics in mind. He is occupied with the "truth" (the term appears five times in the first four verses). This truth is "in us" but is also

---

1. Rudolf Schnackenburg, *The Johannine Epistles*, trans. Reginald and Ilse Fuller (New York: Crossroad, 1992), 267.

2. *Against Heresies* 1.9.3; 3.17.8.

3. Origen (third century), Eusebius of Caesarea (fourth century), and Jerome (fourth century) observe that 2 John and 3 John are considered among the "disputed writings," held to be canonical by some churches but not given full recognition by others.

4. The Syriac church is the one exception: several of the †Catholic Epistles, including 2 John and 3 John, were not accepted into the Syriac canon until the sixth century. For a detailed survey of the reception of 2 John and 3 John in the early Church, see Raymond E. Brown, *The Epistles of John: Translated, with Introduction, Notes, and Commentary*, AB 30 (Garden City, NY: Doubleday, 1982), 5–13.

something in which we "walk." For John, "the truth" is Jesus Christ himself, the truth about him, and the true way of life he has called us to follow. The author also draws attention to the commandment to love one another and urges his readers to walk in love and keep the commandments. Further, he warns his audience against deceivers who teach in the spirit of the †antichrist: they do not acknowledge that Jesus Christ has "come in the flesh." John calls his readers to reject these deceivers and to remain in the "teaching" of Christ the Son. This enables them to abide in the Father and the Son.

All these themes closely reflect the concerns of 1 John.[5] But John gives one further instruction that is unique to this letter: he tells his readers not to provide hospitality or even to greet those who fail to teach truly about the Son. In closing, John writes that he has much more to say, but he will do this through a personal visit, and he ends by offerings greetings from the sister church from which he is writing.

Outline of 2 John

Opening Greeting (1:1–3)
Core Exhortations (1:4–11)
    Walking in Love for One Another (1:4–6)
    Warning against False Teachers and Call to Abide in the True Teaching (1:7–9)
    Directive against Showing Hospitality to False Teachers (1:10–11)
Closing Greeting (1:12–13)

5. Schnackenburg sees the themes of 2 John as closely connected to 1 John, saying that in 2 John the writer's "thought revolves—as in 1 John—around two themes: mutual love and true Christian faith" (*Johannine Epistles*, 276).

Opening Greeting

2 John 1:1–3

[1]The Presbyter to the chosen Lady and to her children whom I love in truth—and not only I but also all who know the truth—[2]because of the truth that dwells in us and will be with us forever. [3]Grace, mercy, and peace will be with us from God the Father and from Jesus Christ the Father's Son in truth and love.

NT: John 14:17; 1 Tim 1:2; 2 Tim 1:2; 3 John 1:1
Catechism: the Church as mother, 2040; living according to the truth, 2465–70

The letter begins with a standard greeting, naming the sender and the recipients: **The Presbyter to the chosen Lady and to her children**. Unlike most New Testament letters, however, John does not give proper names. Instead, he employs a title and a symbolic name. The title "†presbyter" (*presbyteros*), also commonly translated as "elder" (NJB, RSV), identifies a leadership position common in the early Church (see the sidebar, "Presbyters in Israel and the Church," p. 247). But by describing himself as *the* presbyter, John seems to be marking himself out in a special way as having a unique leadership role. He is not just *a* presbyter among many, but *the* presbyter, possessing a special standing and authority for other churches beyond the church in which he resides.

The recipient of the letter is "the chosen Lady" or "the elect Lady" (NRSV). Given that John concludes the letter with a greeting from "your chosen sister," almost certainly he is writing not to an individual woman but to the church as a whole. The "chosen Lady," then, is the church, and "her children" are the

1:1–2

245

Figure 10. Statue of St. John with quill in hand (Lateran Basilica in Rome)

members of the church. The title "children" is John's most common way of referring to Christians throughout the three letters.[1]

John tells his readers that he loves them **in truth**. He sounds the note of love right from the start and will return to this theme in verses 5–6, but for now he gives special attention to the matter of truth. It is not only John who loves them in truth, **but also all who know the truth**. And why? **Because of the truth that dwells in us and will be with us forever**.[2] What, then, is John saying in this opening greeting? He is speaking about the family of Christ, the children of God. Those who know the truth and have the truth dwelling in them are part of the same family and so love one another. Christ and his word dwell within them, and so they share a common truth. And this truth will never fail or abandon them: it lives in them now and will remain with them forever.[3]

1:3   John now gives the greeting: **Grace, mercy, and peace will be with us**. The terms "†grace," "mercy," and "peace" are standard words of greeting in the early Church.[4] The form of the greeting, though, is somewhat unusual. Most commonly the greeting is given in the form of a wish or desire for the readers: "grace and peace be with you." Here John employs the future tense of the verb and says that grace, mercy, and peace "will be with us," including himself in the blessing. He is making a statement rather than expressing a wish. By using the future tense,

1. See 1 John 3:1, 2, 10; 5:2; 3 John 1:4.
2. This closely parallels John 14:17, where Jesus says that the "Spirit of truth . . . remains with you, and will be in you."
3. The Greek word for "dwell" (*menō*) can also be translated as "remain" (NJB) or "abide" (RSV, NRSV). This is a key word throughout the †Johannine literature, occurring forty times in the Gospel of John and twenty-four times in 1 John.
4. Paul typically greets his readers by wishing them "grace and peace," but in the letters to Timothy he employs the triad used here by John, "grace, mercy, and peace" (1 Tim 1:2; 2 Tim 1:2).

Presbyters in Israel and the Church

BIBLICAL BACKGROUND

The term "presbyter" (*presbyteros*), often translated as "elder," means literally "older man," but it came to designate a role of leadership in Israel. In the †Septuagint we first encounter the term in the time of Moses: the leaders of the tribes of Israel were designated "elders" (Exod 24:1; Num 11:16–25), and it seems that they continued to have a leadership role alongside prophets, priests, and kings through the history of Israel (e.g., 1 Kings 12:6; Ezra 6:7–8; Ezek 8:1). At the time of Jesus we hear of "elders" who served on the Jewish ruling council in Jerusalem (the Sanhedrin), but there were also elders in the towns of Israel—probably leaders of the local synagogues—some of whom were more sympathetic to the message of Jesus (e.g., Luke 7:3–5). Though we cannot be certain, it is possible that Paul was following the model of the synagogue when he established "elders" or "presbyters" in the churches that he founded (e.g., Acts 14:23; 20:17; 1 Tim 5:17, 19; Titus 1:5). We also hear of "presbyters" serving in the church in Jerusalem (Acts 15:2–23), and the term is used by James (James 5:14) and Peter (1 Pet 5:1, 5) to designate Christian leaders. By identifying himself as "the Presbyter," John links himself with a long tradition of leadership in Israel and the Church.

John is not putting off the blessing of grace, mercy, and peace to a distant time, but rather is acknowledging that the blessing promised to those who are in Christ is both for now and for the future. In an ongoing way, the fruits of grace, mercy, and peace will be with those who have Christ dwelling within them.

Where do these blessing originate? They come **from God the Father and from Jesus Christ the Father's Son in truth and love**. "The Father's Son" is literally "the Son of the Father" and is the only occurrence of this exact phrase in the New Testament. Here we see the pairing of the Father and the Son so typical of 1 John. The Father and Son are distinct, yet they stand together as the one source of grace, mercy, and peace for the Christian community that receives these gifts "in truth and love."

What can we glean from this opening greeting? The author—the "Presbyter"—is writing to a church that he knows and loves. He identifies his recipients as part of one family, linked together by "the truth" that lives in them, and he is standing with them under the blessings of grace, mercy, and peace that come from the Father and the Son. Evidently John is deeply concerned in this short letter for "the truth." In what way he is concerned for the truth unfolds in the verses that follow.

Core Exhortations

2 John 1:4–11

Walking in Love for One Another (1:4–6)

⁴I rejoiced greatly to find some of your children walking in the truth just as we were commanded by the Father. ⁵But now, Lady, I ask you, not as though I were writing a new commandment but the one we have had from the beginning: let us love one another. ⁶For this is love, that we walk according to his commandments; this is the commandment, as you heard from the beginning, in which you should walk.

OT: Lev 19:18
NT: Rom 13:8–9, 13; Gal 5:16; Eph 2:10; 1 John 2:7; 5:3; 3 John 1:3–4
Catechism: the new commandment of love, 782, 1823, 1970, 2842

1:4 John opens the main body of the letter on a joyful note: **I rejoiced greatly to find some of your children walking in the truth**. We find a very similar expression in the opening lines of 3 John (1:4): "Nothing gives me greater joy than to hear that my children are walking in the truth." "Your children" refers to the members of the church to which he is writing. "Walking in the truth" is a common biblical expression for living the Christian way of life faithfully and actively.[1] What John means by "some of your children" (literally, "from your children") is unclear. He might just be saying that he has encountered *some* of them walking in faithfulness, and this is a cause for

---

1. For parallel uses of "walking" in Paul's writings, see Rom 13:13; Gal 5:16; Eph 2:10 ESV.

great joy. But he could also be implying that he has found *only* some, not all, living faithfully. If so—and I believe that this second meaning best fits the context—this would give John reason to write a cautionary letter, addressing a situation where some of the members of the church are falling short of living according to the truth.

John then adds: **just as we were commanded by the Father**. This way of "walking in the truth" is what the Father himself has commanded through the Son. Jesus' command to his disciples, that they should love one another (John 15:17), directly follows his declaration "I have told you everything I have heard from my Father" (John 15:15). It is the Father speaking through the Son who calls us to love one another by laying down our lives.

Addressing the church once again as **Lady**, John calls his readers to love   1:5–6
one another: **I ask you, not as though I were writing a new commandment but the one we have had from the beginning: let us love one another**. This is very similar to what John says in his first letter (1 John 2:7). He is, in fact, reminding them of what they already know: they are called to love one another as brothers and sisters in the Church. This is the core of what it means to walk in the truth.

In this context, "from the beginning" could refer to the command to love one another found in the Old Testament (Lev 19:18), but more likely it refers to the command to love one another that they received when they first heard the †gospel of Jesus Christ. In other words, it refers to the beginning of their conversion and life in Christ (see commentary on 1 John 2:7–8).

In these verses John goes back and forth between "commandment" in the singular and "commandments" in the plural. He first identifies a "commandment" (singular) that they had from the beginning (v. 5), but then he goes on to say that **this is love, that we walk according to his commandments** (plural, v. 6 [parallel in 1 John 5:3]). "Commandments" in the plural would include the †Decalogue (the Ten Commandments) and also all that Jesus taught us from the Father.

Further on in verse 6 John reverts to the singular form of "commandment": **this is the commandment, as you heard from the beginning, in which you should walk**. What is the commandment here? It is the demand to love one another. John is circling back and restating the same truth from a slightly different vantage point: the command to love one another that they heard from the beginning marks out the way they should live. In sum, the critical feature of love for John here is obedience in action: Christians must "walk" in the way of the commandments and love one another in practice.

John points to a circular relationship between love and keeping the commandments. The primary commandment (singular) is to love one another, but the way we demonstrate our love is by keeping the commandments (plural). This circularity is valid because the command to love one another is a true summary of all the commandments. Paul confirms this: "Owe no one anything, except to love one another; for the one who loves another has fulfilled the law. The commandments, 'You shall not commit adultery; You shall not murder; You shall not steal; You shall not covet'; and any other commandment, are summed up in this word, 'Love your neighbor as yourself'" (Rom 13:8–9 NRSV). Because we have Christ living within us, we can and should keep the commandments, and we keep them preeminently by loving one another.

Warning against False Teachers and Call to Abide in the True Teaching (1:7–9)

---

⁷**Many deceivers have gone out into the world, those who do not acknowledge Jesus Christ as coming in the flesh; such is the deceitful one and the antichrist. ⁸Look to yourselves that you do not lose what we worked for but may receive a full recompense. ⁹Anyone who is so "progressive" as not to remain in the teaching of the Christ does not have God; whoever remains in the teaching has the Father and the Son.**

NT: Mark 13:22; 1 John 2:19; 4:1–3; Rev 22:12

Catechism: denial of the incarnation and humanity of Christ, 465; the deception of the antichrist, 675–76

1:7 John abruptly changes tack by identifying a pack of false teachers who are prowling about and threatening the faith of believers: **Many deceivers have gone out into the world**. What defines them? They **do not acknowledge Jesus Christ as coming in the flesh**. For John, anyone who denies the †incarnation of the Son of God **is the deceitful one and the antichrist**. This closely parallels 1 John 4:2–3 (ESV): "By this you know the Spirit of God: every spirit that confesses that Jesus Christ has come in the †flesh is from God, and every spirit that does not confess Jesus is not from God."

This is the only occurrence of the noun "deceiver" in the †Johannine Epistles, though 1 John warns against "those who would deceive you" (1 John 2:26). By linking the term "deceiver" with "†antichrist," John shows that he almost certainly has in mind the same false teachers and prophets whom he identified in 1 John (see commentary on 1 John 2:18–19). They are the "false prophets" who "have gone out into the world" (1 John 4:1 [see Mark 13:22]), who have departed from the †fellowship of the Church (1 John 2:19) and have gone out to spread their false teaching. "Deceivers," then, occupy the place and role of the antichrist by denying the true appearance of the Son of God in the flesh. For John, to deny that the Son has come in the flesh is to deny the incarnation and by extension to deny all that Jesus did for us by dying on the cross for our sins and giving us new life.

John then turns immediately to exhortation, telling his readers, **Look to** **1:8–9** **yourselves**. This can also be translated as "watch yourselves" (NJB, ESV) or "be on your guard" (NRSV). The simple point is that they should beware of deceivers and their false teaching. Why? So that they **do not lose what we worked for but may receive a full recompense**.[2] By this John shows that he himself has labored among them to teach them the faith—that is, the incarnation of the Son of God, who died to free us from our sins and to give us eternal life. He does not want them to fall prey to deceit and so "lose" what he and they together have worked for, namely, the faith in Christ that he taught them from the beginning (see commentary on 1 John 4:1–3). Rather, they need to remain faithful and so receive the full inheritance of the children of God, which is to have fellowship with the Father and Son (1 John 1:1–3). This is the "recompense" or "reward" that awaits those who remain faithful (see Rev 22:12).

Verse 9 is a remarkable saying. John asserts, **Anyone who is so "progressive" as not to remain in the teaching of the Christ does not have God**. To the contrary, **whoever remains in the teaching has the Father and the Son**. What does John mean by this? Anyone who "runs ahead" (NIV) or "goes beyond" (NJB) the teaching of "the Christ"—that is, Jesus, the †Messiah—simply does not have a relationship with God.[3] But whoever "remains" or "abides" in this teaching has fellowship with both the Father and the Son. John does not spell out here what he means by "going beyond" the teaching of Christ, but given his critique of those who deny the incarnation, we can assume that he is referring to those who are denying or corrupting the true teaching about who Christ is and what he has accomplished for our salvation.

---

2. There is also a strong manuscript tradition for the second person plural, "what *you* worked for." Either reading is possible, and both make sense in the context.

3. The NABRE translation "progressive" is unhelpful in this context, as it carries modern political connotations that may not be aligned with the teaching that John is rejecting.

The term "teaching" (*didachē*) is an important word in both the New Testament and the early Church.[4] Is John referring here to teaching that Christ *himself* gave or teaching *about* Christ that was given along with the preaching of the gospel?[5] Most commentators favor the former interpretation (the teaching *from* Christ), but both are true and fit the context well. Undoubtedly John assumes that the teaching that Christ himself gave is fully consistent with the teaching that the Church offers about him. Crucially for John, teaching is not just an added extra. Knowing and living out the teaching of the Christ is an essential mark of the Christian.

Reflection and Application (1:7–9)

In an age when image is everything and marketability is the name of the game, John recalls us to the crucial importance of sound teaching. If we do not welcome and embrace "the teaching of the Christ," John warns, then we will not have a relationship with the Father and the Son. If instead we seek out and consume teaching that "goes beyond" what Christ has taught and so fails to teach his way of life truly, then we are in danger of losing our inheritance in the kingdom of God. This gives us a strong motivation for embracing and handing on Christ's teaching faithfully and reverently.[6]

What guides our effort to make the teaching of Christ known and loved? Because of our media-soaked society and the intense competition for people's attention, the Church has good reasons for making every effort to present the faith in a way that is interesting, captivating, and up to date. But the temptation to entertain rather than to teach weighs on us heavily, especially when we're working with young people. Entertainment by itself is fleeting and bears no lasting fruit. What people really long for—and respond to energetically—is Christ's own teaching delivered with faith and conviction. Christ's words bring life: "The words I have spoken to you are spirit and life" (John 6:63). If we wish to have fellowship with the Father and the Son—and to help others enter this fellowship—we ourselves need to abide in the teaching of Jesus and pass on this teaching effectively and with conviction.

---

4. In the NT, see Matt 7:28; Mark 1:22; Luke 4:32; John 7:16; Acts 2:42; Rom 16:17. One of the earliest Christian writings (c. 100) that describes the faith and basic practices of the early Church is entitled simply *The Didache* ("The Teaching").

5. The NABRE translation ("the teaching of the Christ") favors the view that this is teaching given *by* Christ, while other translations leave either meaning open ("the teaching of Christ," "the doctrine of Christ").

6. For an explanation of how the Catholic Church has preserved the teaching of Christ faithfully through time, see Catechism 74–95.

Directive against Showing Hospitality to False Teachers (1:10–11)

[10]If anyone comes to you and does not bring this doctrine, do not receive him in your house or even greet him; [11]for whoever greets him shares in his evil works.

NT: 1 Cor 5:9–11; 1 Tim 5:22
Catechism: the meaning of heresy, 464, 2089

What John says here flows directly from his commendation of "the teaching of   **1:10** the Christ" in the previous section. He is warning the church against teachers and prophets who fail to uphold the true teaching of Christ: **If anyone comes to you and does not bring this doctrine, do not receive him in your house or even greet him.**[7] What is "this doctrine"? It is Jesus' own teaching and the truth about him, namely, that he has come in the †flesh for the salvation of the †world (see v. 7).[8] John directs the church not to show hospitality to these false teachers—that is, not to receive them into their homes.

To welcome a brother or sister in Christ into one's home was an important expression—a core practice—of hospitality in the early Church. It was a characteristic mark of fraternal love. The "house" was also the place where the first Christians met for worship, since there were no church buildings in this early period.[9] Thus, to deny someone welcome into the "house" probably was also a way of denying that person access to the common prayer and liturgy of the church.

John adds that they are not even to greet such persons. This seems harsh, but we should realize that, for John, to "greet" them is tantamount to acknowledging them as brothers and sisters in good standing in the Lord. The greeting is not just an act of courtesy; it is a sign of a common family bond in the faith. John is saying that if these visiting teachers are not abiding by and teaching the truth, they should not be given a family greeting.

Why is the local Christian community not to show hospitality to the person   **1:11** who does not teach the truth? Because **whoever greets him shares in his evil works.** If they were to welcome these false teachers as family members in the

---

7. Paul too had to warn the churches that he served against traveling teachers who taught a deficient message about Jesus Christ (see 2 Cor 11:4–6; Gal 1:6–9).

8. For a concise explanation of what Catholics believe about Christ and the †incarnation, see Catechism 430–78. This section expounds the main titles for Jesus ("Christ," "Lord," "Son of God"), clarifies the purposes of the incarnation, and explains the various false teachings about Jesus that arose in the early Church.

9. For early Christian worship held in a house, see Acts 2:46; Rom 16:5; 1 Cor 16:19; Col 4:15.

Lord, John is saying, the church would share in the bad effects of their false teaching. Employing the same verb ("to share"), Paul says something similar to Timothy: "Do not share in another's sins" (1 Tim 5:22).

John is not telling his readers to do evil to these false teachers or to refuse them readmittance to the church if they acknowledge the truth of the faith. He is simply instructing them not to welcome these teachers as if they were faithful siblings in Christ.[10] Because they are bringing teaching that distorts or undermines the faith, they should not be given a platform to propagate their teaching in the church.

The verb translated as "greet" in verses 10–11 is *chairō*; the same verb is translated as "rejoice" in verse 4. John "rejoiced" (*chairō*) to hear that some in the church were walking in the truth; now he instructs the same church not to "greet" (*chairō*) those who fail to teach the truth. The link between "rejoicing" and "greeting" is suggestive. When we share the truth of the faith, we rejoice to see the truth being taught and lived, and we are able to give a full welcome to those who teach and live this same truth.

---

10. For similar directives not to welcome people who are bringing serious disruption to the local church, see Matt 18:17; 1 Cor 5:9–11; Titus 3:10–11.

Closing Greeting

2 John 1:12–13

¹²**Although I have much to write to you, I do not intend to use paper and ink. Instead, I hope to visit you and to speak face to face so that our joy may be complete.** ¹³**The children of your chosen sister send you greetings.**

OT: Num 12:8
NT: 1 Pet 5:13; 1 John 1:4; 3 John 1:13

John brings this short letter to a close by indicating his future plans: **Although** **1:12**
I have much to write to you, I do not intend to use paper and ink. Instead, I hope to visit you and to speak face to face. John has much more to say, but he has decided not to put this in writing.[1] Instead, he will pay them a personal visit in the near future and speak to them, face to face (literally, "mouth to mouth"). This same phrase describes how God spoke directly and clearly to Moses: "With him I speak face to face—clearly, not in riddles" (Num 12:8 NRSV [in Hebrew, literally "mouth to mouth"]).

If John is planning to visit, why write this short letter in the first place? It functions like an advance sentinel, communicating a few basic truths and alerting the audience that a personal visit is imminent. John wished to greet this Christian community, to commend the members for their faithfulness, to remind them of the fundamentals of faith and love, and above all to

---

1. John uses a similar expression in the conclusion to 3 John: "I have much to write to you, but I do not wish to write with pen and ink" (1:13).

Sister Churches

John's identification of the church as "the chosen Lady" and her "children" (v. 1) alongside the reference to "your chosen sister" (v. 13) indicates that these first local churches looked upon other local churches as "sisters"; they were part of the same family. As the Church grew and spread, the phrase "sister churches" came to designate the major sees of the Church that were in communion with one another (e.g., the church in Alexandria, the church in Antioch). In more recent times, the term "sister churches" has been used in †ecumenical settings to describe the relationship between the Catholic Church and the various Eastern Orthodox churches.

The idea of sister churches can serve the unity of the Church in two distinct ways today. First, it can remind Roman-rite Catholics that they are part of a wider communion of Catholic churches that includes many churches in the East (e.g., Maronite Catholics and Chaldean Catholics). All the churches of the Catholic Church are sister churches together and need to support and pray for one another. Second, when applied to the relationship between the Catholic Church and the Eastern Orthodox churches, it can help us recognize that, as sister churches, we already possess a real though imperfect communion together, and it can prompt us to pray and seek for that full unity for which Christ prayed (John 17:11). Pope John Paul II expressed this reality of being sister churches and seeking for full unity: "With the grace of God a great effort must be made to re-establish full communion among [the churches of the East and the West], the source of such good for the Church of Christ. This effort calls for all our good will, humble prayer and a steadfast cooperation which never yields to discouragement. . . . The traditional designation of 'Sister Churches' should ever accompany us along this path."[a]

a. *Ut Unum Sint* 56. For the history of the term "sister churches," see "Note on the Expression 'Sister Churches,'" Congregation for the Doctrine of the Faith (2000).

warn them of false teachers who are on the prowl. All this has been accomplished in a few short verses. The rest of his message will wait until he arrives in person.

One goal of this upcoming personal visit is **that our joy may be complete**. John used the same phrase in 1 John 1:4. There, his joy was made complete by writing to them about the truth; here, his joy will be complete when he visits them and speaks to them face to face.

1:13   In a final greeting, John writes, **The children of your chosen sister send you greetings**. This is a figurative way of saying that the members of the church where John is presently living also send their greetings.[2] Peter gives a similar greeting to close his first letter: "She who is at Babylon, who is likewise chosen, sends you greetings" (1 Pet 5:13 RSV). Because John the apostle is the presumed author of this letter, many conclude that he is writing from his home in Ephesus, conveying greetings from the members of the church there.

2. John uses a traditional word for "greet" here. He uses the same verb twice in the closing verse of 3 John (1:15).

Introduction to 3 John

Third John can boast of being the shortest writing in the New Testament. Though it has been assigned more verses than 2 John, it is slightly shorter in overall length. As with 2 John, the author identifies himself as "the †presbyter," or "elder," but in this case he is writing not to the entire church community but to a single individual, Gaius.[1] In fact, there are four persons who figure in this letter: the author, Gaius, Diotrephes, who opposes the author, and Demetrius, who is commended by the author.

Unlike 1 John and 2 John, this letter is not concerned directly with either the truths of the faith or the admonition to love one another. These concerns undoubtedly lie in the background, but the foreground of the letter concerns relationships, and in particular relationships between leaders in the early Church. When we read 3 John, we are peering into John's personal communication about relationship issues and challenges in one local church.

As we set out to study this letter, we must admit that we have sparse information to work with. We can glean certain facts from John's letter to Gaius, but we do not know the background in any depth and can only make educated judgments about what is really going on between John, Diotrephes, and the itinerant missionaries whom John commends. For example, is Diotrephes one of the false teachers whom John warns about in 1 John and 2 John? Probably not, but it is unclear. Is the conflict between the author and Diotrephes grounded in disagreements over the content of the faith, or is it simply a disagreement about authority and how to work together as leaders? Through a close reading of the text we will attempt to arrive at a reasonable judgment on these and other issues.

1. For the authorship of 3 John, see the general introduction to 1–3 John; for the reception of 3 John in the early Church, see the introduction to 2 John.

At this point, further questions arise: Why do we read 3 John at all? What value does it have for Christian faith and life? First, 3 John casts a spotlight onto pastoral practice in the early Church and offers insight into how to handle relationship problems among leaders. Second, this letter shows us that some influences in the Church are to be opposed and others promoted. What is the criterion for discerning one from the other? John commends those who are "walking in the truth" (vv. 3–4), while he criticizes the one who "dominates," spreads evil rumors, and fails to support those engaged in the mission of the church. Finally, 3 John reminds us that in all circumstances—and especially in the midst of relationship conflict—we are to do good and avoid evil. This reflects God's nature and shows that we belong to him.

Outline of 3 John

Opening Greeting and Commendation (1:1–4)
Requests and Recommendations (1:5–12)
    Request for Hospitality toward Faithful Missionaries (1:5–8)
    Warning against Diotrephes (1:9–10)
    Commendation of Demetrius (1:11–12)
Closing Greeting (1:13–15)

Opening Greeting and Commendation

3 John 1:1–4

---

¹The Presbyter to the beloved Gaius whom I love in truth.

²Beloved, I hope you are prospering in every respect and are in good health, just as your soul is prospering. ³I rejoiced greatly when some of the brothers came and testified to how truly you walk in the truth. ⁴Nothing gives me greater joy than to hear that my children are walking in the truth.

NT: 1 John 2:1; 3:1–2; 2 John 1:1, 4
Catechism: living according to the truth, 2465–70

The opening line of greeting is eminently simple and clear. The author identi- **1:1–2**
fies himself as **the Presbyter** (as in 2 John) and addresses the letter to a certain
Gaius,[1] who is called **the beloved**—a term of affection and friendship that
John uses four times in the letter (vv. 1, 2, 5, 11). As if to underscore this affec-
tion, John adds: **whom I love in truth**. John truly loves Gaius as his brother in
Christ—they share a bond in the truth—and wishes to communicate this clearly.

Verse 2 expresses a standard wish of good health that was typical in ancient
letter writing: **Beloved, I hope you are prospering in every respect and are
in good health, just as your soul is prospering**.[2] The Greek is literally, "I pray
that you are prospering." In his prayer John distinguishes Gaius's physical health

---

1. The name "Gaius" appears several times elsewhere in the NT (Acts 19:29; 20:4; Rom 16:23; 1 Cor 1:14), but there is no evidence that the Gaius addressed here in 3 John is one of these.

2. "The convention of wishing one's reader good health at the outset of a letter . . . is one of great antiquity" (F. F. Bruce, *The Epistles of John: Introduction, Exposition and Notes* [London: Pickering & Inglis, 1970], 147).

and the welfare of his soul. The NJB captures this sense: "I hope everything is going happily with you and that you are as well physically as you are spiritually." John's prayer reminds us that prospering or flourishing, both materially and spiritually, is God's normal will for us and that we should pray for ourselves and for one another that all of us would prosper and be able to give generously to others (2 Cor 9:10–11; Eph 4:28).

1:3–4   John now attends to the reason for his writing. First, he recounts how joyful he was at hearing that Gaius was living a faithful Christian life: **I rejoiced greatly when some of the brothers came and testified to how truly you walk in the truth**. The phrasing of this is a bit awkward: literally, these brothers testified "to your truth, as you are walking in the truth." "Your truth" probably is short-hand for "your faithfulness to the truth."[3] In other words, John is commending Gaius for personally embodying the truth in the way he lives. John received this report from some "brothers" who had come from Gaius and the church in his area, reporting to John how impressively Gaius was living the faith. It is entirely possible that these "brothers" were sent by John in the first place, just as Paul often sent representatives to care for his churches.

John now expresses the joy in his heart at hearing this good news: **Nothing gives me greater joy than to hear that my children are walking in the truth**. Note that John refers to those under his care as "his" children.[4] This displays an important feature of John's relationship to Gaius and those to whom he is writing: John is a spiritual father to them, as they are his children in the faith, and nothing makes him happier than the true welfare of his spiritual children. To "walk" in the truth means to live in a way that is actively faithful to God. It reminds us that life is a pilgrimage: we must continue to walk faithfully toward the goal of full and eternal life with God.

Reflection and Application (1:3–4)

Every year millions of people go on pilgrimage. The Camino de Santiago in northern Spain, for example, has several hundred thousand walkers every year, many of whom are not even Christians—they are just seekers who are walking to find greater meaning in life.

3. The NRSV expresses this meaning: "[They] testified to your faithfulness to the truth, namely how you walk in the truth."
4. In his first letter, John uses the term "children" (*tekna*) only when speaking of God's children (1 John 3:1, 2, 10; 5:2); John employs a diminutive, "little children" (*teknia*), when speaking of his own children in the faith (1 John 2:1).

When we look to the origins of the story of God with his people, we see that it begins with a pilgrimage. God called Abraham to leave his home and go to the land that God was preparing for him. He "went out, not knowing where he was to go" (Heb 11:8). Though God later showed him the land that he would give him, Abraham remained a pilgrim all the days of his life. The people of Israel wandered as pilgrims in the wilderness for forty years, relying on God's provision of water, manna, and quail, led by a pillar of fire and cloud. And Jesus himself wandered up and down the territory of Israel, declaring that he had no permanent place "to rest his head" (Matt 8:20).

As Christians, we are called to embrace our identity as "strangers and nomads" (1 Pet 2:11 NJB). To be a Christian is not just to adopt a set of beliefs and to attend religious services; rather, it is to walk in the truth, as John says here. We are not walking blindly or without clear purpose. We have "tasted that the Lord is good" (1 Pet 2:3), and so we are walking in a way of truth that embraces every aspect of our lives. Going on pilgrimage is meant to express in a microcosm what our whole life is intended to be: a way of walking with God, day by day, toward full and eternal life with God.

Requests and Recommendations

3 John 1:5–12

Request for Hospitality toward Faithful Missionaries (1:5–8)

⁵Beloved, you are faithful in all you do for the brothers, especially for strangers; ⁶they have testified to your love before the church. Please help them in a way worthy of God to continue their journey. ⁷For they have set out for the sake of the Name and are accepting nothing from the pagans. ⁸Therefore, we ought to support such persons, so that we may be co-workers in the truth.

OT: Exod 20:7; Lev 24:16; Deut 5:11
NT: Matt 10:40; Acts 5:40–41; Phil 2:9
Catechism: the name of God and of Jesus, 232–33, 430–35, 2145–46, 2812

1:5–6 John now commends Gaius specifically for his faithful and hospitable reception of visiting fellow Christians, even those who were previously unknown to him: **Beloved, you are faithful in all you do for the brothers, especially for strangers**. It is safe to assume that John has the same "brothers" in mind whom he mentioned in verse 3. John tells Gaius that these brothers **have testified to your love before the church**; that is, they have given public testimony in the church to which John belongs that Gaius received them with true fraternal love.

This is the first appearance of the word "church" (*ekklēsia*) in 3 John (it occurs twice more in this letter, vv. 9–10). It does not occur at all in the other †Johannine Epistles or in John's Gospel. On this basis some scholars conclude that the author of 3 John is different from the author of the Gospel and the other two letters. But given the strong evidence for common authorship of all three letters (see the general introduction to 1–3 John), there is no reason to question John's authorship here. Instead, this third letter shows that John is consistent with other New Testament writings in employing the term "church" to describe the local Christian community.[1]

The request for hospitality and provisioning is then renewed: **Please help them in a way worthy of God to continue their journey**. The NABRE translation gives the impression that these "brothers" are still in Gaius's home and that John is asking that they be sent on their way with provision and care. But this probably is not the case. Rather, John is commending this action in a general way into the future: "You will do well to send them on in a manner worthy of God" (NRSV). He is "praising what Gaius has done in the past, and is doing so in order to invite Gaius to a future manifestation of love."[2] This is especially important because Gaius's hospitality contrasts with the conduct of Diotrephes, who is refusing to welcome and support these traveling fellow Christians (v. 10). By providing care and further provisions for them, Gaius will be acting in a way worthy of the God they mutually serve. He is fulfilling the word spoken by Jesus, "Whoever receives you receives me, and whoever receives me receives the one who sent me" (Matt 10:40).

Why are these fellow Christians worthy of this care and provision? **They have set out for the sake of the Name and are accepting nothing from the pagans**. They deserve this care because they are traveling and visiting the churches for the sake of the Lord Jesus himself and the growth of the Church. "For the sake of the Name" is a way of saying that they are doing this for Christ, the Son of God, in order to advance the kingdom of God. We find a similar expression in Acts 5:41: "So [the apostles] left the presence of the Sanhedrin, rejoicing that they had been found worthy to suffer dishonor for the sake of the name" (see sidebar, "The Name," p. 266).

It is not clear what John means when he says that these visiting believers "are accepting nothing from the pagans." "Pagans" is literally "†Gentiles" (*ethnikoi*) and refers in this case to non-Christian Gentiles.[3] Why would pagans be expected to give financial support to Christian missionaries in the first place? Perhaps, as Peter Jones suggests, these missionaries "were apparently preaching

1:7–8

---

1. For the NT use of the word "church" for the local congregation, see Acts 14:23; Rom 16:1; James 5:14; Rev 2:1. For a broad and more universal meaning of the word "church," see Eph 1:22; Phil 3:6; Col 1:24; Heb 12:23.

2. Raymond E. Brown, *The Epistles of John: Translated, with Introduction, Notes, and Commentary*, AB 30 (Garden City, NY: Doubleday, 1982), 710.

3. For the other NT occurrences of "pagans" (*ethnikoi*), see Matt 5:47; 6:7; 18:17.

The Name

John's phrase "for the sake of the Name" has deep Old Testament roots. In the †Decalogue we are solemnly commanded not to take "the name" of the Lord our God in vain (Exod 20:7; Deut 5:11), and in countless Old Testament passages the people of Israel are exhorted to honor the name of the Lord. The expression "the Name" came to be a placeholder for God's own name, †YHWH, which Jews did not pronounce out of reverence. Even today pious Jews often refer to the Lord God simply as *Hashem* ("the name" in Hebrew). Strikingly, in the New Testament "the name" often refers to Jesus himself, not just to God the Father. In Acts 5:40–41, the apostles are commanded by the ruling Jewish council not to speak "in the name of Jesus," but they left the council "rejoicing that they had been found worthy to suffer dishonor for the sake of the name" (see also 1 Pet 4:14). In Phil 2:9–11, we see that the Father has bestowed on Jesus "the name above every name," so that "at the name of Jesus every knee should bend." In other words, the "name" and honor of God have been bestowed on Jesus, the incarnate Son of God.

Although Father and Son and Spirit are distinct persons, they are honored by the single "name" that belongs to God alone (see Matt 28:19).[a]

a. The Catechism, after noting that "Jesus" means "God saves" (430), states, "The name 'Jesus' signifies that the very name of God is present in the person of his Son, made man for the universal and definitive redemption from sins. It is the divine name that alone brings salvation" (432).

---

to unbelieving Gentiles but were not mendicants begging from them."[4] That is to say, they were sent out to preach to Gentile unbelievers but could not expect to get material support from them; therefore, members of the church must provide support for this mission. In a similar manner, Paul received support from other churches when evangelizing unbelievers (2 Cor 11:7–9; Phil 4:15–16).

And so, John concludes, **Therefore, we ought to support such persons, so that we may be co-workers in the truth**. Because of their noble cause and their need, John urges Gaius to receive and provide for such as these, just as he has recently done. Travel in the ancient world was far more demanding than it is today. Not only were the means of travel rigorous, but also travelers normally had to rely on friends or patrons for food and housing along the way. The supplying of food and shelter to travelers fulfilled a profound need.

The last phrase shows the significance of this kind of missionary hospitality. By aiding those who are working for the †gospel, we become "co-workers"

4. Peter Rhea Jones, *1, 2 & 3 John*, SHBC (Macon, GA: Smith & Helwys, 2009), 270.

with them in the mission—what Paul calls "partnership for the gospel" (Phil 1:5).[5] This is the positive counterpart to John's instruction in 2 John to refuse hospitality to false teachers. Missionary hospitality is not indiscriminate; it ought to serve the advance of the gospel.

As we conclude this first section of the letter, we should recognize the prominence of the term "truth" (used five times in eight verses) and how it permeates the opening of the letter. For John, all is done, or should be done, in service to the "truth" of Jesus Christ and the way of life in which he has called us to walk.

Warning against Diotrephes (1:9–10)   #15

> [9]I wrote to the church, but Diotrephes, who loves to dominate, does not acknowledge us. [10]Therefore, if I come, I will draw attention to what he is doing, spreading evil nonsense about us. And not content with that, he will not receive the brothers, hindering those who wish to do so and expelling them from the church.

NT: 2 Cor 13:2
Catechism: the office of authority in the Church, 861–62, 880–96

John now introduces a concrete problem with an individual in the local church: **1:9** **I wrote to the church, but Diotrephes, who loves to dominate, does not acknowledge us**. Here John seems to be using "us" to indicate himself: Diotrephes is refusing to acknowledge John's personal authority in the church. What is this writing that John penned and sent to the church already? Is he referring to 1 John or even perhaps to 2 John, or the two combined as sent in one package? Perhaps, but it is equally possible that John is referring to another letter that has not survived.

John names a certain person, Diotrephes, and says two things about him. First, he "loves to dominate," literally, "loves to put himself first," or "loves preeminence."[6] Whatever he is doing (and we are told little about his specific actions), he is either seizing an authority that he does not rightly possess or

5. For other requests for material support for mission and missionaries in the NT, see Rom 15:24; 1 Cor 16:6; Titus 3:13–14.
6. The Greek verb that John employs here, *philoprōteuō* ("to love to put oneself first"), is found nowhere else in the Bible or in Greek literature and may be John's own invention. See Judith Lieu, *The Second and Third Epistles of John: History and Background*, ed. John Riches, SNTW (Edinburgh: T&T Clark, 1986), 111.

exercising his rightful authority in an improper way.[7] Second, John says that Diotrephes "does not acknowledge us" (NRSV: "does not acknowledge our authority"). Putting these together, we can reasonably assume that Diotrephes is acting without respect for John's authority and teaching and is exercising authority in a domineering manner.

1:10   A promise of action then follows: **if I come, I will draw attention to what he is doing, spreading evil nonsense about us**. John is giving advance warning that if and when he comes in person, he will bring to the church's attention the works that Diotrephes is doing. Among these, he is slandering John in words (NIV: "gossiping maliciously"). Clearly, then, Diotrephes not only is failing to acknowledge John's authority but also is actively speaking against him maliciously and unjustly. This tells us that John has an authority or enjoys the esteem of the church in a degree that is greater than that of Diotrephes, since John is confident that he will be able to deal with Diotrephes by personally confronting him in the presence of the church.[8]

Further, John charges Diotrephes with failing to receive those who have come from John and obstructing those who would receive them: **And not content with that, he will not receive the brothers**, **hindering those who wish to do so**. He is even taking such an extreme measure as **expelling them from the church**. What exactly is going on here? We cannot tell for sure, but it appears that John sent delegates ("the brothers") to the church whom Gaius warmly received but Diotrephes refused to welcome. Has Diotrephes actually expelled Gaius himself for receiving these emissaries? Possibly, but this is not indicated by John and seems unlikely. In any case, there is strife in the church, for which John holds Diotrephes responsible.

The heart of this controversy concerns authority in the church. John faults Diotrephes for refusing to acknowledge and receive John and his delegates and for unjustly casting from the church those who do. Diotrephes is not linked directly to the false teachers who appear in 1 John and 2 John, but at the very least he has refused to receive all that John is teaching, and his actions show a failure in fraternal love.

7. There has been much scholarly discussion and debate over the actual position or office of Diotrephes in the local church. Was he the properly appointed †bishop who was acting badly, or at least a †presbyter, one of the appointed elders? Was he simply a functional presider over the church that met in his house, taking more authority than was his right? Was he an upstart member of the church acting in his own person? The second option best fits the description John gives, but we do not have enough information to make a clear determination.

8. Paul likewise writes warningly about the action he will take when he comes in person: "I warned those who sinned earlier and all the others, and I warn them now while absent, as I did when present on my second visit, that if I come again I will not be lenient" (2 Cor 13:2).

Commendation of Demetrius (1:11–12)

---

¹¹Beloved, do not imitate evil but imitate good. Whoever does what is good is of God; whoever does what is evil has never seen God. ¹²Demetrius receives a good report from all, even from the truth itself. We give our testimonial as well, and you know our testimony is true.

NT: Matt 7:18–20; John 21:24; 1 John 3:6, 10
Catechism: good and evil acts, 1749–56

John now gives a general principle for action: **Beloved, do not imitate evil but   1:11
imitate good**. How does this fit into the context of the letter thus far? John has commended Gaius for his good and faithful work of hospitality (v. 5), while accusing Diotrephes of evil works (vv. 9–10). By urging Gaius to imitate what is good, John in effect is saying this: Do not follow the bad example set by Diotrephes but continue in the good work that you have already shown to the traveling missionaries.

Why imitate what is good? Because **Whoever does what is good is of God; whoever does what is evil has never seen God**. The contrasting sentences show close parallels with John's first letter (e.g., 1 John 3:14; 4:2), but this is the first time in his letters that John employs the moral categories of good and evil to distinguish those who are of God from those who are not. The terms are different but the message is the same, as we read in his first letter: "In this way, the children of God and the children of the devil are made plain; no one who fails to act in righteousness belongs to God, nor anyone who does not love his brother" (1 John 3:10). For John, to *see* God is to *know* God and to bear the fruit of fraternal love: "No one who remains in him sins; no one who sins has seen him or known him" (1 John 3:6).

John is establishing good and evil action as a criterion for discernment. Diotrephes, by acting wrongly, shows that he is not acting as one who has "seen God"; Gaius, on the other hand, demonstrates that he is "of God" by showing care and hospitality—fraternal love—to the itinerant missionaries. "A sound tree cannot bear evil fruit, nor can a bad tree bear good fruit. . . . Thus you will know them by their fruits" (Matt 7:18, 20 RSV).⁹

Our attention is now drawn to another man, Demetrius, who **receives a good   1:12
report from all, even from the truth itself**—literally, "has received testimony from all." John uses the verb *martyreō* ("to bear witness," "to give testimony," also

---

9. For good and evil works contrasted, see Matt 12:33–35; Luke 6:43–45; John 5:29; Rom 12:9, 21; 1 Pet 3:17.

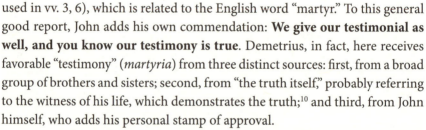

The Imitation of the Saints

LIVING TRADITION

John calls us to imitate those in the faith who do good. In the living tradition of the Church, there is a rich resource of faithful men and women, the saints, who offer us inspiring models to emulate. The Second Vatican Council gave an eloquent invitation to imitate the saints who have gone before us:

> When we look at the lives of those who have faithfully followed Christ, we are inspired with a new reason for seeking the City that is to come (Heb 13:14), and at the same time we are shown a most safe path by which among the vicissitudes of this world, in keeping with the state in life and condition proper to each of us, we will be able to arrive at perfect union with Christ, that is, perfect holiness. In the lives of those who, sharing in our humanity, are however more perfectly transformed into the image of Christ, God vividly manifests his presence and his face to men. He speaks to us in them, and gives us a sign of his Kingdom, to which we are strongly drawn, having so great a cloud of witnesses over us (Heb 12:1) and such a witness to the truth of the Gospel.[a]

a. *Lumen Gentium* 50.

used in vv. 3, 6), which is related to the English word "martyr." To this general good report, John adds his own commendation: **We give our testimonial as well, and you know our testimony is true**. Demetrius, in fact, here receives favorable "testimony" (*martyria*) from three distinct sources: first, from a broad group of brothers and sisters; second, from "the truth itself," probably referring to the witness of his life, which demonstrates the truth;[10] and third, from John himself, who adds his personal stamp of approval.

We are told nothing further about Demetrius.[11] He may be one of the "brothers" whom John refers to in verses 5–8, but it is more likely that he is the personal bearer of this letter (3 John) to Gaius. If so, then by commending Demetrius, John is implicitly calling on Gaius to offer Demetrius the same generous hospitality and support that he previously showed to the itinerant missionaries.

10. "In Demetrius' case the truth that abides in him finds expression in the holiness of his life and the soundness of his preaching, and so constitutes a powerful witness on his behalf" (Brown, *Epistles of John*, 724).

11. The only other reference to a "Demetrius" in the NT comes from Acts 19:24–38, where Demetrius, a silversmith from Ephesus, opposes Paul and rouses the city against him. A fourth-century work, *The Apostolic Constitutions*, reports that the apostle John ordained Demetrius as the bishop of the city of Philadelphia, but most scholars doubt the historical reliability of this account.

Reflection and Application (1:9–12)

John shows us by his example in this letter how important good Christian leadership is for the Church. By commending Gaius and Demetrius for their faithfulness but censuring Diotrephes for putting himself first, John reminds us of Christ's own teaching on servant leadership. Let us recall the famous Gospel scene: James and John approach Jesus privately, asking to be placed in the two highest positions in his government. Jesus tells them that these positions are not his to give, but he takes the occasion to teach all of his followers what it means to lead: "Jesus summoned them and said to them, 'You know that those who are recognized as rulers over the Gentiles lord it over them, and their great ones make their authority over them felt. But it shall not be so among you. Rather, whoever wishes to be great among you will be your servant; whoever wishes to be first among you will be the slave of all. For the Son of Man did not come to be served but to serve and to give his life as a ransom for many'" (Mark 10:42–45).

The call to be a servant leader applies to every level of leadership in the Church: the pope, bishops, priests, deacons, and lay leaders alike. No one gets a pass; no one is above this call. The title "the servant of the servants of God" (*servus servorum Dei*), first used by Pope Gregory the Great and then adopted by later popes, exemplifies the principle that the greatest must be the servant of all. It is easy to sit back and criticize leaders in the Church who fall short of this ideal; it is much more difficult to follow Jesus' example when my turn to lead comes. Am I seeking the good of those I am leading, or am I seeking to please myself? Is my style of leadership domineering, or do I make a place for others (see 1 Pet 5:1–3)? Do I lead with fairness, or am I partial to some who flatter me and provide me with benefits (see Deut 1:17)? Am I rightly under authority as I seek to exercise the authority given to me for the common good? Let us continually pray for all those in leadership in the Church, that they might lead with humility and a servant's heart.

Closing Greeting

3 John 1:13–15

---

¹³I have much to write to you, but I do not wish to write with pen and ink. ¹⁴Instead, I hope to see you soon, when we can talk face to face. ¹⁵Peace be with you. The friends greet you; greet the friends there each by name.

NT: John 15:13–15; 20:19
Catechism: friendship with God and one another, 277, 396, 1395, 1468, 2347

1:13–14   In words nearly identical to the closing of 2 John, this short letter concludes: **I have much to write to you, but I do not wish to write with pen and ink** (see commentary on 2 John 1:12). In place of a longer letter, John tells Gaius, **I hope to see you soon, when we can talk face to face**. John has much more to say, but he has decided not to put this in writing; instead, he will wait and talk through these matters with Gaius at greater length in person.

1:15   John now offers Gaius the greeting of peace: **Peace be with you**. There is an echo here of the first words that Jesus spoke to his disciples when he appeared to them together after his resurrection: "Peace be with you" (John 20:19). This wish of peace is especially poignant in light of the obvious division and strife currently at work in the local church. Despite this disruption of peace in the church, John wishes Gaius the peace of the Lord. One can still know peace even in a situation of objective disorder.

In his second letter, John referred to the church as the "chosen Lady and . . . her children" and to the members of his own church as "the children of your chosen sister." Now he uses a different term, **the friends**, to identify both the

272

faithful of his church and those of the church to whom he is writing. Plainly John knows personally these "friends" who surround Gaius, because he asks that they be greeted **each by name**.

Where else do we find this title "friend" as a means of identifying fellow Christians? The one instance in the New Testament where the disciples are identified as "friends" appears in John 15:13–15, where Jesus calls the disciples his "friends" and links this friendship to laying down one's life in love: "No one has greater love than this, to lay down one's life for one's friends. You are my friends if you do what I command you. I no longer call you slaves, because a slave does not know what his master is doing. I have called you friends, because I have told you everything I have heard from my Father."

The "friends" of Jesus are those who remain with him. They have experienced the fruits of his life-giving death, they keep his commandments, and they know his truth. This is, in fact, an apt description of faithful Christians in the †Johannine Epistles. For John, the term "friend" sums up what the faithful Christian is to be: one who holds to the faith and lays down his or her life for fellow Christians in love. The closing greeting to 3 John, and thus to the Johannine Epistles, reminds us that Christlike friendship is at the heart of what it means to be a follower of Jesus and a fellow believer with other Christians.

Reflection and Application (1:15)

Friendship is a great gift—one of the richest blessings of human life. Even for those who have no faith and who claim no relationship with God, friendship is a great good. Yet friendship with God, and the friendship that we share with one another in Christ, is an even greater blessing. Jesus has called those who follow him his friends. He has elevated us to a great dignity: not just to be servants or hired laborers, but friends who walk as his companions and come to know his mind. More than this, we become true friends to one another, ready to lay down our lives even to death for our brothers and sisters.

At the close of his renowned work on Christian spirituality, *The Life of Moses*, Gregory of Nyssa (d. 395) strikingly presents friendship with God as the perfection of the spiritual life:

> This is true perfection: not to avoid a wicked life because like slaves we servilely fear punishment, nor to do good because we hope for rewards, as if cashing in on the virtuous life by some business-like and contractual arrangement. On the contrary, disregarding all those things for which we hope and which have been

273

reserved by promise, we regard falling from God's friendship as the only thing dreadful and we consider becoming God's friend the only thing worthy of honor and desire. This, as I have said, is the perfection of life.[1]

---

1. *The Life of Moses* 2.320 (*The Life of Moses*, trans. Abraham J. Malherbe and Everett Ferguson, CWS [New York: Paulist Press, 1978], 138).

Suggested Resources

Sources from the Christian Tradition

Augustine of Hippo. *Homilies on the First Epistle of John.* Translated by Boniface
   Ramsey. Edited by Daniel E. Doyle and Thomas Martin. WSA 3/14. Hyde
   Park, NY: New City Press, 2008. A wonderful set of homilies by a theological
   and pastoral master.
Bray, Gerald, ed. *James, 1–2 Peter, 1–3 John, Jude.* ACCS 11. Downers Grove,
   IL: InterVarsity, 2000. A collection of short excerpts from a wide variety of
   the Church Fathers offering brief comments on many sections in James and
   the Letters of John.

Scholarly Commentaries

Brown, Raymond E. *The Epistles of John: Translated, with Introduction, Notes,
   and Commentary.* AB 30. Garden City, NY: Doubleday, 1982. A massive, thorough commentary on the Letters of John covering all questions and issues.
Johnson, Luke Timothy. *The Letter of James: A New Translation with Introduction and Commentary.* AB 37A. New York: Doubleday, 1995. A scholarly
   commentary by a leading Catholic scholar.
Martin, Ralph P. *James.* WBC 48. Waco: Word, 1988. A very thorough, detailed
   work by a leading evangelical scholar.
McCartney, Dan G. *James.* BECNT. Grand Rapids: Baker Academic, 2009.
   Excellent exposition by a Presbyterian scholar.

Painter, John. *1, 2, and 3 John*. SP 18. Collegeville, MN: Liturgical Press, 2002. A fine scholarly commentary often providing an interpretation different from or complementary to that of Raymond Brown.

Schnackenburg, Rudolf. *The Johannine Epistles*. Translated by Reginald and Ilse Fuller. New York: Crossroad, 1992. Originally published as *Die Johannesbriefe* (Freiburg: Herder, 1963). An in-depth commentary from a renowned German Catholic scholar, especially strong on explanatory notes.

Smalley, Stephen S. *1, 2, 3 John*. WBC 51. Waco: Word, 1984. A sound, in-depth commentary from an evangelical perspective.

Popular and Pastoral Works

Bruce, F. F. *The Epistles of John: Introduction, Exposition and Notes*. London: Pickering & Inglis, 1970. An accessible and reliable commentary from a renowned evangelical scholar.

Hahn, Scott, and Curtis Mitch. *The New Testament*. 2nd ed. ISB. San Francisco: Ignatius Press, 2010. The notes on the Letters of John from this study Bible provide excellent short comments from a Catholic perspective on the main issues in these letters.

Jones, Peter Rhea. *1, 2 & 3 John*. SHBC. Macon, GA: Smith & Helwys, 2009. A refreshing evangelical commentary that provides thoughtful application of each main section of the Letters of John to modern life.

Martin, Francis. "1 John." In *The International Bible Commentary*, edited by William R. Farmer, 1823–32. Collegeville, MN: Liturgical Press, 1998. A short commentary full of insight on the overall message of the Letters of John from a renowned Catholic biblical scholar.

Motyer, J. A. *The Message of James: The Tests of Faith*. BST. Downers Grove, IL: InterVarsity, 1985. A literary and theological analysis with pastoral reflections from an Anglican scholar.

Royster, Dmitri. *The Epistle of St. James: A Commentary*. Yonkers, NY: St. Vladimir's Seminary Press, 2010. A brief and spiritual commentary from an Orthodox archbishop containing many patristic references.

Glossary

antichrist: a human figure who will appear in the last days, doing wonders through the power of Satan and leading many astray from Christ. In 1 John the "spirit" of this figure who is still to come is already at work attempting to deceive the faithful.

antithesis: the placing of a sentence or one of its parts in opposition to another.

beloved disciple: title for "the disciple whom Jesus loved" in the Gospel of John (see John 13:23; 19:26; 20:2; 21:7, 20), traditionally understood as a reference to the apostle John.

bishop (Greek *episkopos*): literally, "overseer"—from *epi* ("over") and *skopos* ("one who watches or looks out"). Sometimes used synonymously with "presbyter" or "elder" in the New Testament (e.g., Phil 1:1; Titus 1:5–7). This office came to designate the overall ordained leader of each local Christian community.

canon (canonical): the list of the books discerned by the Church as belonging to sacred Scripture.

Catholic Epistles: the collection that designates seven New Testament letters: James, 1–2 Peter, 1–3 John, and Jude. The name "catholic" was given to these letters by the ancient Church because it was presumed that they were written not to individual churches but to the wider "catholic" or "universal" Church.

Cerinthus: a second-century heretical teacher who was reputed to teach that the Spirit descended upon Christ at his baptism but then fled from him before his passion and death. He denied that the incarnate Son actually shed his blood and died for our sins.

conditional sentence: a sentence that states a condition ("If . . .") and the consequence ("then . . ."). It expresses a hypothetical situation.

covenant: a solemn agreement that creates a bond between the parties, involving a mutual commitment of love and fidelity. In the Bible, the word is used mostly to describe the solemn, sacred promise between God and his people whereby God freely and graciously invites his chosen people Israel to form a special relationship with him. This invitation is later extended to the Gentiles (the new covenant) through Jesus Christ.

Dead Sea Scrolls: a collection of ancient manuscripts discovered in the caves near Qumran on the shore of the Dead Sea between 1947 and 1977. The scrolls contain many fragments of Old Testament texts as well as other Jewish religious texts from the period approximately 250 BC to AD 50.

Decalogue: the Ten Commandments (see Exod 20:2–17; Deut 5:6–21).

deification: a Christian doctrine that describes our new life in Christ in terms of our sharing in the life and power of God, both now in this age and fully in the life of the age to come. Deification does not mean that we become God by nature, but that we share in his life by grace as sons and daughters of God.

ecumenism (ecumenical): the set of activities and efforts by Christian churches and ecclesial communities directed toward making the partial unity that Christians share grow toward full communion.

evangelist: (1) one who proclaims the good news of salvation; (2) a designation for each of the authors of the four canonical Gospels.

expiation: the act of making amends or making reparation for sin, through which the guilt of sin is put away and extinguished.

fellowship (Greek *koinōnia*): communion with God and with one another, marked by a sharing of life and bonds of love.

flesh: (1) the condition of our bodily life in this world, used as a synonym for "body"; (2) the condition of our sinful humanity with its disordered desires.

Gentiles (Greek *ethnē*), also translated as "nations": (1) people of non-Jewish descent; (2) people who are not a part of God's people, who do not know God, and who live immorally and unjustly ("pagans").

gnosticism: a second-century movement that posed a threat to Christianity by assimilating Christian elements into its ideas of a secondary creator god responsible for material creation.

gospel: the message (literally, "good news") about salvation through the life, death, and resurrection of Jesus Christ preached by the apostles to Jews and Gentiles, summoning all to faith and repentance. "Gospel" later came to refer to one of the four canonical narratives of the life of Jesus.

grace (Greek *charis*): (1) an attitude of favor, generosity, or magnanimity; (2) a gift, benefit, or other effect that results from this attitude. The distinguishing character of grace is that it is freely given, not earned.

incarnation (from Latin *incarnatio*, literally, "enfleshment"): the eternal Son of God's taking on of human nature in the womb of Mary (John 1:14).

intertestamental: a term referring to the period between the writing of the Old Testament books and the writing of the New Testament books (roughly between 200 BC and AD 50), though there is some overlap in time between the latest books of the Old Testament and the earliest writings of the intertestamental period.

Johannine: a term used to refer to the writings or the theology of the apostle John.

Johannine shorthand: a technique found in the Fourth Gospel and the Letters of John whereby John compresses a truth or set of ideas into a short phrase.

Lord: the form (in small capital letters) that most English Bibles use to translate the divine name "**YHWH**" in the Old Testament. According to ancient custom, Jews refrain from pronouncing the divine name out of reverence when reading the Scriptures aloud, substituting the title "the Lord" (Hebrew *Adonai*).

LXX: the Roman numeral for 70, used as an abbreviation for the **Septuagint**.

messiah (from Hebrew *mashiah*, "anointed one"; Greek *Christos*): the descendant of King David promised by God, whom many Jews of Jesus' day hoped would come to restore the kingdom to Israel. The early Christians recognized Jesus as the Christ, the Messiah promised in the Jewish Scriptures.

New Evangelization: The effort to proclaim the gospel and bring people into a living relationship with Jesus Christ in the midst of a post-Christian global culture. It is directed both to the full conversion of those who are already baptized and to those who are not Christians.

parousia: from the Greek meaning "presence" or "arrival." It refers to the return of Jesus Christ in glory, when he will raise the dead, conduct the last judgment, and establish the kingdom of God.

presbyter (Greek *presbyteros*, "elder"): a term literally meaning "older man" that came to designate those appointed by the apostles to lead local churches (see, e.g., Acts 14:23; 20:17; 1 Tim 5:17, 19; Titus 1:5). This term gradually came to be understood as signifying a share in Christ's priestly ministry; the English term "priest" derives from the term "presbyter."

propitiation: the act of conciliation by which our sins are forgiven and we are restored to a right relationship with God.

sanctification: the process of being made holy or set apart for God through the work of the Holy Spirit.

Satan (Hebrew for "adversary"): in the Old Testament, a member of the heavenly court who accused or opposed God's people (1 Chron 21:1; Job 1:6–12). In the New Testament, Satan is the prince of demons, the invisible spirits who oppose God's plan and seek to destroy humanity.

scandal: an action that causes offense and has the potential to lead others to become skeptical of their faith or to engage in sinful behavior.

Septuagint (abbreviated LXX): the Greek translation of the Old Testament produced around the third century BC. The name comes from the Latin *septuaginta* ("seventy"), based on a legend that seventy scholars uniformly translated the Hebrew text into Greek. It is the version most often used by New Testament authors when they quote from the Old Testament.

Torah (Hebrew for "instruction" or "law"): the first five books of the Old Testament, also called the Pentateuch (Greek) or the law of Moses. It can also refer to all God's instructions for a holy life for those who live in a covenant relationship with him.

type: a person, place, institution, or event in an earlier stage of God's plan that foreshadows God's action at a later stage in Christ, the Church, the sacraments, or the future kingdom.

world (Greek *kosmos*): (1) creation or the universe and all it contains; (2) all human beings; (3) human society as opposed to God and under the sway of the devil.

YHWH: God's holy name revealed to Moses at the burning bush (Exod 3:14). The form "YHWH" (called the Tetragrammaton, meaning "four letters") is used because Hebrew script has no vowels. According to ancient custom, Jews refrain from pronouncing the divine name ("Yahweh") out of reverence, substituting the title "the Lord" (Hebrew *Adonai*).

Index of Pastoral Topics

This index indicates where topics that may be useful for evangelization, catechesis, apologetics, or other forms of pastoral ministry are mentioned in James or in 1–3 John.

James

anger, 1:19–20
anointing of the sick, 5:13–15
care of the poor, 1:27; 2:1–4, 15–17
confession, 5:16
desire, 1:14–15; 4:1–4
eternal life, 1:16–18; 5:19–20
faith, 1:2–7; 2:5, 17–26; 5:15
faith and works, 1:22–25, 27; 2:1–4, 14–26
good works, 1:21–25, 27
humility, 1:21; 3:13; 4:6, 10
jealousy, 3:16
judgment, 2:12–13; 5:9, 19–20
law, 1:25; 2:8–13; 4:11b–12
mercy, 2:13; 3:17; 5:11, 15
oaths, 5:12
patience, 5:7
peace, 3:18
persecution, 5:1–5
perseverance, 1:2–7, 25; 5:8, 11
prayer, 1:5–7; 4:2–3, 7–10; 5:13–15, 16–18
prayer, intercessory, 1:5–7; 5:14–15, 16b–18
prayer, petitionary, 4:2–3
poverty, 1:9–11, 27; 2:5–6; 5:1–4
slander, 4:11
speech, 1:26; 3:1–13; 4:11; 5:9
speech, blessing, 3:10
speech, cursing, 3:8–12
teachers, 3:1–2
temptation, 1:12–15
wisdom, 1:5; 3:13–18

First, Second, and Third John

abiding (remaining) in God, 1 John 2:6, 10, 17, 24, 27–28; 3:6, 9, 17, 24; 4:12–16
children of God, 1 John 3:1–3
communion (fellowship), 1 John 1:1–10
confession of Christ, 1 John 2:23; 4:2–3, 14–15
confidence in God, 1 John 2:28; 3:21; 4:17; 5:14
conquering (the devil and the world), 1 John 2:12–14; 5:4–5
deification of the Christian, 1 John 3:1–2
devil, 1 John 3:6–10; 5:18–19
discernment of spirits, 1 John 4:1–3; 5:20
doing the will of God, 1 John 2:17; 5:14
doing what is good, 3 John 1:11

Index of Sidebars

42 Parables of Jesus